MY **KIND**
OF PLACE

*Also by Susan Orlean
in Large Print:*

The Bullfighter Checks Her Makeup

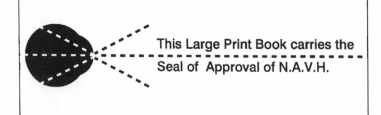

This Large Print Book carries the
Seal of Approval of N.A.V.H.

MY KIND OF PLACE

—TRAVEL STORIES—
from a Woman Who's Been Everywhere

Susan Orlean

Thorndike Press • Waterville, Maine

Published in 2005 by arrangement with
Random House, Inc.

Thorndike Press® Large Print Core.

The tree indicium is a trademark of Thorndike Press.

The text of this Large Print edition is unabridged.
Other aspects of the book may vary from the original edition.

Set in 16 pt. Plantin.

Printed in the United States on permanent paper.

Library of Congress Cataloging-in-Publication Data

Orlean, Susan.
    My kind of place : travel stories from a woman who's been everywhere / by Susan Orlean.
        p. cm.
    ISBN 0-7862-7289-9 (lg. print : hc : alk. paper)
    1. Orlean, Susan — Travel.   2. Voyages and travels.
    3. Large type books.   I. Title.
    G465.O75 2005
    910.4—dc22   2004024864

For John

As the Founder/CEO of NAVH, the only national health agency solely devoted to those who, although not totally blind, have an eye disease which could lead to serious visual impairment, I am pleased to recognize Thorndike Press* as one of the leading publishers in the large print field.

Founded in 1954 in San Francisco to prepare large print textbooks for partially seeing children, NAVH became the pioneer and standard setting agency in the preparation of large type.

Today, those publishers who meet our standards carry the prestigious "Seal of Approval" indicating high quality large print. We are delighted that Thorndike Press is one of the publishers whose titles meet these standards. We are also pleased to recognize the significant contribution Thorndike Press is making in this important and growing field.

Lorraine H. Marchi, L.H.D.
Founder/CEO
NAVH

* Thorndike Press encompasses the following imprints: Thorndike, Wheeler, Walker and Large Print Press.

CONTENTS

PART THREE: Everywhere

Introduction

I travel heavy. This is probably something of a surprise, since you might well assume that someone who travels as much as I do would be the sort to throw a T-shirt and a toothbrush into a paper bag and go. Unfortunately, this is not the case. I deliberate endlessly before I travel; I pack and repack; I am shamed by how much I've packed, and then, as penance, I force myself to remove a few items; then I capitulate, put everything back in, add one or two more things just to be safe, and at last, burdened and beaten, limp to the airport or the train station or the parking garage with my gross overload. Why do I do it? I've decided that it is a sort of passage I have to make before making my true passage — it's my ritual of clinging to the familiar before entering the unfamiliar, my resistance to leaving the comforts of home for the displacement of travel, of being a stranger embarking on exploration.

This might make me sound like a reluctant traveler, but I'm not at all; I'm only a reluctant packer. I'm a passionate voyager, and as soon as I can force the locks shut on my overstuffed suitcase, I'm eager to head out the door. I love the jolt you get from travel. I love the freshness and surprise of being in a new place, the way it makes even the most ordinary things seem extraordinary and strange. It makes me feel extra-alive. The things that are routine in a familiar place are thrilling somewhere new; things I don't notice at home jump out at me when I'm traveling. As soon as I get out of town, I love stopping for gas so I can poke around the gas station minimarket; besides the usual, ubiquitous junk food and cigarettes, there are always odds and ends that reveal the character of the place. Those serendipitous discoveries are my addiction. I found a real raccoon-skin Davy Crockett hat for sale in a gas station in Tennessee; a hand-printed pamphlet — the biography of a famous local giant — among the mass-market magazines in a convenience store in Florida; homemade barbecue beside the Doritos and Slim Jims in a minimart in Missouri. These are little tokens of what make all journeys seem so promising, so loaded with possibility — full of the yet unseen, the impossible to imagine, the still unknown.

I'm a sucker for going places that sound wonderful, of course, but I'm even enthusiastic about places that don't. This quality sometimes vexes the people around me. Years ago, I had some reporting to do in Houston. I was, as usual, excited about the trip. I mentioned it to a friend of mine who had lived in Texas for a few years, and he warned me that Houston was a drag. I said that I couldn't imagine how it could be, since it was a major city in an interesting state full of interesting industries like oil and gas, and in my opinion that guaranteed that it would be a great place to explore. My friend was disgusted. "Believe it or not," he said, "there *are* places in the world that even you wouldn't find interesting." I will confess that he was almost right: Of all the places I've been, Houston was one of the hardest to love, but its blankness and shapelessness fascinated me and made a great backdrop to the story I had gone there to see.

This is a collection of pieces about journeys. With one or two exceptions, they aren't what are ordinarily described as "travel writing"; they are not prescriptive or advice giving, and they don't review whether or not you get your dollar's worth

11

out of the local hotels. In some cases, these are stories that came about because I was interested in the place itself. For instance, I got the idea to write about Khao San Road in Bangkok — the street where all the backpackers and hitchhikers and hair braiders in the world converge — because I was in Bangkok changing planes (coincidentally, I happened to be on my way back from reporting another one of these pieces, "Fertile Ground," in Bhutan) and had some time to kill. A young couple I had met on the plane had told me a little bit about Khao San, and on a whim I hopped in a cab to take a look. I found it such an amazing scene that as soon as I got home and emptied my suitcase, I packed again and returned to Bangkok to spend a week walking up and down the road. I decided to write about Midland, Texas, because it was being mentioned so often — and so significantly — as a building block in George W. Bush's personality that it seemed like a place worth understanding and describing in order to have an idea of what sort of building block a place like Midland might be. Likewise, Mt. Fuji loomed: It is so embedded in Japanese semiotics and symbolism that it has always struck me as being less a place than an al-

12

most living thing, yet I had no real idea of what it was like as a physical place. When my editors at *Outside* asked me where in the world I'd like to go, Mt. Fuji was the first thing that came to mind. It was also nice to climb a mountain that sounds a lot bigger and more challenging than it really is; of all my travels, it is the one that has afforded me the most extravagant and undeserved bragging rights.

Other stories included here started with narratives, and the places emerged as characters only after my reporting began. When I set out to write about a woman in New Jersey who had twenty-seven or so tigers in her backyard, the operative concept seemed to be "tiger," not "New Jersey." The tigers were certainly the centerpiece of the story, but I found myself equally interested in the setting and in the idea that when the Tiger Lady had first moved in, her corner of southern New Jersey was wild and empty and remote — in other words, the sort of place where you might indeed have a few dozen tigers in your backyard without anyone noticing — and that the arc of her troubles followed the arc of the area's development, drawing an almost perfect picture of how rapidly and dramatically a rural place can change. Or take the story about the two Cuban oxen Carbonaro and Primavera. This is a piece about the Cuban economy and a small portrait of the man who farmed with these oxen, but it was also a chance to capture the feel of the Cuban countryside and how *little* and how slowly a rural place sometimes changes. I'm not good at fitting my stories into categories, and many of them can be described as any number of things — profiles, essays, reporter-at-large, whatever — but these are stories that I think of most in the context of place. When I wrote these pieces, the sense of where I was — of where the stories were unfolding — seemed to saturate every element of the experience, to inform it and shape it, and to be what made the story whole.

To be honest, I view all stories as journeys. Journeys are the essential text of the human experience — the journey from birth to death, from innocence to wisdom, from ignorance to knowledge, from where we start to where we end. There is almost no piece of important writing — the Bible, the *Odyssey*, Chaucer, *Ulysses* — that isn't explicitly or implicitly the story of a journey. Even when I don't actually *go* anywhere for a particular story, the way I report is to immerse myself in something I usually know very little about, and what I experience is the journey toward a grasp of what I've seen. I picture my readers having the same expedition, in an armchair, as they begin reading one of my pieces and work their way through it, ending up with the distinct feeling of having been somewhere else, whether it's somewhere physically exotic or just the "somewhere else" of being inside someone else's life.

The farthest I've ever gone for a story was Bhutan, which is on the other side of the world. In fact, since it is literally on the other side of the world, I used one of my trips there to satisfy a lifelong desire: Instead of doing a round trip there and back, I flew around the entire world, stopping in Bhutan in between. The closest "travel" story I've ever done is the piece called "Homewrecker," in which the roles of visitor and visitee were reversed — it is a story about how someone (almost) made a journey into my own home, which was a peculiar experience for someone like me, whose professional life involves going into other people's houses. The most difficult trip I've ever taken for a story was probably one that was just a few blocks from home, to Martin Luther King Jr. High School in

Manhattan. Even though the person I wrote about — the president of the student body — was a buoyant and witty young woman, the school struck me as a harsh, hard place, ground down and depleted, and what made it difficult was reconciling this with the fact that it was just a few blocks from my very comfortable apartment. The easiest trip I've taken for a story, hands down, was the one I took to visit three lavish spas in Thailand. I prefer going on my reporting trips alone, and since I often go to unglamorous places like Midland, Texas, and Jackson, New Jersey, I rarely have to fend off friends and family who want to keep me company. In the case of the spa trip to Thailand, though, I had a waiting list of volunteers who told me they were very, very concerned about my taking such a long, difficult trip all alone.

A few years ago I was asked to speak on a panel about travel writing. A week or two before the panel, the catastrophic attacks on the World Trade Center took place. During the weeks and months that followed the attacks, nothing seemed to matter — or at least nothing except those things that could be shown to matter even through the heavy shroud of that event. The panel on travel writing went on as scheduled, and one of the first questions we were asked was what we thought would happen to travel writing in the new world that 9/11 seemed to have brought forth. I thought it was a legitimate question. Should anyone write about — or read about — what it's like to snowshoe through Alaska or raft in Costa Rica when the world seemed to be falling apart? Would anyone in his or her right mind have any interest in leaving home when the universe seemed so threatening? What I said then, and still believe, is that human beings are stubbornly and persistently curious and that I can't imagine we will ever lose our desire to know about what lies beyond our immediate horizon. At a time when the world feels chaotic and frightening, writers who go out to see it and describe it seem more important, not less. Even fluffy, expository stories about pretty places matter if people are less inclined to travel, since then the writer acts as the reader's proxy, bringing back the world that most people might be reluctant to go out and see for themselves. At the most elemental level, the world's troubles are the result of people turning inward and turning away from whatever and whoever is different and unfamiliar. If a writer can make even one reader feel more open to someone or someplace new, I think he or she has accomplished something well worth doing.

What do you get for all this travel? Lots of frequent-flier miles, of course. I've ended up with a passport that is stamped, ink stained, dog-eared, creased, and in need of supplemental pages to accommodate the piling on of seals and visas. Also, I am seized repeatedly by epiphanies (or what I mistake for epiphanies) about how to travel well: how to conquer jet lag (stay up until the proper time to sleep, no matter how bad you feel); how to master suitcase selection (I'm now very big on wheelie bags and down on soft luggage); how to pack (never go anywhere without a sweatshirt, a string of pearls, and a big, elegant scarf, which can be used as a dress, a shawl, a skirt, a shrug, a blanket, or a tent, and try, try, *try* not to overpack); and how to find my bearings in a new place (hang out in a coffee shop, strike up a conversation with anyone willing to talk, read the local papers, spend a day walking around downtown, stop in at garage sales and open houses and flea markets and fairs). Travel quietly.

Probably the most valuable lesson I've

learned after these years of travel is how to bear being lonely. There is nothing that has quite the dull thud of being by yourself in a place you don't know, surrounded by people you don't recognize and to whom you mean nothing. But that's what being a writer requires. Writing is a wonderful life — a marvelous life, in fact — but it is also the life of a vapor, of floating in unseen, filling a space, and then vanishing. There are times when I'm traveling, when I'm far from home, that I am so forlorn that I can't remember why I chose this particular profession. I yearn to be home so fiercely that I feel as though my heart will pop out of my chest. And then I step out and see the world spread out around me. I know where I'm heading: I am heading home. But on the way there, I see so many corners to round and doors to open, so many encounters to chance upon, so many tiny moments to stumble into that tell huge stories, that I remember exactly why I took this particular path. The journey begins again; the story starts over; I gather myself and go out to see what I can see and tell it as best I can, and the beckoning of home is always, forever, there, just over the next horizon.

HERE
Part One

Lifelike

As soon as the 2003 World Taxidermy Championships opened, the heads came rolling in the door. There were foxes and moose and freeze-dried wild turkeys; mallards and buffalo and chipmunks and wolves; weasels and buffleheads and bobcats and jackdaws; big fish and little fish and razor-backed boar. The deer came in herds, in carloads, and on pallets: dozens and dozens of whitetail and roe; half deer and whole deer and deer with deformities, sneezing and glowering and nuzzling and yawning; does chewing apples and bucks nibbling leaves. There were millions of eyes, boxes and bowls of them, some as small as a lentil and some as big as a poached egg. There were animal mannequins, blank faced and brooding, earless and eyeless and utterly bald: ghostly gray duikers and spectral pine martens and black-bellied tree ducks from some other world. An entire exhibit hall was filled with equipment, all the gear required to bring something dead back to life: replacement noses for grizzlies, false teeth for beavers, fish-fin cream, casting clay, upholstery nails.

The championships were held in April at the Springfield, Illinois, Crowne Plaza hotel, the sort of nicely appointed place that seems more suited to regional sales conferences and rehearsal dinners than to having wolves in the corridors and people crossing the lobby shouting, "Heads up! Buffalo coming through!" A thousand taxidermists converged on Springfield to have their best pieces judged and to attend such seminars as "Mounting Flying Waterfowl," "Whitetail Deer — From a Master!," and "Using a Fleshing Machine." In the Crowne Plaza lobby, across from the concierge desk, a grooming area had been set up. The taxidermists were bent over their animals, holding flashlights to check problem areas like tear ducts and nostrils and wielding toothbrushes to tidy flyaway fur. People milled around, greeting fellow taxidermists they hadn't seen since the last world championships, held in Springfield two years ago, and talking shop:

"Acetone rubbed on a squirrel tail will fluff it right back up."

"My feeling is that it's quite tough to do a good tongue."

"The toes on a real competitive piece are

very important. I think Bondo works nicely, and so does Super Glue."

"I knew a fellow with cattle, and I told him, 'If you ever have one stillborn, I'd really like to have it.' I thought it would make a really nice mount."

That there is a taxidermy championship at all is something of an astonishment, not only to the people in the world who have no use for a Dan-D-Noser and Soft Touch Duck Degreaser, but also to taxidermists themselves. For a long time, taxidermists kept their own counsel. Taxidermy, the three-dimensional representation of animals for permanent display, has been around since the eighteenth century, but it was first brought into popular regard by the Victorians, who thrilled to all tokens of exotic travel and especially to any domesticated representations of wilderness — the glassed-in miniature rain forest on the tea table, the mounted antelope by the front door. The original taxidermists were upholsterers who tanned the hides of hunting trophies and then plumped them up with rags and cotton, so that they reassumed their original shape and size; those early poses were stiff and simple, the expressions fairly expressionless. The practice grew popular in this country, too: By 1882, there was a Society of American Taxidermists, which held annual meetings and published scholarly reports, especially on the matter of preparing animals for museum display. As long as taxidermy served to preserve wild animals and make them available for study, it was viewed as an honorable trade, but most people were still discomfited by it. How could you not be? It was the business of dealing with dead things, coupled with the questionable enterprise of making dead things look like live things. In spite of its scientific value, it was usually regarded as almost a black art, a wholly owned subsidiary of witchcraft and voodoo. By the early part of the twentieth century, taxidermists such as Carl E. Akeley, William T. Hornaday, and Leon Pray had refined techniques and begun emphasizing artistry. But the more the techniques of taxidermy improved, the more it discomfited: Instead of the lumpy moose head that was so artless that it looked fake, there were mounts of pouncing bobcats so immaculately and exactly preserved, they made you flinch.

For the next several decades, taxidermy existed in the margins — a few practitioners here and there, often self-taught and usually known only by word of mouth.

Then, in the late 1960s, a sort of transformation began: The business started to seem cleaner and less creepy — or maybe, in that messy, morbid time, popular culture started to again appreciate the messy, morbid business of mounting animals for display. An ironic reinterpretation of cluttered, bourgeois Victoriana and its strained juxtapositions of the natural and the man-made was in full revival — what hippie outpost didn't have a stuffed owl or a moose head draped with a silk shawl? — so, once again, taxidermy found a place in the public eye. Supply houses concocted new solvents and better tanning compounds, came out with lightweight mannequins, produced modern formulations of resins and clays. Taxidermy schools opened; previously, any aspiring taxidermist could hope to learn the trade only by apprenticing or by taking one of a few correspondence courses available. In 1971, the National Taxidermy Association was formed (the old society had moldered long before). In 1974, a trade magazine called *Taxidermy Review* began sponsoring national competitions. For the first time, most taxidermists had a chance to meet one another and share advice on how to glue tongues into jaw sets or accurately measure the carcass of a squirrel.

The competitions were also the first time that taxidermists could compare their skills and see who in the business could sculpt the best moose septum or could most perfectly capture the look on a prowling coyote's face. Taxidermic skill is a function of how deft you are at skinning an animal and then stretching its hide over a mannequin and sewing it into place. Top-of-the-line taxidermists sculpt their own mannequins; otherwise they will buy a ready-made polyurethane foam form and tailor the skin to fit. Body parts that can't be preserved (ears, eyes, noses, lips, tongues) can be either store-bought or handmade. How good the mount looks — that is, how alive it looks — is a function of how assiduously the taxidermist has studied reference material (photographs, drawings, and actual live animals) so that he or she knows the particular creature literally and figuratively inside out.

To be good at taxidermy, you have to be good at sewing, sculpting, painting, and hairdressing, and mostly you have to be a little bit of a zoology nerd. You have to love animals — love looking at them, taking photographs of them, hunting them, measuring them, casting them in plaster of

Paris when they're dead so that you have a reference when you're, say, attaching ears or lips and want to get the angle and shape exactly right. Some taxidermists raise the animals they most often mount, so they can just step out in the backyard when they're trying to remember exactly how a deer looks when it's licking its nose, especially because modern taxidermy emphasizes mounts with interesting expressions, rather than the stunned-looking creations of the past. Taxidermists seem to make little distinction between loving animals that are alive and loving ones that are not. "I love deer," one of the champions in the Whitetail division said to me. "They're my babies."

Taxidermy is now estimated to be a five-hundred-and-seventy-million-dollar annual business, made up of small operators around the country who mount animals for museums, for decorators, and mostly for the thirteen million or so Americans who are recreational hunters and on occasion want to preserve and display something they killed and who are willing to shell out anywhere from two hundred dollars to mount a pheasant to several thousand for a kudu or a grizzly bear. There are state and regional taxidermy competitions throughout the year and the world championships, which are held every other year; two trade magazines; a score of taxidermy schools; and three thousand visits to Taxidermy.net every day, where taxidermists can trade information and goods with as little self-consciousness as you would find on a knitting website:

"I am in need of several pair of frozen goat feet!"

"Hi! I have up to 300 sets of goat feet and up to 1000 sets of sheep feet per month. Drop me an email at frozencritters.com . . . or give me a call and we can discuss your needs."

"I have a very nice small raccoon that is frozen whole. I forgot he was in the freezer. Without taking exact measurements I would guess he is about twelve inches or so — very cute little one. Will make a very nice mount."

"Can I rinse a boar hide good and freeze it?"

"Bob, if it's salted, don't worry about it!"

"Can someone please tell me the proper way to preserve turkey legs and spurs? Thanks!"

"Brian, I inject the feet with

Preservz-It. . . . Enjoy!"

The word in the grooming area was that the piece to beat was Chris Krueger's happy-looking otters swimming in a perpetual circle around a leopard frog. A posting on Taxidermy.net earlier in the week declared, "EVERYTHING about this mount KICKS BUTT!!" Kicking butt, in this era of taxidermy, requires having a mount that is not just lifelike but also artistic. It used to be enough to do what taxidermists call "fish on a stick" displays; now a serious competitor worries about things like flow and negative space and originality. One of this year's contenders, for instance, Ken Walker's giant panda, had artistry and accuracy going for it, along with the element of surprise. The thing looked a hundred percent pure panda, but you can't go out and shoot a panda, and you aren't likely to get hold of a panda that has met a natural end, so everyone was dying to know how he had done it. The day the show opened, Walker was in the grooming area, gluing bamboo into place behind the animal's back paws, and a crowd had gathered around him. Walker works as a staff taxidermist for the Smithsonian. He is a breezy, shaggy-haired guy whose hands are always busy. One day, I saw him holding a piece of clay while waiting for a seminar to begin, and within thirty seconds or so, without actually paying much attention to it, he had molded the clay into a little minklike creature.

"The panda was actually pretty easy," he was saying. "I just took two black bears and bleached one of them — I think I used Clairol Basic. Then I sewed the two skins together into a panda pattern." He took out a toothbrush and fluffed the fur on the panda's face. "At the world championship two years ago, a guy came in with an extinct Labrador duck. I was in awe. I thought, What could beat that — an extinct duck? And I came up with this idea." He said he thought that the panda would get points for creativity alone. "You can score a ninety-eight with a squirrel, but it's still a squirrel," he said. "So that means I'm going with a panda."

"What did you do for toenails, Ken?" someone asked.

"I left the black bear's toenails in," he said. "They looked pretty good."

Another passerby stopped to admire the panda. He was carrying a grooming kit, which appeared to contain Elmer's glue, brown and black paint, a small tool set, and a bottle of Suave mousse. "I killed a blond bear once," he said to Ken. "A two-hundred-pound sow. Whew, she made a beautiful mount."

"I'll bet," Ken said. He stepped back to admire the panda. "I like doing re-creations of these endangered animals and extinct animals, since that's the only way anyone's going to have one. Two years ago, I did a saber-toothed cat. I got an old lioness from a zoo and bleached her."

The panda was entered in the Re-Creation (Mammal) division, one of the dozens of divisions and subdivisions and sub-subcategories, ranging from the superspecific (Whitetail Deer Long Hair, Open Mouth division) to the sweepingly colossal (Best in World), that would share in twenty-five thousand dollars' worth of prizes. (There is even a sub-sub-subspecialty known as "fish carving," which uses no natural fish parts at all; it is resin and wood sculpted into a fish form and then painted.) Nearly all the competitors are professionals, and they publicize their awards wherever possible. For instance, instead of ordering just any Boar Eye-Setting Reference Head out of a taxidermy catalog, you can order the Noonkester's #NRBERH head sculpted by Bones Johnson, which was, as the catalog notes, the 2000 National Taxidermy Association Champion Gamehead.

The taxidermists take the competition very seriously. During the time I was in Springfield, I heard conversations analyzing such arcane subjects as exactly how much a javelina's snout wrinkles when it snarls and which molars deer use to chew acorns as opposed to which ones they use to chew leaves. This is important because the ultimate goal of a taxidermist is to make the animal look exactly as if it had never died, as if it were still in the middle of doing ordinary animal things like plucking berries off a bush or taking a nap. When I walked around with the judges one morning, I heard discussions that were practically Talmudic, about whether the eyelids on a particular bison mount were overdetailed, and whether the nostrils on a springbok were too wide, and whether the placement of whiskers on an otter appeared too deliberate. "You do get compulsive," a taxidermist in the exhibit hall explained to me one afternoon. At the time, he was running a feather duster over his entry — a bobcat hanging off an icicle-covered rock — in the last moments before the judging would begin. "When you're working on a piece, you forget to eat, you

34

forget to drink, you even forget to sleep. You get up in the middle of the night and go into the shop so you can keep working. You get completely caught up in it. You want it to be perfect. You're trying to make something come back to life."

I said that his bobcat was beautiful and that even the icicles on the piece looked completely real. "I made them myself," he said. "I used clear acrylic toilet plunger handles. The good Lord sent the idea to me while I was in a hardware store. I just took the handles and put them in the oven at four hundred degrees." He tapped the icicles and then added, "My wife was pretty worried, but I did it on a nonstick cookie sheet."

So who wants to be a taxidermist? "I was a meat cutter for fifteen years," a taxidermist from Kentucky said to me. "That whole time, no one ever said to me, 'Boy, that was a wonderful steak you cut me.' Now I get told all the time what a great job I've done." Steve Faechner, who is the president and chairman of the Academy of Realistic Taxidermy, in Havre, Montana, started mounting animals in 1989, after years spent working on the railroad. "I had gotten hurt and was looking for something to do," he said. "I was with a friend who did taxidermy and I thought to myself, I have got to get a life. And this was it." Larry Blomquist, who is the owner of the World Taxidermy Championships and of *Breakthrough*, the trade magazine that sponsors the competition, was a schoolteacher for three years before setting up his business. There are a number of women taxidermists (one was teaching this year's seminar, "Problem Areas in Mammal Taxidermy"), and there are budding junior taxidermists, who had their own competition division, for kids fourteen and younger, at the show.

The night the show opened, I went to dinner with three taxidermists who had driven in from Kentucky, Michigan, and Maryland. They were all married, and all had wives who complained when they found one too many antelope carcasses in the family freezer, and all worked full-time mounting animals — mostly deer for local hunters, but occasional safari work for people who had shot something in Africa. When I mentioned that I had no idea that a person could make a living as a taxidermist, they burst out laughing, and the guy from Kentucky pointed out that he lived in a little town and there were two other full-time taxidermists in business right down the road.

"What's the big buzz this year?" the man from Michigan asked.

"I don't know. Probably something new with eyes," the guy from Maryland answered. "That's where you see the big advances. Remember at the last championship, those Russian eyes?" These were glass animal eyes that had a reflective paint embedded in them, so that if you shone a light, they would shine back at you, sort of like the way real animals' eyes do. The men discussed those for a while, then talked about the new fish eyes being introduced this year, which have photographic transfers of actual fish eyes printed on plastic lenses. We happened to be in a restaurant with a sports theme, and there were about a hundred televisions on around the room, broadcasting dozens of different athletic events, but the men never glanced at them and never stopped talking about their trade. We had all ordered barbecued ribs. When dinner was over, all three of them were fiddling around with the bones before the waitress came to clear our plates.

"Look at these," the man from Kentucky said, holding up a rib. "You could take these home and use them to make a skeleton."

In the seminars, the atmosphere was as

sober and exacting as a tax law colloquium. "Whiskers," one of the instructors said to the group, giving them a stern look. "I pull them out. I label them. There are left whiskers and there are right whiskers. If you want to get those top awards, you're going to have to think about whiskers." Everyone took notes.

In the next room: "Folks, remember, your carcass is your key. The best thing you can do is to keep your carcass in the freezer. Freeze the head, cast it in plaster. It's going to really help if your head is perfect." During the breaks, the group made jokes about a T-shirt that had been seen at one of the regional competitions. The shirt said PETA in big letters, but when you got up close you saw that PETA didn't spell out People for the Ethical Treatment of Animals, the bane of all hunters and, by extension, all taxidermists; it spelled out "People Eating Tasty Animals." Chuckles all around, then back to the solemn business of mounting flying waterfowl: "People, follow what the bird is telling you. Study it, do your homework. When you've got it ready, fluff the head, shake it, and then get your eyes. There are a lot of good eyes out there on the market today. Do your legwork, and you can have a beautiful mount."

It was brisk and misty outside — the antler vendors in the parking lot looked chilled and miserable — and the modest charms of Springfield, with its mall and the Oliver P. Parks Telephone Museum and Abraham Lincoln's tomb, couldn't compete with the strange and wondrous sights inside the hotel. The mere experience of waiting for the elevator — knowing that the doors would peel back to reveal maybe a man and a moose, or a bush pig, or a cougar — was much more exciting than the usual elevator wait in the usual Crowne Plaza hotel. The trade show was a sort of mad tea party of body parts and taxidermy supplies, things for pulling flesh off a carcass, for rinsing blood out of fur — a surreal carnality, but all conveyed with the usual trade show earnestness and hucksterism, with no irony and no acknowledgment that having buckets of bear noses for sale was anything out of the ordinary. "Come take a look at our beautiful synthetic fur! We're the hair club for lions! If you happen to shoot a lion who is out of season or bald, we can provide you with a gorgeous replacement mane!" "Too many squirrels? Are they driving you nuts? Let us mount them for you!" "Divide and Conquer animal forms — an amazing advance in small-mammal mannequins, patent pending!"

The big winner at the show turned out to be a tiny thing — a mount of two tree sparrows, submitted by a strapping German named Uwe Bauch, who had grown up in the former East Germany dreaming of competing in an American taxidermy show. The piece was precise and lovely, almost haunting, since the more you looked at it, the more certain you were that the birds would just stop building their nest, spread their wings, and fly away. Early one morning, before I left Springfield, I took a last walk around the competition hall. It was quiet and uncanny, with hundreds of mounts arranged on long tables throughout the room; the deer heads clustered together, each in a slightly different pose and angle, looked like a kind of animal Roman forum caught in mid-debate. A few of the mounts were a little gruesome — a deer with a mailbox impaled on an antler, another festooned with barbed wire, and one with an arrow stuck in its brisket — and one display, a coyote whose torso was split open to reveal a miniature scene of the destruction of the World Trade Center, complete with little firemen and rubble piles, was surpassingly weird. Otherwise, the room was biblically tranquil, the lion at last lying down with the Corsican lamb, the family of jackdaws in everlasting, unrequited pursuit of a big green beetle, and the stillborn Bengal tiger cub magically revived, its face in an eternal snarl, alive looking, although it had never lived.

A Place Called Midland

In Midland, Texas, it's not the heat, it's the lack of humidity. Almost total lack of it, or so it seems, especially when you first arrive and step out of the chilled Midland International Airport and into the dry-roasted air. Midland has the kind of air that hits you like a brick. After a few minutes, your throat burns. After a few days, your skin feels powdery, your eyelids stick, your hair feels dusty and rough. The longer you spend there, the more you become a little bit like the land — you dry out and cake and crack. Not until I spent time in Midland did I fully appreciate the fact that the earth has an actual crust, like bread that has been slowly baked. I became convinced that if I stayed for a while, I would develop one, too.

Midland is a city of ninety-nine thousand, in the middle of the region known as the Permian Basin, a platform of sediment and salt capped with a wedge of rock that covers roughly a hundred and twenty-five thousand square miles of West Texas. Most people, if they know about Midland at all, know that it is where Baby Jessica McClure was rescued from a well thirteen years ago and where George W. Bush grew up and later started his business career. ("I don't know what percentage of me is Midland," he once said in an interview, "but I would say people, if they want to understand me, need to understand Midland and the attitude of Midland.") Both associations suggest a city that is innocent, idyllic, congenial — the kind of place where people fish fallen babies out of wells and young men make fortunes in old-fashioned ways. But Midland struck me as weirder than that — its simplicity deceiving, its character harder to uncover and know.

Being inconspicuous is Midland's most conspicuous feature. It used to be called Midway, because it was halfway between Fort Worth and El Paso. When it was determined that there was already a Midway in Texas, it was renamed Midland, as if nothing else about it could inspire a name. A current city slogan is "Midland: In the Middle of Somewhere." Previous slogans have included "Midland: Most Ambitious City Between the Oceans" and "Midland: Oil, Livestock, and Financial Center of the Permian Basin." Recently, the more buoyant seventies slogan "The Sky's the

Limit" has been revived, since Bush has said that it embodies the Midland he knew.

Originally, Midland was a depot on the Texas & Pacific Railway. It outlived and outgrew the other flyspeck towns in the basin — now vanished cotton and cattle outposts like Boone and Slaughter and Toad Loop and Fighting Hollow and Bounce — by wooing oil companies to locate there after the first West Texas gusher, the Santa Rita, was tapped in 1923. In the late twenties, a hopeful businessman built an ornate office tower to enhance Midland's prestige and named it the Petroleum Building. And in the thirties, houses were literally picked up and moved from the neighboring town of McCamey to Midland in order to attract employees of Humble Oil. By the mid-fifties, Midland was where the oil company engineers, geologists, leaseholders, and attorneys lived; its sister city, Odessa, was home to the tool pushers and roughnecks.

The only measure of time that really matters in Midland is oil time. Recent history is divided into two periods. There was the mid-seventies through the early eighties, when OPEC was controlling the market and crude went up to an unimaginably high thirty-five dollars a barrel and was expected to go as high as a hundred: a Rolls-Royce dealership opened in town; Midland Airpark had a waiting list for private hangars; and powerboats were beached in nearly every driveway. And then there was 1986, and the years after that, when OPEC flooded the market, the price per barrel dropped to nine dollars, and the FDIC became the biggest employer in the county.

A popular local joke is to say that the city is in the middle of the finest fishing and hunting in the Southwest. The first person to try the joke on me was an engineer named Richard Witte. Like everyone else I met, he warned me that I'd never see the real Midland on my own, and he offered to show me around. We took his pickup and rode out of the city on razor-straight roads to the oil fields — an ocean of gray dirt, unmarked, parched, spectacularly monotonous, not a ripple in it except for the occasional sunken spot of a former buffalo wallow, until you get to the edge of the Permian Basin caprock and fall off into the rest of the world. We skirted ranches on which little sprouted except for shrubby mesquite and rows of skeletal pump jacks bobbing for oil, and zigzagged across square miles so wide and empty that, even when we raced along, we seemed to be standing still. It looked like nothing, except that there were millions of dollars underneath us, sacks of money banked in stone.

Witte then took me to see the Clay-Desta Center, an office building with a fountain of silvery water and a life-size sculpture of a mother and baby giraffe in its atrium. It was a beastly day, and the gurgling sound of the water was so pleasant that we lingered for a bit; Witte said that people often came to the Clay-Desta Center just to be near the fountain. The idea of going to an office building to be near water seemed so peculiar that I asked whether there was a more natural source around. "Sure there is," Witte said. "In fact, we're in the middle of the finest fishing and hunting in the whole Southwest." Once Witte was satisfied by the look of shock on my face, he grinned. "Drive five hours in any direction and you'll find great fishing and hunting and boating," he said. "We're right in the middle of it. It's just that none of it's here." The second time I heard the joke — from a real estate broker, as I recall — I pretended to fall for it out of politeness; the third time someone — a lawyer — tried it on me, I delivered the punch line myself.

The first day I was in Midland, I stopped in an antiques store to see what passed for an antique in West Texas, which had pretty much been unpopulated until the 1920s. I dug through old copies of *Sunset* magazine and empty Avon perfume bottles while the only other customer, a heavy, red-faced woman, talked to the store clerk. "The president made a lot of people mad," the customer was saying, and I turned to listen.

"A lot of presidents do," the clerk replied.

"Well, he shouldn't have been in a convertible," the customer went on. "That was a big mistake. But, okay, let's forget about the convertible, even. My feeling is that JFK was a goner no matter what."

I had come to Midland expecting that everyone would be talking about the presidential campaign, but it was the dead of summer and little was stirring; there were no local discussions of whether Midland might become the next Hope, Arkansas, or whether there would be house tours of Bush's former residences. It wasn't for lack of partisanship: Another local joke is to say that you can name more than ten Democrats in town. It was just that the Bush candidacy seemed predestined and expected, a natural ascendancy. While I was in Midland, the big news stories were that one of the longest horizontal wells ever drilled in the area had been completed, reaching from its starting point, near Interstate 20, to a spot twelve thousand feet below the Midland Kmart; that the Midland RockHounds had beat the Tulsa Drillers, 4–3, putting them back at the .500 mark for the season; and that oil prices were creeping up to thirty dollars a barrel.

Midland is such a small city and the Bushes are so woven into it that most people seem to have had some contact with them — lived down the street from them, or belonged to the same country club, or known Laura Bush when she was a girl. The Bush family first moved to Midland in 1950, when a lot of East Coast entrepreneurs were coming to Texas and looking for oil. It was a great moment to be punching holes in the Permian Basin: Within nine years, George H. W. Bush had made his fortune and moved the family to Houston. In the mid-seventies, when George W. Bush came back to Midland and founded Arbusto Oil, it was still a good time to be in the business. But only half of Arbusto's wells hit oil or gas; eventually, the company faltered and merged with another dying company, which was then bought out by Harken Energy, and Bush moved to Washington, D.C. Virtually every oilman I met remembered George W. from his Arbusto days. The comment I heard from most of them was, "George W. was the nicest young man you ever will meet. Just the nicest. But, you know, he never did earn a dime."

I was hot the whole time I was in Midland and dying to see anything green. When I could bear the heat, I walked around the deserted downtown, or through the neighborhood called Old Town Midland, or to the Permian Basin Petroleum Museum, Library, and Hall of Fame, over by the interstate. Everything seemed bleached and lifeless. Then, one afternoon, I drove out to the Racquet Club — which used to have George W. Bush as a member — to attend a party hosted by a local mortgage company. The clubhouse was cool and whitewashed, the lawns were silken and lush, and when the kids did cannon balls into the swimming pool, the water roared like applause. All the other guests at the party were in real estate, and they gathered in the shade of a live oak tree, snacking on hors d'oeuvres and chatting about the annual performance of Summer Mummers, the local vaudeville troupe, and the upcoming season of high school football, which is by far the biggest sport around.

It is a pretty nice time to be a real estate broker in Midland. It is not as nice as it was in, say, 1980, when you could show people only two or three houses and know they would snap one up at any price. "This was not the real world back then," Kay Sutton, who owns Century 21 in Midland, explained to me. "My daughter would shop and have lunch at the country club, and she didn't know that there was any other way people lived." Back then, so many new houses were going up that contractors were brought in from all over the country and had to camp out in RVs and tents.

These days are middling; still, the agents were feeling easy and the mortgage company was flush enough to have ordered shrimp. "It's the high price of oil," Kay Sutton said. "It makes people optimistic." When people are extremely optimistic, they want to live in a fancy development like Saddle Club North or Green Tree Country Club Estates, with maybe an attached three- or four-car garage and a view of the golf course. The best houses have swimming pools and lawns that are as soft as lamb's wool — real luxury in a place where a gallon of drinking water can cost more than a gallon of gas. "Of course, everyone dreams of mature trees," Kay Sutton said. "But it's just a dream. You can't have both a new house and mature trees."

Right next to my hotel was a café called the Ground Floor, the unofficial clubhouse of a different Midland. The Ground Floor was opened in 1996 by a real estate investor from Seattle named John Nute; he put in free Internet access, sponsored live music and poetry readings, and made the restrooms available to anyone who walked in the door. The Ground Floor is across the street from Centennial Plaza, one of those sterile brick-and-concrete urban parks, and once the café opened, the two places quickly filled with kids. "A lot of us misfits sort of found each other by hanging out at Centennial Plaza and the Ground Floor," a seventeen-year-old named Barbara Lawhon explained to me one afternoon. "We'd sit around writing poetry and playing music. It was a really big deal."

By 1997, Nute says, Friday night crowds at Centennial Plaza had grown to two hundred teenagers. Some of them were skateboarders and in-line skaters, who began doing a move on the park benches called grinding, which tears the benches to shreds. By the next summer, a city ordinance forbidding skateboarding and in-line skating in Centennial Plaza was being strongly enforced, and Nute's business dropped off by more than two-thirds.

The year before the ordinance was enforced was one of the only times Barbara liked living in Midland. "Growing up here sort of sucked for me," she explained. "We were basically poor. Midland is all about money. All the rich kids get into upper-level classes, even though they can't spell. In the first day of honors English in eighth grade, our teacher made us stand up and say our names and why we wanted to be in an honors class, and then say what our parents did for a living. And your parents' occupation is listed on the roster for band and for some of the other clubs, too. It's gross." In Midland, the nickname for spoiled preppies is "white hats," because of the fashion for wearing white painter hats with college logos. I told her I'd gone to the Midland Park Mall earlier in the week and had overheard a young guy in a white hat talking to two girls who were working at the Athlete's Foot. "Midland has a lot, a lot, of money," the young guy was saying as the girls nodded enthusiastically. "There are more Mercedeses here than anywhere in the country. In other places, when kids get cars it's something like, you know, a Toyota."

"There are all these rich kids here," Barbara said. "They're doing coke, drinking, partying. They're totally into football and cheerleading and into trashing cars — just trashing them, for no reason. Everything here is about being trendy. There's even a trendy church, Kelview Heights Baptist Church, which is trendy because the pastor is on TV." Barbara said that her mother was a housecleaner. For a while, she had worked at a private club in the Clay-Desta Center, and she told Barbara that many of the younger rich men who were members behaved in a disgusting way. I was lucky to have met Barbara at all, because it turned out that she was planning to move to Austin in a couple of days, and she thought she would be a lot happier there. "It'd be great to live in Midland if you were rich," she said.

After a few minutes, Barbara and I were joined by Midge Erskine, one of the few environmental activists in town. Midge is an elegant, silver-haired woman who grew up in the East but came to Midland thirty years ago with her husband, a geologist. In the late seventies, she became unpopular with local oil companies when she protested their practices of dumping contaminated water and keeping their oil tanks uncovered — both of which killed thousands of birds and other wildlife. Recently, Midge began videotaping city council meetings and set up a website, Truthmidlandtx.com, raising questions about local power. In general, the café seemed to be the place where people's dark suspicions about their hometown surfaced: Why was the Midland Airpark, which has no control tower, still operating? Who was so eager to come in and out of Midland sight unseen? Were police reporting the real crime statistics? How did So-and-so get his money, make his deals, and avoid getting busted? But if the Ground Floor is the meeting place for Midland's local hippies, poets, folksingers, and Democrats, there may not be enough of them to keep it afloat; these days, the establishment is barely breaking even. Nute blames the city, for having scared away teenagers, and the economy, for having failed to bring a spark back to the city's downtown. To keep the café going, he was forced to liquidate his investments, and now he has lost hundreds of thousands of dollars.

I went to Midland expecting to find an ordinary small city, but nothing about it was ordinary: not its weather or its topography or its history or its economy. People in Midland take in huge amounts of money, they lose huge amounts of money — then they move on to the next day. It's a manic-depressive city, spending lavishly and then suffering desperately. One afternoon, I was out with Richard Witte, looking at the fanciest neighborhoods in town. "Here's a fella who lost millions," he said, passing one sprawling Italianate ranch. "And see that house over there?" He pointed to a white-brick confection with skylights and Palladian windows. "They lost all their money, had to sell every single piece of furniture, the TV, everything. You drive past these houses and you see a big, expensive home, but you don't know how the people might be living inside."

There's a saying in Midland that whenever you strike oil you go out and get a boat, a plane, and a mistress, and when you lose your money you get rid of them one by one, starting with the mistress. No one mentioned anything to me about mistresses, but several people I met in Mid-land had been forced to sell their boats and planes. No one seemed ashamed about having lost money: It was like catching a cold — common and widespread and out of your control. According to Texas law, it used to be slanderous to say someone was bankrupt, but then, in the late eighties, it became part of the vernacular, so the law was changed. One day, I was talking to a local lawyer, Warren Heagy, who himself had owned and then had to sell a couple of planes. On the way out of his office, he in-troduced me to a colleague, who said, "I don't understand all these Internet people whining about losing money. My husband and I lost seven million dollars and you don't see us in the newspaper complaining!"

Now oil prices are cresting again, but the buzz that always follows — "like being near a beehive on a spring day," Richard Witte says — is missing. There are still thirteen pages of oil listings in the Yellow Pages — Oil Marketers, Oil Well Casing Pullings, Oil Well Log Libraries, Oil Re-finers, Oil & Gas Lawyers — and there is still a special oil-and-gas section in the newspaper every week, and every day I saw pickup trucks downtown with pieces of pump riggings bouncing around in the back. But the bust in 1986 was something no one had ever seen before, and Midland has not been the same since. When oil prices dropped from twenty-seven dollars to nine dollars a barrel, as much as seventy-five percent of the rigs were shut down, and roughly ten thousand people left Midland and never returned. Mobil, Texaco, Chevron, Conoco, and other companies scaled back their Midland operations and consolidated elsewhere, taking hundreds of administrative and executive jobs out of town.

More important, there is little exploration left to do in the Permian Basin. Most of the entrepreneurial gamble is gone: All you can do these days is work on how to draw every last drop of oil out of the ground. Some scientists speculate that in the next half century or so the Permian Basin will actually run out of oil and gas. The phrase "economic diversification" — probably unheard of in town twenty years ago — was on the front page of the *Midland Reporter-Telegram* nearly every day I was in Texas. Midland may not become one of those forgotten towns that popped up on the cap rock, never took hold, and then simply vanished, as if a high dry wind had blown it away, but these days the city is trying to market itself as a retirement haven and a convention site, just in case.

It's not hard to imagine that in Midland you are seeing the end of something. The pump jacks dipping up and down in the distance look prehistoric, and the hot wind bangs on the empty windows of the now defunct Midlander Athletic Club and the long-gone Rockin' Rodeo. You even sense it in the Petroleum Club, an exclusive organization that caters to local oil executives. It must have been a great place to make an entrance in the days when oil was big and Big Oil was invincible: The club has an enormous open staircase, and when you walk up to the dining room, you feel as if you are rising to the top of the world. The day I visited, though, the club was a little vacant; the empty stairway seemed to stretch forever, and half the dining room had been sectioned off and filled with artificial palm trees. It was my last day in Midland: I was having lunch with John Paul Pitts, the oil-and-gas editor at the *Reporter-Telegram*, and he seemed to know everyone in the room. This one had been worth millions, and that one worth billions, and that one was the founder or the president of this or that oil concern. But the dining room was subdued, and many of the fellow diners who walked by were ancient, skinny men wearing string ties.

The Petroleum Club has always been for the money people in the oil business, and the money people have almost always been white. Early on, even the oil-field workers were white, but after 1986, many of them left Midland or left the industry, and in the last fifteen years or so, a majority of the people digging and servicing and repairing the rigs have been Hispanic. The population of Midland has changed as well: Now only sixty-five percent of the residents are white, and nearly all the rest are Hispanic. There are very few Hispanics at the upper reaches of the oil industry — and few Hispanic geologists or engineers — and none were in evidence in the quiet dining room at the Petroleum Club. Pitts said that he expects the next generation of Hispanics in the business to end up in the offices downtown, rather than out on the oil patch; and some Midlanders believe that in twenty years the city may be mostly Hispanic. The question is how much longer there will be oil for them to tap.

George W. Bush has said that he would like to be buried in Midland. This will not necessarily be easy to do. When you first see it, the soil here looks loose and crumbly, and you'd think digging a hole in it would be as easy as sticking a knife in a cake. But nothing in Midland, not even burial, is as simple as it first seems. The tender soil conceals a calcium deposit called caliche that is as thick and hard as bone, and it takes a tempered-steel drill bit to break through.

Beautiful Girls

The Holiday Inn in Prattville, Alabama, is on a grassy rise beside a wide gray highway across from a Waffle House and a McDonald's and several different places to buy gas. One Sunday this spring, the hotel lobby was especially crowded. Some of the people had come straight from church for Sunday lunch: mild-faced women in pastel dresses and men in gray suits and dull blue ties; boys in white shirts and oxfords and girls in Sunday school dresses and black Mary Janes. The rest of the people had come for the Universal/Southern Charm International Children's Beauty Pageant being held at the hotel. They were wearing stonewashed jeans or leisure outfits, and they were carrying babies or pushing strollers or rushing around leading little girls by the hand, and with a spare finger some of them were balancing hangers that held tiny dresses with ballooning skirts covered by dry cleaners' plastic bags. A few of the littlest babies were fussing. Mothers hurried through the lobby and bumped their strollers into other mothers' strollers. A miniature dress of green chiffon slid off its hanger and settled onto the carpet with a sigh, and as soon as the woman holding the empty hanger noticed it she yelled, "Nobody move! Don't step on that dress!" Then a few three-year-olds started horsing around and squealing, and a cosmetic case slipped out of someone's hand, and, when it landed, out shot a dozen cylinder-shaped things — hair curlers, hairbrushes, lipstick tubes, eyeliner brushes — that rolled in every direction across the floor. A few fathers were sent back to the parking lot to retrieve the shoes or hat or Wet Ones or entry forms that had been left in the car by accident. One mother had spread her baby out on the lobby sofa and was changing her into a lavender Western outfit. In the ladies' room, small dresses and hats were hanging from every ledge they could hang from, and white anklet socks and white shoes and pairs of children's size 2 rhinestone-studded cowboy boots were scattered on the floor, and there was the tangy metallic smell of hot curling irons in the air. In the middle of the room, four women were adjusting the bows in their daughters' hair and smoothing blusher on their cheeks. Across from them, three other women were lined up elbow to elbow. Each one held a Great Lash mascara wand poised like a conductor's baton, and each was facing a lovely little girl in a glittering pageant dress sitting quietly in a sink.

I had never been to a beauty pageant before I went to Prattville. For the longest time, the world of children's beauty pageants was invisible to millions of people like me, who don't read *Pageant Life* and *Pageant World*, and don't plan their vacations around the big state finals, and don't have a little girl who has dozens of trophies and crowns and pageant banners in her room. Probably all of that would have remained invisible if someone hadn't murdered JonBenet Ramsey. Once the footage of her in pageant clothes and wearing makeup appeared on the TV news, the world of children's beauty pageants came into sight and a horrible association was made — not just that a beauty pageant girl was murdered, but that the pageants themselves were depraved and had maybe even contributed to the murder in some way. It was as if you'd never heard of the game of football until the O. J. Simpson trial, and then you'd never be able to separate the crime from the game.

But pageants have been taking place all over the country for decades, and in the South, especially, they are as common as barbecue. Pageants are held nearly every Sunday — Sunburst Pageants and Moonbeam Pageants and Miss American Starlet and Glamour Dolls USA Pageants — in meeting rooms at Holiday Inns and Comfort Inns and Best Westerns in places like Florence, Alabama, and Jackson, Mississippi, and Jackson, Tennessee. Every Sunday, pageants have been making winners and losers, inspiring and dashing hopes, wasting some people's money and making some little girls rich. As I left for Alabama, I guessed that I would see some overcompetitive parents and some parents who would insist on winning even if their kids didn't want to be in a pageant — the same bad things you sometimes see at junior tennis matches and gymnastics meets. I knew that I wasn't going to enjoy seeing three-year-olds wearing eyeliner and crying when they weren't named Supreme Queen. But in spite of what most of the stories that followed JonBenet's murder led me to expect, what I saw in Prattville were not people like the Ramseys, with lots of money and mobility. They were ordinary people: They were dazzled by glamour, and they believed truly and uncynically in beauty and staked their faith on its power to lift you and carry you away. It may be

embarrassing or naïve to believe
Miss America will lead you som
life, unless it happens to be you
your daughter's life, and the work
life that has been assigned to you a
baby feels small and flat and plain.
are only so many ways to get out of a
like Prattville. The crown you wil
Sunday might be the chance for your b
tiful baby to get a start on a different
so that someday she might get ahead a
get away.

Darlene Burgess, who founded th
Universal/Southern Charm Internationa
Pageant seventeen years ago, told me that
ever since JonBenet, people who don't know
anything about pageants are peering into the
pageant world and then condemning it
because they're shocked by the makeup
and the dressy dresses and the sexy sophis-
tication of some of the girls. There have
been magazine stories and television shows
about children's pageants before, but most
of them have been for foreign press and
TV, so this has really been the first time
that the pageant world has been shoved
into view. It's not that anyone has anything
to hide; it's just that they feel scrutinized
and criticized by people who haven't been
to a single pageant — people who can't see

w proud mothers are when their daughters n and don't see how pageant people are actically a family, in which everyone nows one another and watches out for ne another.

Darlene got into pageants purely by accident. She grew up on a farm in Arkansas in the fifties; her mother drove a grain truck, and Darlene lived on her own in town starting at the age of fifteen. She didn't know a thing about pageants and wouldn't have had the money to compete in them even if she had. When she got married, she and her husband, Jerry, who was a pilot for Oral Roberts University, lived in Tulsa. They started their little girl, Becky, in dancing classes at the age of three. Becky was a natural onstage, and Darlene learned to coax out her best performances by waving a flyswatter at her. After a while, Becky's dance teacher entered her in a competition that turned out to be part of a children's pageant. Becky came home that day with a trophy, and Darlene was hooked.

Darlene learned about pageants as she went along. One thing she learned was makeup. The dance teacher used some on the girls in their recitals, and Darlene didn't like it at first, but then she agreed

66

that for pageants Becky needed it. "She was just so pale," Darlene said to me recently. "I just had to cake her. Otherwise, she would have been invisible onstage. If you have a baby who's a true blonde, not a browny blonde, and you put her under those lights, it'll kill her." Darlene herself is tall and substantial and has fair skin and clay-colored hair. She wears big rimless glasses and warm-up suits. She has an Arkansas accent, rolling and drawly, and a light, chiming laugh that can put you in an instant good mood. She is self-possessed and capable in a way that is slightly intimidating. When she needed a dress for Becky, she sewed one; when she saw that there was no good pageant dress business in the area, she started one; when she discovered that no one manufactured mannequins small enough to use for her clients, she built one; and then, when she decided that the pageants Becky was entering were poorly run, she started her own. "I'd hear talk in dressing rooms," Darlene told me. "Like 'If they know you, you win; if they don't, you don't.' And then I was at a pageant and found out that one of the judges was the grandmother of one of the babies, and I thought, I'm going to do my own pageant and do it right." She picked a date, made up flyers, and rented a room. To break even, she had to attract at least fifty kids. She ended up with a hundred and twenty. After a few years, she was able to expand Southern Charm into North Carolina, Mississippi, New York, and Maryland, and she told me that she might soon be adding Virginia and Florida. In each state, Darlene appoints a director to run preliminary pageants and the state finals, and she herself takes care of the national finals. All beauty pageants are owned privately, and most use state directors, as Darlene does. State directors can make money running a pageant, but unless they own a pageant system they need a full-time job. Recently, Darlene's Tennessee directors, a married couple, had to resign, because the man, a Baptist minister, had just got his own church and wasn't free on Sundays anymore.

Stacie Brumit, Southern Charm's Alabama state director, arrived at the hotel around noon, loaded down with boxes and bags. The mothers in the lobby hurried with their daughters into a line that started in front of Stacie's registration table and curled down the hall and out the door. Stacie is round faced and round shouldered and has a bleached blond pageboy.

She was already heavily into pageants when she signed on to be Darlene's Alabama director — she had competed herself when she was little, and so far she has entered her two-year-old daughter, Brianna, in thirty pageants, starting when Brianna was five months old. "I see how much being in them is giving Brianna, even at her age," she said. "I think she's going to be a great public speaker because of her pageant experience. She's learning poise. She's going to end up being . . . being like the president! I mean, he's not shaky when he's up there speaking." Before becoming a pageant director, Stacie worked at Wal-Mart. This was when she was expecting Brianna, and she says that even though directing a pageant is hard work, it's nothing compared with sitting on a stool out in the cold in front of a Wal-Mart greeting shoppers when you're six months pregnant and sick as a dog.

The kids in line to be registered ranged from six months old to almost but not quite four, and they were beautiful or cute or plain, and they were wearing white satin dresses covered with matching satin capes trimmed with feathers, and peach dresses with beaded bodices and heart-shaped cut-outs in the back, and powder blue dresses with leg-o'-mutton sleeves. The girls who were old enough to have some hair had it swept up, prom style, or left loose and sprayed into curvy shapes, and the bigger girls wore foundation, blusher, eye shadow, and mascara, and the babies wore no makeup except maybe a little pink gloss on their lips. Some of the mothers wore attractive clothes and had their hair blown smooth, but many were too fat or too thin or looked tired and frayed next to their dazzling daughters. While the mothers were waiting to register, the fathers dawdled in the parking lot, having a smoke. The babies napped, and the bigger girls practiced pageant modeling: eye contact with the judges; a wide smile showing one row of teeth; "pretty hands," which means holding your arms straight and slightly lifted, with your hands bent at the wrist and parallel to the floor; and "pretty feet," the pose for the beauty lineup, right heel pressed to left instep, toes wide and apart.

To put on a proper pageant, you need trophies and banners and crowns and plaques, and judges who aren't related to any of your contestants, and a master of ceremonies to run the event, and masking tape to make X's on the floor showing the kids where to do their modeling turns. If you're giving prize money, you need your prize money, but otherwise you don't need anything else — except in Tennessee and Arkansas, where directors need to post a ten-thousand-dollar bond. Tennessee instituted this practice about twenty years ago, after a pageant director in Nashville was shot and killed by her husband the night before one of her pageants and none of the contestants ever got their entry fees back. Some pageants are scams. Some issue bad checks to the winners or promise scholarships and never come through, and others say they will give you your prize money only if you come to another pageant, and by the time you do that, you've spent more money than you would have ever won. There have been occasions when a pageant went bankrupt before any of the winners could collect their money, but not before the pageant director had collected a lot of entry fees. Some pageants start late and are run sloppily, and the kids are kept up until all hours and are expected not to complain. Many pageants, though, like Universal/Southern Charm, have been around a long time and are considered quality pageants. Darlene Burgess is strict, and her rules are exacting:

Contestants should stand still in lineup, no exaggerated poses. Mothers should

71

have control of their children at all times. Baby through six years old should wear short dresses. Dresses do not have to be loaded with rhinestones. After thirty-six months of age, no waving or blowing kisses. *Sportswear:* This is a garment of your choice but should be dress sportswear such as a jumpsuit . . . something they would wear when dressing up, but not sports related. Black is a very good fashion color now. It is permissible in all age groups if the color is becoming to the contestant. *Braces and Missing Teeth:* This is just a part of growing up, and as long as the contestant smiles and acts naturally, you are not to count off. . . . This same principle applies to scratches and similar childhood mishaps. We expect our judges to conduct themselves in a ladylike (gentlemanly) fashion at all times. Judges, no drinking at any time while you are at this pageant. No exceptions. You must keep in mind that this is a children's pageant and conduct yourselves accordingly.

In a stroller in the lobby was Nina from Montgomery, who had a tiny pink face and tiny gold earrings and a scramble of fine red hair. Her pageant dress was still on its hanger. She was napping in a pink sleep suit and a pair of Tweetie Bird shoes. Her mother, Kris Ragsdale, had a long dark braid and a steady, sobering gaze. While she talked, she moved Nina's stroller back and forth, the way you move a vacuum cleaner. Kris told me that she was eighteen and Nina was eight months old. She'd got into pageants this past winter, when she took Nina to the Jefferson Davis Pageant and the Christmas Angel Pageant in Montgomery at the urging of a friend. Kris had never been in a pageant when she was a kid. She lived mostly in foster homes or on her own since she was little, and she got married when she was sixteen. Her husband, James, was dressed in a loose, heavy-metal-band T-shirt and an Orlando Magic hat, and he said he worked in Montgomery as a saw sharpener. "He's got a pretty good job," Kris said, rocking the stroller. "Still, I mean, we can hardly save a penny." Until recently, Kris and James shared an apartment with James's ex-girlfriend, James's little son, David, and James's ex-girlfriend's daughter, to save on rent. It cost thirty-five dollars just to enter today's beauty competition, and there were extra fees to enter the contests for Most Photogenic, Most

Beautiful, Best Dress, Dream Girl, and Western Wear. There was also the Supreme Special — fifty dollars for all categories except Dream Girl and Western Wear. The fees for national pageants are higher. It costs a hundred and seventy-five dollars to register for the Southern Charm national, and between fifty and a hundred dollars to enter each special category, like Superstar Baby, Talent, Additional Talent, and Southern Belle. Kris said she'd bought the Supreme Special for Nina today. "You save money with the Supreme," she explained. "You don't get the Western Wear, but we don't do Western Wear with her yet anyway. The hats are too big for her." She lifted Nina out of the stroller and started changing her carefully into a stiff royal blue dress. "My mom got this for me," Kris said. "It was guess how much. Sixty dollars reduced to forty."

A woman nearby who heard us talking came over and said to Kris, "Honey, you have to meet Joni Deal. She rents out all sorts of dresses and Western clothes and everything. She'll rent you something nice for the pageants." The woman was here with her granddaughter Rhiannon, who was named for a Fleetwood Mac song and was three years old and big for her age.

Rhiannon had been in dozens of pageants and usually won everything except fashion. "We're doing something about that, though," her grandmother said. "We've got something really nice now for her dress. We're not talking about a Kathie Lee off-the-rack-from-Wal-Mart dress, either. I bought her a plain old dress, and then I went to the bridal section at a fabric store and bought a whole lot of trim and beading, and I got out that glue gun and did it myself." She looked at Kris and then said, "For us, losing is not an option."

"If we take Nina to the nationals, we're going to have to get her something that's more elegant," James said. "Something more frilly. The judges kill for frilly." In the meantime, Kris said, they had to save for future entry fees, although James hopes they will be able to find a local business that will sponsor Nina; someone told him that a business could claim beauty pageant fees as a tax deduction. He mentioned that both Nina and David, his little boy, had been offered modeling contracts. "It sounded good," he said, "but it cost about six hundred and fifty dollars just to sign up, and then you had to buy all the makeup and the modeling kit, too, so we decided not to do it." He brightened for a moment. "Something good is definitely going to happen for Nina and David, I think," he said. "Nina's got the pageants, and my ex-girlfriend's talking to some guy right now at Extra Model Management who says he thinks he might be able to get a sitcom for David. That would really be great, but I think it would mean moving to New York, and I don't know how I feel about moving."

"It's hard doing pageants, because of the money, but it's worth it," Kris said. "I mean, everybody likes to show off their daughter, right? It's fun for us, and she really enjoys it. It's mother-daughter time, and I know someday we won't have that as much. We're putting all her pageant pictures and scorecards in a scrapbook so she can have it, and someday she'll be able to see it and all her trophies and say, 'Gee, I did that!' It gives her something she can be proud of."

The pageant was about to start, and Kris stood up and attached a bow to Nina's wisps of hair. Nina didn't have enough hair to hold a regular barrette, so Kris had devised something clever with a piece of a zipper she'd cut from a Ziploc bag. She said she realized that some people might not like pageants, because they thought children shouldn't be exposed to competition this early in their lives, but she and James thought it would be good for Nina — it would give her a head start, especially if Nina wanted to try for Miss America someday. Kris said, "I know it's a lot of pressure, but, I mean, you know, you're under some kind of pressure your whole entire life."

Darlene likes her pageants to start with the babies, because they're at their best in the morning. "You have to do it that way," she said. "Babies just will not put up with an all-day pageant." The room for the competition looked festive. A blue-and-white Southern Charm banner was hanging on the back wall, and beside it was a table loaded with crowns and trophies of all different sizes. The crowns were as big as birthday cakes and were studded with rhinestones. The biggest ones cost almost two hundred dollars apiece. "When Becky was in pageants, she was always getting these so-so crowns," Darlene had complained to me. "I don't want that reputation, so I spend a fortune on my crowns."

The judges were two big-boned women with layered haircuts and soft faces. For a few minutes, they murmured to each other and then looked at Stacie with solemn expressions and nodded. The mothers brought their babies forward one by one and held them facing out toward the judges, fluffing the babies' skirts into meringues of chiffon that billowed up and over the mothers' arms and the babies' dangling legs. Displayed this way, the babies looked weightless and relaxed and sublime, suspended in midair. The judges studied them and scored them in the individual categories while Stacie read introductions: "This is Cheyenne. Her hobbies are playing and cooing. . . . Her favorite food is pears. . . . Her favorite TV show is *Barney*. She is sponsored today by her friends and family. . . . This is Kayle. . . . Her favorite food is macaroni and cheese. . . . Her hobby is exploring new-found things. . . . This is Taylor. . . . She loves horseback riding and taking her baby cat, Patches, out for walks." One baby picked her nose during her moment at the judging table. Another flailed her arms at the balloons floating above the judges and started to cry. Kris bounced Nina and clucked at her until she finally cracked a gummy smile, but just at that moment both judges happened to look away. Everyone in the audience was standing and waving and aiming toss-away paper cameras at the babies onstage, and every time a camera flashed, the crowns on the table flashed, too.

The older girls were divided into age groups of twelve to twenty-three months, twenty-four to thirty-five months, three- and four-year-olds together, five- and six-year-olds, and so on. Southern Charm accepts girls up to twenty-one years old, but the oldest girl at the Prattville pageant was probably seven. These older children walked onstage by themselves, and some of them even turned the way they were supposed to when they got to the masking-tape X's, and a few remembered to do "pretty hands" and "pretty feet" and the grimacing pageant-girl smile. The two-year-olds tended to wander. A blonde from Eclectic named Kendall stood twirling a piece of her hair around her finger and then roamed off the stage. Her mother was standing next to me, and she said that this would probably be Kendall's last pageant because she hated wearing dresses and was much happier barrel-racing her pony at home.

The Southern Charm rules say, "Remember, if you coach from the audience, the child will not have eye contact with the judges and they will deduct points for not having eye contact." In spite of that, nearly all the parents were on their feet during the rest of the pageant, making wild hand signals to their daughters that meant "Smile" and "Blow a kiss at the judge" and "Smile much bigger." They pushed to the front of the room, nearly leaning over the judges' shoulders. It was as if someone had set them on a table and then tipped it forward. Just a few minutes after the pageant started, hardly anyone was left sitting in the back of the room.

Darlene has forty thousand people on her mailing list, and they are spread out all over the nation. JonBenet Ramsey was one of those names, although she never particularly stood out. Darlene says that in spite of what the papers have said, not that many people in the pageant world had heard of JonBenet until she got killed. Right after the murder, Darlene looked up JonBenet's name on her computer and deleted it, so that the Ramseys wouldn't get any upsetting Southern Charm mail.

Darlene and Jerry Burgess live about ten miles from downtown Jackson, in an old farmhouse that has been renovated since the days when their daughter, Becky, was at home. (Becky is married and lives in

Nashville, where she is studying to go to medical school, and she has a two-year-old daughter, who is just starting on the pageant circuit.) Now the Burgess house is pure pageant. In the outbuildings is a trophy shop and a silk-screening shop where the banners are made and a photography studio where Jerry shoots portfolios of contestants. In the basement is Glitz & Glamour, Darlene's mail-order pageant dress business, and in the front room are four computers containing all the mailing lists, and eight video machines for copying Jerry's official tapes of the pageants, and Federal Express labels and boxes for the dozen or so Glitz & Glamour dresses and Southern Charm videos they ship out every day.

The phone rings all day without stopping, so it is nearly impossible to have an uninterrupted conversation with Darlene. One of the days I was in Jackson, I asked her why she thought people outside the pageant world objected to it so adamantly. "I don't know why they even have an opinion about it at all," she said. "I look at pageants like I look at any other hobby, like golf. I sure wouldn't hit a little white ball around on a lawn, and I don't know why anyone else would want to, but that's their business and not mine. Hold on a minute.

"Hello, Glitz. . . . Yes, this is Darlene Burgess. . . . Okay, I can send you an entry form. How'd you find out about us? . . . Well, if you want to go to New York, that's a mininational. Who's crowning in New York? . . . Let me think. . . . Oh, fiddle! Jerry, who's crowning in New York? Well, I can't remember. . . . So now give me your name and address."

Vicki Whitehead, who works at Glitz & Glamour part-time, came upstairs. "Darlene, I have a lady on the phone who has an eight-month-old she says is really tiny and she needs something very dainty for her to wear. And do we have any Ultrasuede in an animal print in pink and black? Because I have a lady who's dying for some."

Another call for Darlene: "I see. . . . Do you have videos of her in pageants? . . . Okay, send it and I'd be glad to critique it for you." Darlene covered the mouthpiece and said to me, "I'm offering to do it because this lady's up in Illinois and really needs help. They're not too pageant wise up in places like Illinois. I really think the kids up north are afraid to compete with the kids down south. I remember once

82

Becky said to me, 'Mom, the New York kids are beautiful, but they don't know how to model and they don't know how to dress.' "

When Darlene had a break from the phone, she said that nearly every day since JonBenet's murder she has been called by some reporter. So have most of the best-known coaches and the owners of the other big pageant systems. Since JonBenet, Darlene has had mothers tell her they weren't going to come to the pageants if reporters would be there, and some mothers have said they had stopped answering their phones because they were sick of being asked to comment on the murder. She is rankled by how dismissive nonpageant people are of everything that she loves about pageants and of how much they mean to these little girls. Some people in pageants have difficult lives and work hard all the time and lose out on a lot, but on any Sunday at a pageant somewhere they have their chance to win. This seems so obvious that Darlene thinks there must be some other reason that pageants have been so maligned. She has finally decided that people who don't appreciate children's pageants probably just don't have their own pretty little girls.

From all appearances, Darlene has been a very successful entrepreneur. It happens that most of her state directors are women, and many other pageant systems and pageant-related businesses, like the dress shops, are owned by women. Some of the best-known coaches are women, too. It seems odd that these are the very same women who are certain that a girl's best path in life is to learn how to look good onstage. It's as if they had never noticed that they've made something of themselves by relying on other talents.

The first day I was in Jackson, Darlene and I sat in her living room to watch some tapes of last year's Southern Charm national finals, while Jerry was in the other room labeling FedEx boxes with Glitz dresses inside, bound for Irving, Texas, and Lawrenceville, Georgia, and Leesville, Louisiana. To me, all the kids on the tape looked the same — cute, awkward, stiff in their frothy dresses, a little uncertain when they got to the X's on the stage. Most of them stared anxiously at their mothers for directions. Darlene used to judge pageants, and she still has a judge's eye: As we watched the tape, she pointed out winners and losers and which girls had pushy coaches and which girls were wearing makeup that didn't do justice to their skin tone. "This girl, she's beautiful, but her sportswear doesn't do a thing for her, it's too boxy," Darlene pointed out. "I don't like this one's hair all sprayed up like that. I swear, she looks like a Pentecostal! Oh, here's the Southern Belle category. You have to wear something that's historically accurate. My judges get so ticky about it that they'll come up onstage and check your dress and make sure you don't have any zippers. . . . Now, look at this baby with her belt sagging. I don't know why these mothers don't realize that a little Velcro under the belt would hold it up. Babies don't have any hips and they have that little potbelly, and a belt just isn't going to stay up on its own."

In her personal philosophy, Darlene doesn't like too much eyeliner, and this year she's going to allow only classic Miss America–style modeling in the Swimwear competition. She blames coaches for teaching sexy poses to the girls. "Ten years ago, it wasn't like this," she said. "Now, with the coaches, things are getting out of control." On her granddaughter, Shelby, she likes to see simple makeup and a gorgeous dress, and since Shelby is doing well, this appears to be working. But some girls do need help to be really big in pageants, according to Darlene. They need coaching, they need advice on their clothes, and, in a few exceptional circumstances, they might even need surgery, although as a rule she doesn't approve. "There was one girl, about thirteen, and it was a special case," Darlene said. "She was a very pretty girl, except she had a really big old honker and it just killed her in the pageants. Even if she hadn't been a pageant child, she was actually better off with a new nose." She has seen kids who are miserable but have been pushed onstage by their mothers, and mothers who yell at their kids when they don't win, and kids falling asleep on their feet because the pageants went on late into the night. "I don't compete the kids at night, but some pageants do," she said. "I remember once Becky had to do her talent at one in the morning. One in the morning! She was exhausted! But the pageant directors insisted on going late. I think that's child abuse."

While we talked, Darlene got up to check the chicken in the oven and the fresh bread rising in her bread maker for lunch. Before we ate, she wanted to show me the winners' speeches at last year's Southern Charm nationals. On the tape, a knock-kneed girl with tawny curls placed a rhine-stone Supreme Queen crown on another girl's head. Then the new Supreme Queen started her speech: "I want to say thanks to the Lord Jesus Christ, and thanks to Jerry and Darlene, the directors of the pag-eant. . . . I want people to know that pag-eants are about the whole girl, not about who has the best makeup and hair."

By the time the Western Wear competition began in Prattville, it was the end of the afternoon. The room was chaotic: People were coming in and out with snacks from a vending machine outside; a lot of the ba-bies were fretting, and a few were yelling as if it were the end of the world. Stacie cast her eye on one of the loudest babies and said into her microphone, "Sounds like we got someone who's not ready for Western Wear!" I was sitting next to this particular loud baby, who was on her mother's lap, and a man behind us was the loud baby's grandfather. He tapped me on the shoulder. "What do you think of this?" he said. "I mean, they're exploiting these kids! Dressing them up, keeping them up all day!"

"Daddy, you're supposed to be supporting me, not criticizing me," the baby's mother said. "Look, it's our first pageant and probably our last, but I think it's good to try things. I don't know how I feel about spending so much money. But I like it. It's fun. It's just . . . maybe she's not ready."

She glanced at her daughter, who was about a year old and was dressed in a satin cowgirl outfit. The outfit looked scratchy. The baby was squirming and weeping. The man said, "Come on, look at her crying, Jeannie! I think it's crazy. And it's a waste of money besides."

Stacie Brumit had told me that she'd seen "a lot of mamas dragging their babies kicking and screaming onto the stage." She doesn't like that sort of thing, but she says that some children need extra encouragement. Even Brianna Brumit, who is a veteran, pulls back a little before she has to go onstage. "Once I get her up there, though, she's totally different," Stacie said. "She's just in another world. And it's special for me. For Brianna to go up and win Queen, that's the best thing in the world to me."

Nina Ragsdale didn't win Most Photogenic; when Kris asked the judges later, they told her that Nina's pictures needed to show more personality. Nina didn't win Dream Girl, which is based on pure facial beauty; that went to a baby with a peachy face and dark, sleepy eyes. She didn't win Most Beautiful, which is subtly different from Dream Girl, and she didn't win Best Dress; the judges said that blue didn't work for her and that Kris should get her something in turquoise or white. Then the final categories were announced. Nina didn't win Queen or Supreme Queen, and when there were hardly any prizes left to be given out, my heart started sinking, but then Nina was named first runner-up and got a medium-size trophy, and Kris had a moment in which to display her with the trophy on the stage. The baby who won Supreme Queen got a trophy that was taller than any of the children at the pageant. Someone called out, "Honey, if you live in a trailer, you're in trouble! You won't be able to get that into your home!"

I went back to Alabama a few weeks later to see Nina in another pageant. This one was also at the Prattville Holiday Inn. The pageant was called Li'l American Beauty, and the trophies and the crowns and the backdrop were different, but the feeling in the air was the same. I recognized some of the kids from Southern Charm. There were only about a dozen girls, so the judging went fast, and just as at the first pageant, I could hardly bear to watch the crowning. Kris Ragsdale stood up there with Nina, who was asleep, her bow sliding out of her hair. The other mothers were also lined up with their babies, shifting them around in their arms like bags of groceries, and they had a little tightness in their faces as they waited to hear what the judges had to say. Most of the babies had curled up and were lost in the folds of their puffy dresses, and suddenly all I could really see were the mothers, wearing their plain outfits and their plain makeup, their husbands and parents standing a few feet away, ready to take the picture they were all waiting for, of their beautiful daughters being crowned.

Party Line

If you're one of those people who have three phone lines at home, plus a pager, plus a CDMA trimode cellphone with a Web browser and SMS, and you still want to upgrade your telecommunications system, you should meet Pat and Jim Bannick. Better yet, you should give them a call. Chances are they won't be on the phone.

"We're not really phone people," Pat said when I called her the other day at her home in Dimondale, Michigan. "By the way, I couldn't believe Jim answered when you called. He never answers the phone. Once, I bought him one of those nice phones that you can walk around with —"

"A cellphone?"

"Yes, I think that's it. The kind so you don't need a long cord on it?"

"Oh, you mean a cordless phone?"

"That's right. The kind without a cord. Anyway, a while ago I got Jim one of those, but he wouldn't even look at it, so I ended up returning it."

The Bannicks are among the last people

in the state of Michigan, and possibly in the entire known universe, who still have their telephone service on a party line. A party line is not a current telecommunications option. SBC Ameritech, the Bannicks' phone company, has only a handful of them left, all of them in Michigan. (The Nevada division took its last party line out of service in 2001; the Southwestern Bell division shut down its last one in 1996; and Pacific Bell took all but one of its party lines out of service in 1997.)

Party lines are not to be confused with chat lines, party planners, or escort services: They are a prehistoric phone technology of copper-loop circuits that can be shared by as many as twenty telephones in separate locations, predating by several decades such advancements as three-way conferencing and the quack-ringing Mallard Duck Phone. On a typical party line, all the phones in all the houses sharing the line have the same phone number, and all the phones in all the houses ring whenever a call comes in for any one of them. Each household would be assigned a distinctive ring, so you could tell if the bell was tolling for you or for another one of the houses on your line. "Ours was a three-ringer," Pat said. "Or was it first a two-ringer? No, I think it was a three-ringer, and then we were a two-ringer."

"What year did you get your phone?"

"It was 1955," Pat said. "It was the year that we built the house."

"In 1955? That was the year Mary L. Kayes, of Dutchess County, New York, was convicted of refusing to yield her party line to someone wanting to report a fire."

"My goodness."

"What was it like sharing a phone?"

"Well, honestly, it was awful. We'd never get to use the phone, because someone was always on it. Plus, the phone rang and rang and rang all the time, since you had ten families sharing it. We did get into counting the rings, though. You'd hear the phone and you'd stop and wait and count to see if it was for you. That was kind of fun."

"Did you know that in 1950 three-quarters of all the phone service in the United States was by party line?"

"No," Pat said.

"Pat, can you hold on a minute? I've got a call on my other line."

"I suppose so."

"Okay, I'm back. Sorry. So you were saying it was hard to share the phone."

"Well, it was a pain. When we were on a ten-party line, you could hardly get a word in. And whenever we would pick up the phone to use it, there would already be someone on it. We would pick up the receiver and hear voices —"

"I'm sorry, I have another call again. Can you hold for one second?"

"I guess so."

"Okay, I'm back. So you were saying you'd pick up the phone and listen sometimes."

"Sure," Pat said. "I wouldn't listen a long time, just for a minute or so. But the same thing would happen to us. We'd be on a call and suddenly someone would pick it up and hang up a bunch of times, so there would be click-click-clicking the whole time you were on the phone. This one lady would listen for a long time before she'd hang up."

"Did people observe any kind of etiquette about party lines? Did they observe the Emily Post suggestion that if you share a party line and you have an emergency, you should pick up the phone and first say, 'Emergency,' in a loud voice and then say, 'Our barn is on fire'?"

"No, nothing special like that," Pat said.

"Did you know who any of the other people on your line were?"

"We called once and tried to find out who they were, but the phone company wouldn't tell us. We could tell that a lot of the families we shared the line with had teenagers. We were getting pretty disgusted, because they would never get off the phone. Sometimes we'd have to make an important call and they'd be on for ages, and finally we'd pick up the phone and say, 'Can you please just get off for five minutes and let us make the call, and then you can have the phone back?' And usually they'd say no. This one lady in particular, she would say, 'Well, I can't get off. I'm in the middle of a long-distance call.' "

"You said that the number of people on the line went from ten to four or five?"

"In the sixties or seventies, we were down to sharing with just four other families. Then it was just two, and then finally just one. Now we have a party line, but we're on it all by ourselves. Every once in a while, the phone company — it used to be Michigan Bell, but now it's Ameritech, I think — the phone company calls us and says, 'Well, guess what, we can give you a nice new line of your own,' but we tell them we don't want it! This is fine for us. And it's cheap. We pay fifteen dollars a month and that's it. We can't have an answering machine or anything on it, for some reason, but that doesn't really matter. The only problem we have isn't with the party line; it's with our phone. We have a rotary phone, and I don't know what to do when you get these recordings saying, 'Push this number, push that button.' We don't have any buttons. When I really need to use a Touch-Tone, I go to my mother's. She's ninety years old, but she has a Touch-Tone."

"How many phones do you have?"

"Are you kidding? Just one."

This was when Jim got on.

"I don't really know why we got a phone to begin with," he said. "I think Pat wanted one. I didn't grow up with a telephone. The first time I ever used one was after I graduated from high school. I'm seventy-three, and I grew up without electricity or running water or even a refrigerator, and certainly without a phone."

"Do you use the phone now?"

"I have a need occasionally."

"And what kind of equipment do you have now?"

"We used to have a black one, I believe, and now we have an ivory one."

Jim then recounted the incident of the telephone without a cord with some discomfort. "I think Pat tried one of those touch phones or wireless phones," he said. "I don't know where she secured it, but I think she took it back."

Pat is more open-minded. "I was with my sister a while ago, and while we drove around she used her cellphone in the car, and it was great," she said after Jim had turned the equipment back over to her. "The trouble is, if I had a cellphone, I'd probably call people."

"Do you wish you'd kept the phone without the cord?"

"Yes, definitely. See, I thought it would be nice to have when Jim's out in the garage working, and it's time for dinner, and I have to scream and yell like a banshee to let him know that dinner's ready. I thought if he had the phone, I could just call him."

"So are you still screaming and yelling?"

"No, we've got something better now," Pat said. "We just installed a really nice dinner bell."

Madame President

Tiffanie Lewis, the current student body president of Martin Luther King Jr. High School in Manhattan, wrote a campaign slogan for herself and her running mate, Crystal Belle, that went something like "If You're Not Down with Voting for Tiffanie and Crystal, Then I Have Two Words for You: Suck It." The slogan would certainly have been popular, since "Suck It" is the motto of the eminent wrestler Stone Cold Steve Austin, or maybe of the eminent wrestlers D-Generation X — at the time Tiffanie was telling me this story she couldn't remember which — and in either case it would have thrown some votes her way. But she didn't use the "Suck It" slogan. She decided that it was too rude, which is not at all what she and Crystal are like as candidates, or as people, and not at all the image they wanted to put forward in connection with Martin Luther King Jr. High School. When you're proud of your school but know that it once had a reputation for chaos and violence, and is stuck with the nickname Horror High, you pay attention to these things. Tiffanie ended up using three other slogans. One was "Time for Some Women to Be in Charge!," which referred to the fact that all past student body presidents of King had been male. She had also considered pointing out that she and Crystal would be the first black students to run the school in four years. But "we thought that wasn't a good approach," she says. "I mean, everyone's supposed to be united." Another slogan was "Drop the Zero and Get Down with the Heroes." This was an oblique poke at two other presidential candidates, who had academic and attendance problems and were gaining support by arguing that they were better representatives of the average, imperfect King student than Tiffanie and Crystal, who came to school and earned good grades. Tiffanie's most popular poster had a colorful background and the slogan "And You Don't Know? Vote for Tiffanie Lewis and Crystal Belle." The line "And You Don't Know?" was the refrain from a hit song by rapper Cam'Ron; it didn't actually mean anything, but everyone loved it.

When Tiffanie talks about winning the election, she chokes up. "I'm a very emotional person," she says. "I don't know why, but I just am. I cry at a lot of things. I cried at *Titanic*, and I cried at the lunar eclipse." She cried like mad when she found out that she had won the presidential election. I almost made her cry when we first met and I mistakenly wrote her name down as "Tiffany," like the jewelry store, rather than "Tiffanie."After she corrected me, I asked if people made that mistake often. "All the time," she said, sounding melancholy.

Tiffanie is not a tall person, but she has a big body and a cute, booming voice. Her face is sweet and bright and has absolutely no angles. She keeps her hair chin length and chemically straightened and usually wears it down, but when she sweeps it up in a mini-chignon, she looks regal and much older than seventeen. I spent last Christmas Day with her family, and her mother and her sisters and her aunts are all beautiful, and I got the feeling that Tiffanie grew up being told that she was good-looking, but, more important, that she was smart. Her mother, Cynthia Tillman, is a supervisor at an insurance company. Tiffanie doesn't know much about her biological father. Her stepfather, Anthony, is a store detective, but he isn't working currently. Their house in Brooklyn is the first one the Tillmans have ever owned. It is a small two-family, with a little spit of a front yard, on a tranquil side street in Canarsie, a working-class neighborhood that used to be strictly Italian and Jewish but now has a growing black population. They had been eager to leave their apartment in Crown Heights, because the building had got run-down and drugs were sold on their street.

Everything inside the Tillmans' house is gleaming and large — a large television set, a large dining table, large chairs — squeezed into smallish rooms. Tiffanie's room has an oversize black lacquer bedroom set, a computer, and very little space for anything else. Because she is president of the student body, head of the school Step Team, and taking extra courses to prepare for her Regents' exams, Tiffanie spends very little time at home. When she is home, she is often in her room, e-mailing her friends or talking to them on the phone. A lot of her friends are boys, but she doesn't have a boyfriend and says that this is because she doesn't have time. She says that she isn't that interested in guys right now anyway, but the most annoyed I've ever seen her was when someone suggested that her favorite male R&B group was gay.

President Lewis is self-possessed, and often quite bossy, as in: "Are you-all going to help me move the tables, or are you-all going to just sit there?" (To her cabinet members, before a Student Life meeting.)

"Crystal, I really, really like you, and you know you're my homegirl, but we got to get back on topic right now." (To her vice president, who had lapsed during a meeting into a discussion about reading her poetry at the talent show.)

"First, how about you say the idea, and then we'll decide if it's bangin'." (To the chairperson of the school store, who announced that he had a really bangin' idea.)

"So you're on the seven-year plan? Let me ask you, Chickenhead: Are you proud of that?" (To a student known familiarly as Chickenhead, who asserted that he knew more about King than she did, because, as he had put it, "I been at this school since before you were in eighth grade.")

One recent school day, I visited Tiffanie at the student affairs office at King, and she told me the story of her campaign. "It was very controversial," she said. Her voice started inching up her throat. "First, my friend Wellinthon and I were going to run together, but then he decided to run with Crystal, and everyone thought Crystal should run for president, because she's such a beautiful person and everyone loves her, but she didn't want all the pressure, so then Crystal and I decided to run together, and, oh God, candidates were tearing down each other's posters and writing obscenities on them, and it just got very intense."

A young man who had been sitting nearby listening to a Walkman took off his headphones and said, "Yo, I was Tiff's campaign manager."

"Robert, you were not," Tiffanie said. "I mean, okay, you were my manager at the end. But, first, Cherie Starling was my campaign manager. Then I had to fire her, because she was slacking." Robert frowned and then told me that his name was Robert Benton and that he was the chairperson of the school store and also a master rapper named Spade, and that he was available for interviews. A moment later, Cherie walked into the room. Tiffanie waved her over and said, "Hey, Cherie, remember when I fired you?" Cherie is one of her many best friends and is now the chairperson of the School Improvement Committee.

"You did?" Cherie asked. She looked puzzled.

"From my campaign, girlfriend," Tiffanie said. "Remember? You were slacking."

"Oh, yeah," Cherie answered. She shrugged her shoulders and glanced at the wall clock. "Come on, Madame President. Let's go bust it out in gym."

There are nearly three thousand students at Martin Luther King Jr. High School, but on the best possible day fewer than three hundred of them will turn out to vote in the student government elections. The others probably don't remember to, or don't care, or don't get around to it because of a million different reasons, like schoolwork or job work or family problems or love trouble; many of them might just assume that it doesn't matter if they vote or not. King is one of the biggest high schools in New York City. It is in a gloomy rectangular brown brick building resting on an elevated concrete deck at Amsterdam Avenue and Sixty-sixth Street — a structure that in an architectural drawing might have looked monumental but in real life looks like a giant rusting lunchbox teetering on a rock. Maybe because it is set so high above the sidewalk and so far back from the street, it is almost invisible; I had walked by it at least once a month for ten years without even noticing it. Fiorello H. LaGuardia High School of Music & Art and Performing Arts is right across Sixty-fifth Street, at sidewalk level. King is also within earshot of Lincoln Center, but it is more attuned to the odd, lonesome neighborhood of looming windowless buildings with sealed loading docks and metal doors to the west. The area has always been a hodgepodge. The 1955 Manhattan Land Book map shows a wide band of railroad sidings along the river, an enormous Consolidated Edison property, blocks of dinky brick row houses, a College of Pharmacy, a High School of Commerce, New York City Public School 94, and a flop called Hotel Marie Antoinette. By 1976, when Martin Luther King Jr. High School was built on some of the Con Ed property, much of the area had been razed to make room for Lincoln Center and the American Red Cross headquarters and the eventual site of LaGuardia High.

LaGuardia is one of New York City's prestigious specialized schools: Interested students have to pass a competitive audition to get in. King is a general high school. Any student in Manhattan is eligible to attend, and students from the other New York City boroughs can apply. As it happens, thousands of high school students who live right nearby choose not to go to King — they attend private schools or other New York City public schools, including the specialized schools — and many kids at King come from far away. Tiffanie, for instance, lives an hour and a half by subway from King, but she wanted to go to high school in Manhattan rather than in Brooklyn and heard that King had a good science program. A classmate of hers who lives an hour away, in Flatbush, told me she applied because she liked the idea of going to a school named after Reverend King. Someone else, from the Bronx, wanted to come to King because her best friend was enrolled, and a few others said they were at King because their own neighborhood schools were scary.

According to the most recent New York City Board of Education annual school report, for the 1997–1998 school year, more than half the students at King are African American, forty percent are Hispanic, and four percent are Asian. Only one percent of the school's 1997–1998 student population was white — compared with fifteen percent citywide — and Tiffanie said she didn't think there were any white students at King anymore. She did remember one from last year, a guy whose name was Lucas, and he was Polish or something like that, but definitely white.

King has never really been a lucky place. A swimming pool built as part of the gym facilities couldn't open because of flubbed engineering. A small Martin Luther King Jr. museum on the plaza in front of the school was shut down. There were fights, gang rumbles, declining enrollment, rumors that King students were harassing the junior ballerinas at Lincoln Center's School of American Ballet. In 1990, a student was shot in the stomach at lunchtime. In 1997, a thirteen-year-old girl was sexually assaulted in the boys' bathroom, after another female student ordered her to perform oral sex on several boys. The number of "incidents" and suspensions at King is double the citywide average. About ten years ago, King became one of the many New York City public schools to install metal detectors, and since last fall all students have been forbidden to leave the building during the day. At the same time, there are kids earning scholarships to college and outscoring students at similar schools in New York. This year, there is a popular and enthusiastic new principal, Ronald Williams Wells; and all the time there are toy drives and penny drives and bake sales and student committees decorating the halls and the lunchroom, and there are fashion shows and cheerleader tryouts and student elections — the kinds of cheerful, innocent things that you always picture when you think about high school but that are hard to imagine when what you hear about a school makes it sound like the end of the world.

One recent Wednesday, I went to King to sit in on a student government meeting. It was a wickedly cold, blowy day, and the big concrete plaza in front of the school was bleak and vacant. The front door creaked open. A woman walked out, followed by a dallying teenager in a red puffball coat.

"Honey, I just want you to graduate," the mother was saying. "Please. That's all I want. Please." I found Tiffanie in her senior economics class, taught by Mr. Borak, a wiry man with grizzled hair and rounded shoulders who has been teaching at King for twenty-three years.

The class was studying free enterprise. On the chalkboard, Mr. Borak had written,

"Explain the reasoning for the turnaround in the male black-white wage gap between the 1980s and the 1990s." There were about thirty students in the class; a few stared into middle space and a few were doodling in their books, but the rest were busy debating the difference between a stockholder and a shareholder. It was noisy but contained, like popcorn. At one point, a student chewing gum blew a huge bubble. "Please cancel the bubble," Mr. Borak warned. "This is an economics class. We don't want any bursting bubbles."

The weekly cabinet meeting is attended by the four student body officers and the committee chairpeople. Today was the monthly Student Life meeting, which meant that this group was joined by the principal; the head of school security, Sergeant Murray; and an assistant principal. The meeting wasn't scheduled to start for an hour, but there were already half a dozen kids in the student affairs room. Kiesha Lawhorne, the chairperson of the Hospitality Committee, and Shakira Jones, the student body secretary, were working on computers along one wall; two kids were listening to a new Jay-Z CD by sharing a single set of headphones, one ear apiece. Someone else was braiding cornrows into the hair of a student. A recent graduate had also come by to visit. He introduced himself as Osiris Flores and said that he had been president of King last year and was now a freshman at Ithaca College. "Being president," he said, shaking his head slowly, "it was beautiful."

The student government office is bright and cluttered and randomly furnished. A long white erasable calendar on the side wall listed the month's student government–sponsored events: Pep Rally, Homecoming Game, Twin Day, Mismatch Day, Decade Day, Any Celebrity Day, and Pajama Day. After a few minutes, Tiffanie breezed in. She was wearing a DKNY T-shirt and DKNY jeans and had a couple of books in her hands. "I'm hungry," she announced. She was in a great mood because she had heard the night before that she had won a partial scholarship to Pennsylvania State University. Her other first choice for college is Spelman, a predominantly black school in Atlanta, but getting the money for Penn State was big news.

She saw Crystal and hugged her. Crystal is a slender girl with long, glamorous eyelashes and a husky laugh. She recently was awarded a full scholarship to Middlebury College.

"Can I tell you something, Tiff?" Crystal asked. "You are just a beautiful person." Behind Crystal was Nesia Mathias, the student parliamentarian. She is another one of Tiffanie's best friends and had been planning to drop over the day I visited Tiffanie and her family.

"Sorry I didn't show up," she said. "I had to go with my daddy. He was meeting his daddy for the first time in his life. You know how that is."

"I'm hungry," Tiffanie said again.

"Okay, we ordering right this minute, Mr. President," someone said.

"Let's get on it, people," Tiffanie said. "You all are chilling and being late for the meeting, and that's mad rude."

The student being cornrowed nodded at her. "That's right, baby, you're the president," he said. "You enforce your laws."

"Don't you be braiding hair in here," Tiffanie said. "I told you, you can't be doing that in here. This is the student government room. I'm being mean to you, but it's for a good cause."

Ordering lunch became a feature of student government meetings when King became a completely closed campus. Since students could no longer go out to get lunch, they either had to eat in the lunchroom, which was a madhouse, or they could order food from nearby restaurants and have it delivered to them at school. The restaurant delivery boys sign in with the police officer on security detail and bring the food to the kids. There was hardly a fact of contemporary New York City school life that I found more astonishing than this. Student government officials at Martin Luther King Jr. High School seemed to favor Chinese food, particularly chicken with broccoli and pork fried rice, and they tip modestly but not pitifully. That afternoon, they argued briefly over which of the two nearby Chinese places they should order from and then scraped together the necessary money by figuring out who was rich that day and who wasn't, and by the time that was finished the food had arrived.

Mr. Wells, the principal, strode in. He is strapping and handsome, in his early forties, and he has a glossy brown shaved head, fine features, and deep dimples. His smile is lingering and foxy. This is his twentieth year in education and his first at King. Before coming to King, he was assistant principal at Queens Gateway to Health Sciences High School, in Jamaica. He was raised in New York and went to high school in Far

Rockaway, a scruffy beach community that was disintegrating while he was growing up. He never ran for student government, but he participated in lots of school events. I once asked him which he had been most involved in, and he said that when he was a senior a girl in his class was raped and murdered and he organized a march of a majority of the student body in protest. He is extremely charming, even when he is doing uncharming things, like suspending students, which he does with some frequency. One day, I watched him cajole three sour-looking freshmen whom he was sending home for fighting. "I want you to know something," he said, looking each of them hard in the face, one at a time. "I am going to take good care of your ID cards while you're gone. I'm going to keep them right here with me" — he patted his chest pocket — "and I promise you I won't let anything happen to them."

"But Mr. —" one kid grumbled.

"I hear you," Mr. Wells said. The kids realized by then that they were beaten and started out of the room. "I'll be seeing you soon."

When Mr. Wells walked into the student affairs office, everyone stopped eating. "Are we doing this, people?" he asked. "I understand there is a meeting going on here." One of the electronic things he was wearing — a walkie-talkie, a pager, and a cellphone — bleated: "King One to Base, we're at North Four. Do you copy?"

"Copy," Mr. Wells said. He turned to Tiffanie and said, "Madame President, I have to speak to you about your attendance at gym."

"I know," she said. "But Mr. Wells —"

"But Ms. Lewis," he said.

By tradition, the student body president runs all meetings except for the Student Life meeting, which is run by the vice president. "The meeting is called to order," Crystal said. "The first issue on the agenda today is school unity. This is on the agenda because a lot of students are saying kids are segregated. Now, is there any way we could start a club or something so we could just talk to each other?"

One of the student representatives raised his hand. "You know, I was walking up the stairs the other day, and I saw this Spanish girl crying and I was, like, Are you all right? And she was, like, No, but thanks for asking. So I think we just got to reach out like that."

Another: "How come Asians don't come

to any of the school parties and Hispanics don't come? Maybe we should hang posters about parties in more languages. How about in Chinese, too? And in French?"

Mr. Wells raised his hand.

"I'd like to recognize Mr. Wells," Crystal said.

"I would respectfully offer these suggestions," Mr. Wells said. His walkie-talkie squawked again, and both he and Sergeant Murray twiddled with their volume control, and then Sergeant Murray excused himself for a moment.

"As I was saying," Mr. Wells went on. "How about a multicultural Sadie Hawkins Day dance on Valentine's Day? By empowering females to do the interaction — that is, to invite a male from another culture to the dance — we could engender some cross-cultural contact. And how about an international food festival?"

"Thank you very much, Mr. Wells," Crystal said solemnly. "Now, bathrooms. Every student complains about the bathrooms. There's no soap most of the time and no paper, and the only bathroom open now is on the second floor, and we're wondering what is the deal?" Sergeant Murray had returned by this point. He explained that the bathrooms had to be patrolled, and he didn't have enough staff to monitor one on each floor. This was a sensitive issue, since King's most notorious recent crime, the gang rape, took place in a fifth-floor bathroom.

They next talked about something called the "sweeps" — the patrolling of the school hallways after the start of each period. Anyone caught without a pass during the sweeps is relocated for the rest of the day in the Attitude Readjustment Center, a dreary room on the lower level of the building. Now, during classes, the halls at King are deserted except for the occasional student dashing downstairs with a bathroom pass. Mr. Wells implemented ARC at the beginning of his term. It is one more partition between the kids at King who are falling away and the kids who are moving ahead. When you are in the student affairs office, planning the Fashion Show and the Talent Show and the mini pep rally for Martin Luther King Jr. Week, it's as if there were no metal detectors in the lobby and no school superintendent politics and nothing but the exigencies of being sixteen or seventeen. I asked Tiffanie how she got along with the kids at King who are always in trouble. "I don't really ever see them," she said. "They're always suspended or in ARC or something. I don't end up having much to do with them." I once stuck my head into ARC, just to see what it was like, and the pent-up annoyance and disaffection and peevishness, the teenage fury of the fifty or so kids inside the room, almost blew me out the door.

The president slams her gavel and then nibbles a piece of Chinese broccoli. "Meeting is called to order," she says. "First of all, Robert. So what's up with the school store?"

ROBERT: "Me and Juanita made a huge effort and cleaned it up. I still don't know what kind of stuff we're going to be selling —"

PRESIDENT: "We need to see more progress in the store. Next issue, school unity. Ibrahim, what's up?"

IBRAHIM: "We'll have Culture Day in May."

PRESIDENT: "Why is it so far away? We don't want to be waiting on this forever. Let's get on this, people."

KIESHA: "In May, I'm gonna be really concentrating on getting outta here. How about if we do another 'Be Easy' week sometime sooner? You know, when we pledge time to be easy and stay calm and love our fellow man, like, not to yell at someone because they stepped on your sneaker."

PRESIDENT: "Okay, let's do 'Be Easy' for Dr. King's birthday. And we should change the morning announcements then, too. Make them really cool. Not real ghetto, just something cool."

ROBERT: "You should be doing them, then. You're the president."

PRESIDENT: "Well, I'm not going to lie to y'all. You all know the truth. Sometimes I'm a little late getting out the door, so sometimes I'm not here exactly on time to do the announcements."

KIESHA: "You ain't lying."

PRESIDENT: "Can I say this, people?" She pauses and looks around the room. "You know what? This is not a perfect world."

All Mixed Up

The people who shop at Sunshine Market, a grocery store in Jackson Heights, Queens, are thin and beautiful. They are also fat and plain, relaxed and frantic, Colombian, Italian, Jewish, Indian, African American, Bolivian, Uruguayan, Vietnamese, young, middle-aged, elderly, rowdy, meek, cheerful, world-weary, rich, and broke. They buy health food. They buy Ding Dongs and Diet Coke. They have just come to America. They have lived in America, in Jackson Heights, in the same apartment, with the same furniture in the same arrangement, for sixty years. They are in a big hurry. They are in no rush and hoping to bump into their neighbors for a chat. They are in minks. They are in their pajamas, wearing stacks of hair curlers and no makeup. They are buying the works for a dinner party. They are buying a Lean Cuisine Chicken Fettucini to eat alone. They come in every single day and buy the same three things: a gallon of bottled water, a banana, a skinless boneless chicken breast. They come in once a week and weave up and down every aisle and arrive at the cash register, exhausted, with a tipsy heap of groceries. They are immigrants hunting for Goya Guanabana Nectar or Manischewitz Low Calorie Borscht or Trappey's Indi-Pep Pepper Sauce. They are immigrants who desire Planters Cheez Balls, Salerno Scooter Pies, Maxwell House Coffee, Chef Boyardee Pac-Man Pasta in Spaghetti Sauce with Mini-Meat Balls, Count Chocula, Pringles potato crisps, Frank Sinatra's Marinara Sauce, Newman's Own Olive Oil and Vinegar Dressing, and a copy of the *Sun* (WORLD'S SMALLEST MOM! SHE'S JUST 34 INCHES TALL — BUT HAS A 6-FOOT SON!). They do their shopping with their own red pushcarts, or with eco-conscious green string bags, or with their napping babies in Graco strollers, in which, if the baby is average size, they can also fit a small package of lean ground beef, half a dozen peaches, and two bars of Dove.

The people who shop at Sunshine Market are in touch with their needs. They march up to Toney Murphy, the store's manager, dozens of times a day and express themselves. This candidness has inspired Herb Spitzer, who owns Sunshine Market, to declare that the grocery business is the easiest business in the world, because the

"I am the manager."

Now she freezes with surprise. He does look a little young and a little informal for the job. A light-skinned black man of thirty-five, Toney is slight and slump shouldered, with a foxish, fine-featured face, a wispy mustache, a slicked-back ponytail, and a daily uniform of blue jeans, old tennis shoes, and a beat-up semi-official-looking blue smock. However, this is not the time to point out to Mrs. Potential Heart Attack that Toney has spent twenty years with Herb Spitzer — ten at Sunshine and, before that, ten at Food Pageant, Herb's previous store — and that he knows the store backward and forward. Instead, this is the time to expedite the encounter, because standing behind the woman now is a deliveryman with seventeen boxes of De An's pork products on a hand truck and the look on his face of a guy who is double-parked and is due some money.

"Hey, Toney," the pork man says. "Let me know when you have a minute for us lowly delivery guys."

Toney counts out six dollars, and the woman leaves, trembling but not yet fibrillating. Watching her walk out, he mutters, "My first beer tonight is on her."

Crazy people gravitate toward Toney. He

is often accosted by neighborhood schizo-phrenics, who ask him to inspect their gro-ceries for embedded alien messages or government-authorized concealed poisons before they risk the checkout line. In part, this is because Toney is very approachable. But it's also true that crazy people just gravitate toward supermarkets, because even though supermarkets are private busi-nesses, they provide a sort of semipublic sanctuary where anyone can do what a crazy person might want to do — that is, show up frequently, behave idiosyncrati-cally, and spend untold hours roaming around. Supermarkets are complicated but simple, totally familiar but also strange, and full of big, orderly displays of discrete and interesting items — conditions partic-ularly appealing to an eccentric mind, and ones that I found myself appreciating after spending several weeks at Sunshine Market.

Philosophically, Toney takes the position that the store has to tolerate things other businesses do not. In a place that provides something as basic as groceries, nearly every variety of customer and habit has to be accommodated. People who run super-markets can, if they choose to, make some-thing of this. They can attain a position of stewardship in their neighborhoods. Everyone knows them. Everyone sees them all the time. Everyone relies on them. They know weird details of everyone's lives — who is on a diet and who has company for dinner and who has a fetish for Chuckles Jelly Rings. Everyone is affected by a supermarket's failure or success: A neighborhood without a supermarket is on its way to not being a neighborhood anymore. Often the first places that people break into or burn down in riots are supermarkets — the rioters break in because supermarkets are full of desirable products, and they burn them down because grocery stores are so vital to a neighborhood that if they are run badly or exploitatively or meanly, they are manifestly despised. Toney and Herb are of the stewardship school, which explains Toney's forbearance regarding nearly everything he encounters in the course of his workday, including messages from Mars in the groceries. "What are you going to do?" he once said to me. "Crazy or sane, everyone is entitled to have a grocery store."

North of Thirty-seventh Avenue, two miles from Sunshine Market, is La Guardia Airport. Airplanes sometimes circle over the store as they make their final landing approach. South of Thirty-seventh, one block away, is the number 7 train, which runs on elevated tracks from Flushing to Manhattan, twenty-five feet in the air. Thirty-seventh Avenue is entirely earthbound. It is a main thoroughfare in Jackson Heights, but two people could play catch across it without getting winded. A cardiologist examining the avenue might recommend a bypass operation. There is a lane of traffic in each direction, a lane on each side for on-street parking, where there is usually a buildup of double- and triple-parked cars and trucks, and clots of pedestrians breaking apart at intersections and flowing into the street.

Almost all the buildings that line Thirty-seventh are squat, block-long commercial rectangles that were built in the 1920s. Except for a few blocks here and there that were leveled during the sixties and then re-built with largish modern structures, the buildings on Thirty-seventh remain pleasingly uniform and old-fashioned, but over the years they have acquired plate-glass windows and aluminum façades; grates and security bars; long strings of multi-colored plastic flags; and neon, plastic, and cardboard signs in English, Hindi, Korean, Vietnamese, Spanish, and Chinese. The array is dazzling. On most blocks, the boxy buildings are divided into several little businesses, so they end up looking like those long eight-packs of assorted Kellogg's cereals. Traveling on Thirty-seventh from the western edge of Jackson Heights (the Brooklyn-Queens Expressway) to the eastern edge (Junction Boulevard), among the places you would pass are Subzi Mandi Indo-Pak Grocery, Top Taste Chinese, Pizza Boy, La Uruguaya Bakery, the Ultimate Look, Oh Bok Jung Korean Restaurant, La Gata Golosa, Luigi's Italian Restaurant, Growing Farm, Chivito d'Oro, Different Ladies' Fashion, Familiar Pharmacy, and a store that is called Hello Kids on one sign, Hola Bebé on another, and something in Korean above the door.

Sunshine Market is on the block between Eighty-fifth and Eighty-sixth streets. Next door is Kenny's Fish, which used to be run by a young Korean family and is now owned by Pakistanis but has a sign out front advertising PESCADO FRITO. Two doors down is Anita Cassandra's Botanica La Milagrosa — a one-stop religious shop that sells Blessed Spray, Good Luck Bath, and Double Fast Luck Spray with Genuine Zodiac Oil. Next to the Botanica is Crystal Furniture. Up the block are J. C. Appliances, which is owned by Pakistani immigrants; Gemini II bar, which has one little dark window, mostly blocked by a neon Budweiser sign; and Winston Bagels, which has been on the corner since 1960. Across the street are Quality Farm, a Korean-owned greengrocer; Pic-a-Pak, an Italian butcher shop; Cavalier Restaurant, which has been open since 1950 and offers CONTINENTAL CUISINE AND ROMANTIC LIVE PIANO MUSIC; Fermoselle Travel, which offers DIVORCIOS, INCOME TAX, NOTARIO PUBLICO, INMIGRACION, TICKETS; Charles' Unisex Hairstylist, where you can get something done to you called "dimensional hair coloring"; and A. Wallshein, DDS.

Sunshine is the biggest store on the block. It looks like just about any grocery store anywhere: a big, unadorned, flat storefront, with two inset doors, divided by a thin metal handrail, and with huge plate-glass windows, which are always covered with paper signs advertising the week's specials. One week, some of the signs said:

USDA CHOICE SHELL STEAK (WITH
    TAIL) $2.99 LB.
HARD SLICING TOMATOES "RIPE"
    69¢ LB.

SWEET, RED WATERMELON 29¢ LB.
EDY'S ICE CREAM QT. CONT. ALL
    FLAVORS $1.99
FRESH PORK CALAS (PERNIL) 69¢ LB.
MAZOLA CORN OIL 48 OZ. BOTTLE $1.99
SCOTT PAPER TOWELS "BIG ROLL"
    69¢ EA.
BREAKSTONE BUTTER QUARTERS,
    SWEET OR SALT, 1/2 LB. PKG. 78¢

Supermarket doors seem to have a magnetic field around them. At Sunshine, there are always a couple of people at the door, waiting for the bus, or looking for a taxi, or staying out of the rain, or thinking about going in, or thinking about coming out, or reading the bulletin board, which is along the outside wall to the left of the doors. The bulletin board makes good reading. This same week, there were notices for a lost pit bull ("Friendly Gentle 1-Yr. Old Male"), an available baby-sitter ("Señora Responsable Cuida Niños"), two tickets to Ecuador, and an entire collection of Bruce Lee posters and memorabilia for sale ("Includes Many Items Too Rare to List Here").

One Monday morning, I got to the market at seven forty-five — fifteen minutes before opening time. There were already trucks from Polaner/B&G Pickles, Ingegneri & Son, Pepsi-Cola, Damascus Bakery, and Star Soap and Prayer Candle parked out front. The B&G driver, Wally Wadsworth, had started his morning at B&G's warehouse in Roseland, New Jersey, and was delivering sweet gherkin midgets and kosher dills. Jimmy Penny, the Ingegneri driver, had come from a warehouse in the Bronx with fifty cases of assorted groceries. Ronnie Chamberlain and Chris Laluz had started in Long Island City and had Pepsi liters. Jim Hazar had come from the Damascus Bakery in Brooklyn, with fresh pita bread. Manny Ziegelman, of Star Soap and Prayer Candle, had also come from Brooklyn. This particular morning, he had a mixed case of Miraculous Mother, Lucky Buddha, and Fast Luck prayer candles for Sunshine Market in his truck.

Traffic along most of Thirty-seventh was blocked. The delivery trucks took up all the parking spaces in front of the store. A solid line of cars sat in each traffic lane. Across the street, cars were parked at every meter, and a man double-parked in a piebald Mustang was reading the *News* in a state of leisurely repose; the cars moving down the street were forced around him, like a stream diverted around a rock. Another man was walking in the street between the parked cars and the moving cars, leading a scrawny, needle-nosed dog wearing a jeweled collar. On the sidewalk, five Asian kids were running toward Winston Bagels, which has pumpernickel bagels, garlic bialys, and five video games. Two elderly women were crossing from the entrance of an apartment building on Eighty-fifth Street toward the market. Both women were pushing Kadi-Carts — those fold-up rolling grocery carts that people in New York use, to make up for not having houses with driveways, large cars with trunks, or grocery stores with boys to carry the bags for them.

The man with a clipboard waiting for the deliveries at Sunshine was Bruce Reed. He has a silver crew cut and a poker face. Clustered behind him was a group of small Peruvian men. Bruce is the grocery manager. The small men are known among the people at Sunshine as the "Peruvian Army." A few days a week, when Sunshine is receiving large grocery deliveries, the Peruvian Army is brought in to help open the boxes and put things on the shelves — to do what grocery people call "packing out." Some Mondays, if the weekend was particularly busy, Bruce could use an airborne division.

On this Monday, Bruce walked over to the Ingegneri truck and peered in. Ronnie Chamberlain, walking past him with a loaded hand truck, craned his neck around his cases of Pepsi and said, "Hey, Bruce, help me out here. I got stuck with a million singles today. Everybody's giving me singles."

Bruce ignored him. Wally, the pickle man, walked over and thrust at Bruce a batch of papers to be signed, acknowledging acceptance of delivery of five cases. Bruce scribbled on the forms, said goodbye to Wally, who would be back next Monday with more pickles, and then turned to the Ingegneri truck and began glancing at his clipboard. Jimmy Penny, the Ingegneri driver, stood inside the back of his truck, looking down at Bruce. The boxes were stacked higher than his shoulders. He had one elbow resting on a case of Mazola and one on a case of paper towels. Finally, Bruce cleared his throat and said to Jimmy, "Well, well, well. Okay. Let's go."

As Jimmy started unloading cases, two more trucks pulled up — one from Coca-Cola and one from Wonder Bread. Jimmy kept unloading. The Peruvian Army moved into position. The piebald Mustang pulled out, made a U-turn, and disappeared down the street. The store opened. Two more trucks pulled up — Coors and Hostess Cakes. The Wonder Bread guy and the Hostess Cakes guy waved to each other. Jimmy kept unloading cases.

Monday is the biggest delivery day; Friday is the second biggest. On a typical Monday, Krasdale, the wholesaler that is Sunshine's biggest supplier of groceries, delivers fifteen hundred cases; on a Friday, it delivers nearly a thousand. A store without enough stuff on its shelves is a store that isn't making money. Because Sunshine is small — only seven thousand square feet, compared with the industry average of at least thirty thousand — and has a limited amount of storage for extra inventory, it relies more than the average store on its orders and deliveries; what it has, it has on display.

It was a quarter to nine. Within a few minutes, Jimmy had to be on the road to Port Jersey to pick up another load from a grocery distribution center. He hauled one more case of Mazola off the truck and was finished. The result was a prodigious pile. People walking down the sidewalk had to inch their way around it. Jimmy pulled off his work gloves, stuck them under his arm, smoothed his hair under his cap, shifted his weight to one hip, put his gloves back on, sighed, looked at the pile, looked at Bruce, looked back at the pile, and then said, "Sorry, pal. I didn't mean to smother you with so much stuff."

Anything in a supermarket that doesn't go away doesn't come back. This is especially true at a store like Sunshine, where each item has to be stocked, get sold, and be reordered regularly to make it worth having around. In grocery language, this process of coming and going is called a "turn." Herb likes the whole store to average thirty turns a year, which means that every single thing in the store is ordered, unloaded, price-tagged, placed on a shelf, rung up at the cash register, bagged, and reordered an average of thirty times in fifty-two weeks. Different things turn at different rates. At Sunshine Market, milk makes three hundred and sixty-five turns a year. Ketchup, twenty-four bottles to a case, turns three cases a week.

At Sunshine Market, you can buy Hershey's Kisses, Kellogg's Corn Flakes, La Cena Ground Garlic, Manischewitz Dietetic Matzo-Thins, Goya Gandules Verdes, peaches, potatoes, beets, bananas, Charms

Blo-Pops, Hellmann's Real Mayonnaise, Hellmann's Light Reduced Calorie Mayonnaise, Krasdale Cranberry Juice, Advanced Action Wisk, Ultra Bold, Sun-Maid raisins, Redpack Whole Tomatoes, Campbell's Cream of Chicken soup, Mighty Dog Sliced Chicken in Gravy, No-Cal Chocolate Soda, Luigi Vitelli Linguine, Charmin Free, Polly-O Lite Reduced Fat Ricotta, Hotel Bar butter, Wonder Bread, Hunt's Ketchup, French's Mustard, Morton's Salt, Brawny paper towels, Hungry-Man frozen dinners, Kleenex Man Size tissues, and Chore Boys, among many other things. In theory, if you took the number of things in the store and multiplied that number by the number of turns each item made in a year, you would know how many discrete units of stuff go in and out of the store in that year. This is only a theory. The truth is, no one knows exactly how many things there are inside Sunshine Market, so the math can't be done. Herb Spitzer once said that he thought there were about thirty-five hundred different items in the store. Bruce Reed once guessed ten thousand. Later, he revised his guess down to five thousand. You could drive yourself crazy trying to count all this stuff, because as soon as you started, something would be sold or would be thrown away, and you'd have to start over. Counting items in a supermarket would be like trying to count molecules in a river.

If you go into a supermarket under normal circumstances, you find what you need, you buy it, you take it home. But if you went into a supermarket sometime and just stood still, you would, in the space of a minute or so, see someone coming in the door pushing a hand truck of full boxes; you would see someone in the aisles slicing open boxes and putting things on display; you would see customers putting in their baskets things that had just been packed out and arranged on the shelf; you would see someone in the back room feeding empty boxes into a trash compactor and then lugging them to a Dumpster; you would see people moving their things through the checkout line and then carrying them away. In other words, you would be standing still in the middle of the river of things that flow in and out of the store all day.

It doesn't really matter how modern a store's refrigerators or its cash registers or its aisle displays are. On some level, the grocery business is just a clumsy, bulky, primitive enterprise that involves a great deal of stuff — stuff that weighs a lot, and takes up a lot of room, and has to be picked up and moved around a lot, and put in boxes, and taken out of boxes and put on shelves, and then put in bags, just so someone can take some of it home and eat it. A manager of a grocery store once said to me that his store was like a house that was constantly being torn down by outsiders, and his job was to keep trying to rebuild it in the face of these hostile destroyers. I told this story to Herb, who said, "That's a man who doesn't love his job."

Three hundred vendors bring things to Sunshine Market. Some of them own their own businesses. The nut guy is named Joseph Woo. He owns Bon Ami Nuts and Candy in Flushing. Joseph drives his own truck to his accounts; he takes his own orders; he packs out his nuts at each store. Some of the vendors are franchisees. The Coors and Canada Dry guy, Bobby Flynn, owns the franchise for Canada Dry in Queens and is the distributor for Coors. Like Joseph Woo, he drives his own truck; he takes his own orders; he packs out his cases at each store. Bobby Gonzales drives the Queens route for Coca-Cola — he is known at the store as Coke Bobby, to distinguish him from Coors and Canada Dry Bobby. Coke Bobby drives, packs out, and takes orders for his boss, the local franchisee for Coke. There is also the Archway Cookies guy, the light-bulb-and-battery guy, the Pepperidge Farm guy, the Arnold's Bread guy, the Damascus pita bread guy — scores of guys who work for companies that want to make sure that their goods get into the store and are set up the way they want them to be. Other companies sell their products through big grocery wholesalers like Krasdale and White Rose. Their products are included on a list of thousands of items that a store can order from the wholesaler, and they are delivered along with thousands of other things that the store orders every week.

Grocery stores love the companies that have guys who run their own routes. These guys work for their company, but in a sense they also work for the store. In fact, the drivers probably know the people at Sunshine and their other accounts better than they know the brass at Coke or Pepperidge Farm or Archway. Some of the drivers have been delivering to Sunshine since it opened — coming by once a week, or even once a day, for ten years. Most of the regular delivery guys knew when the wife of

Angel Ruiz, who used to be the assistant manager, was pregnant and asked after her. Sometimes a driver will meet somebody who works at a supermarket and they fall in love. This is what happened with the Pepperidge Farm guy and Rose Mary Cervantes, Sunshine Market's head cashier. They met while he was delivering a case of Mint Milanos. Some of the drivers who are on similar schedules also get to know one another. One day, I was standing near the Archway display, which is right next to the battery display. The Archway guy and the battery guy were both in the store that day, checking their merchandise. I heard the Archway guy saying, "So the guy sideswiped me, and I knew by just looking at him that he didn't have any insurance."

The battery guy said, "Hey, they never do."

The Archway guy said, "Seriously, this is going to cost me a fortune." They both finished restocking their displays and left. Two days later, they were back in the store — apparently, Archway Cookies and batteries turn at approximately the same rate — and I heard them pick up the conversation as if they'd never gone away.

"Anyway, I'm going to check with my insurance company."

"Yeah, maybe they can do something for you. Where were you when he hit you?"

"Right in the way."

At one time, Herb knew the name of every single thing in the store. The most modern supermarkets now have electronic scanning cash registers, which record what has been sold and automatically note when something needs to be reordered. Sunshine doesn't have scanning cash registers, so Bruce walks the aisles with a scanner, which he runs across the bar code of anything that looks sparse. Then he plugs the scanner into a computer modem and transmits his orders to the computer at the wholesaler's. The scanner notwithstanding, Sunshine Market is still rather old-fashioned; for instance, José Aguilar, who orders the Goya products, the beer, and the dog food, and Toney, who orders everything else that the wholesalers don't carry, both do their ordering by the traditional clipboard method. Toney once said that what he liked about the grocery business was the way you had to stash millions of details in your head, so that when you were faced with a decision — whether three Miraculous Mothers at $1.59 apiece were enough to last until Manny Ziegelman of Star Soap and Prayer Candle came back, for example, and whether $1.59 was a price attractive enough for the item to sell and also roomy enough to allow for a profit — you could rummage through your millions of details and come up with the right answer. The only way to learn these things is by being in the store day after day and learning them from someone like Herb, who has millions of such details already stashed away. Like all folklore, this information can't be recorded, really, because it's made up of details too particular and tiny; it can only be passed on, and in a cumulative way. For years, Toney spent his days at Herb's side, taking in everything Herb said. Someday, according to Herb, all supermarkets will have scanning cash registers, and the registers will transmit orders automatically to one central warehouse, and all products will be distributed from there. Then there will be no more Coke Bobbys and no more grocery owners who know what they sell and what isn't turning. There will just be one gigantic truck that will come every morning and drop cases and cases of groceries on the sidewalk and then drive away.

Standing where Toney stands — the manager's elevated cockpit, which is to the right of the cash registers — you can see the eight aisles of the store splayed out in front of you, each topped with bright orange-and-yellow signs and lined with shelves packed with jars and boxes and bottles and bags and cans of every color and shape. Herb sits in an office above the dairy case at the back of the store. From the small window over his desk, he has the same view of the store that Toney does, but in reverse.

Toney and Herb met in 1972, when Toney was in high school and was bagging groceries for pinball money. Toney quickly showed aptitude for bagging and a knack for the business. Toney's father was an air force man who divorced Toney's mother and then disappeared from their lives. Herb has two sons: One is a landscape architect; the other is a writer. Maybe they were interested in the grocery business, or maybe they weren't; in any case, Herb was not interested in their being interested, because he considers the life of a grocery man to be harder than the life he worked so hard to provide for his sons. Upward mobility means giving your children the means to break away from you. But if you have nothing, your children might also break away: Most of the people who work at Sunshine come from places where money and opportunity were scarce, and, in looking for them, they had to leave their families behind. Herb's sons will never have pieces of paper on the wall over their desks saying BANANA PRICE CHART and EGG DEAL; Toney, on the other hand, came to Herb ready for adoption. For the last twenty years, the daily lives of Herb and Toney have been conjoined at the egg deals and the banana price charts and the millions of other details that flesh out a grocery man's life. Other than what they do all day, how they do it, what they know, what they worry about, and what they hope for, Herb and Toney have nothing in common. Toney often explains why he does things in the store the way he does by saying, "That's the way Herb does it, and I do it his way."

On the wall in his office, next to the banana chart, Herb has a plaque from the Harvest Lodge B'nai B'rith honoring his father, Louis: "A Founder and Pillar of the Food Industry." Louis Spitzer was a butcher in the Bronx. When Herb came out of the army in 1952, he went to work for his father, not out of any special love of meat, but because he knew the business, thanks to his father, and getting in would be easy. "This industry has chapters and chapters of generations," Herb says. "It has always been an industry of bloodlines." At that time, the grocery business in New York was dominated by Italians and Jews, many of them immigrants. By 1962, the Spitzer father and son owned five meat markets, called either Commodore Market or Monarch Market. By 1971, Herb had parlayed the meat markets into a fifteen-store supermarket chain called Food Pageant, in Manhattan, Queens, and the South Bronx, where Herb ran the stores, Louis ran the produce and business departments, Herb's brother, Jerry, was in charge of the meat departments, and Herb's mother, Gertrude, mediated whenever they got in one another's way.

Jerry still works with Herb — he is the perishable operations manager at Sunshine — but otherwise the Spitzer food business lineage ends abruptly with Herb. A new lineage starts up with Toney Murphy, whose roots are in black South Carolina, whose mother and brother and sister are all nurses, and who came into the business more or less by accident but found in it an opportunity to work at a place he might someday have a chance to own. Herb is now sixty years old. He is a medium-size man with a smooth, pinkish, egg-shaped face and a scramble of graying hair. He has a soothing, precise manner, which suggests benevolence and intelligence and absolutely no patience for goofing around. It is entirely possible to imagine that for years he worked like a dog. Since he turned sixty, he has kept shorter hours, has left more and more decisions to Toney, and has discovered the world of lunch. Once, he described Toney to me as his heir apparent; another time, he used the words *surrogate son*. Some time ago, the two men made arrangements that will, when Herb is ready, transfer ownership of the store to Toney. Toney's wife, Donna, is a travel coordinator for an ad agency. When they met, she was working as a part-time cashier at Sunshine. They live in Jamaica Estates and have two sons and a daughter. The oldest, Jason, is ten. He likes coming to the store. Now that he is big enough, Toney is teaching him how to bag.

Arnie the Singles Guy comes to Sunshine Market once or twice a day and is rarely dressed for the weather. He is grizzle haired, oldish, nutty looking, and apparently tough as nails. The day I met Arnie the Singles Guy, he was wearing a cotton fatigue jacket and cotton twill hot pants. It was pouring outside. He bounded into Sunshine, fished around in his fatigue jacket, and finally pulled out a loaf-size wad of singles. Toney weighed the loaf on a scale in his office and then traded him a set of ten- and twenty-dollar bills for it. Arnie is the Stonehenge of Thirty-seventh Avenue: He has a clearly discernible function, but no one can quite explain how he got there or why. It is generally assumed that he lives in the neighborhood and is retired from some other job. Currently, he is in the financial services business. Once or twice a day, he travels a two-block route from Kelly's Luncheonette to Winston Bagels and then doubles back to Sunshine, collecting singles from the stores that have too many and trading them to the stores that don't have enough.

Tons of money come in and out of a supermarket in the course of a day. This is a figure of speech. Literally, though, pounds and pounds of it accumulate, and eventually everyone working in the store gets sick of fanning through it and counting it and managing the sheer bulk of it. Confronted with so much money — that is, the raw physical actuality of cash — people working in a supermarket often develop a rather cavalier manner with it, bunching it up, whipping it out of the cash registers, snapping rubber bands around it as if it were trash. I had the feeling that Toney gets a particular charge out of tossing the bales of dollars onto the scale as if they were hay rather than the most important thing in the world. This is not to say that every dollar isn't counted, and carefully — just that in these quantities money seems like nothing special, merely another product that arrives at the store in bulk. The only other people in this neighborhood who are equally unceremonious about money are drug dealers, who come into the store wearing hand-tooled Tony Lama cowboy boots and Gianni Versace blazers and buy their little bags of Doritos and single-serving guava nectars with five-hundred-dollar bills.

In truth, very little of the money that comes into a supermarket stays. The industry standard for gross profits is twenty-three and a half percent, and for net just one-half of one percent. Markups on most things are tiny. Money made is quantified in terms of pennies and dollars per cubic foot of shelf space, or cubage. Prepared foods and salad bars and extra nonfood services are the new big moneymakers in the grocery business, but there is no room for these at Sunshine; in fact, there is barely room for the small, freestanding chicken rotisserie, which is in the back, beside the Jell-O shelves.

Most of the thirty-one thousand grocery stores in this country are part of chains. Sunshine is an anachronism — a single-location, independently owned and operated grocery store. When Herb started in the business, more stores were independently owned. "I'm from a past generation," he says. "Nowadays, I have less in common with the guy who runs a chain supermarket, whose ordering and decisions are made for him at some central office, than I do with the little fellow who runs his own bodega."

When Sunshine opened in 1982, it took over a space vacated by a store called King Kullen, which had gone out of business. Since then, fifteen other grocery stores in the neighborhood have either closed or changed hands. There are still lots of supermarkets. These days, there are a Shop Wise and four Key Foods within a ten-block radius of Sunshine. Directly across the street are Pic-a-Pak and Quality Farm. Everything they sell, Sunshine sells, too.

There are about fifty thousand households in the neighborhood. The trick in the grocery business is to get most of these people in the door and not to allow spoilage and theft and taxes and employee costs and competition to eat up the one-half of one percent net profit. Herb, having presided over the rise and fall of Food Pageant, knows that it is not an easy trick. "As the economy of Queens and the South Bronx soured, so did the fortunes of Food Pageant," Herb says. He is now content with one busy store, as long as it remains busy. Sunshine has one of the highest sales-per-square-foot ratios in the city. "We rely on volume," he says. "We pump an incredible number of people through. There is never a hassle here. Also, we understand refrigeration."

Everything about a supermarket looks plain and uncontrived, because everything is commonplace and staple. But if you ran a business that had a profit margin of one-half of one percent, you would prefer that the customer coming in with plans to buy only a gallon of milk ($2.59) leave with a gallon of milk ($2.59), a can of Nestlé Quik ($4.19), a bag of Chips Ahoy ($3.19), a half gallon of Pride & Joy vanilla fudge ice cream ($2.49), and a week's supply of Ultra Slim-Fast Strawberry Supreme ($3.99). There is a science to doing this. You put the produce in front, because studies show that produce is the most important factor in determining where people shop. The milk is in the back, because everyone buys milk, and having it there ensures that everyone traverses the entire store. Cheap things that don't make much money for the store are on the bottom shelves; moneymakers — which might have a markup of twenty or thirty percent — are on the shelves at eye level, a position that can increase sales by fifty percent. People are drawn to the big displays at the ends of the aisles, which are usually made up of goods that the manufacturer has sold to the store at a promotional price. Some stores pack their shelves to the edge and have stock boys roaming the aisles all day and filling in every hole. Herb believes that items sell better when the shelf is a little ragged. Toney is constantly walking through the aisles, disarranging a few cans and boxes here and there. "If it's too neat, no one wants to be the one to mess it up," he says. "The only thing that pretty sells is dresses."

Most of the time, people who work in grocery stores do not suffer from inferiority complexes. They don't look around the store and wonder if they happen to be carrying the things people want. Americans visit grocery stores more than they visit any other kind of retail establishment — almost two and a half times a week, for between thirty-five and forty minutes per visit, which is an hour and a half every week, total, and three full days, cumulatively, each year. According to Toney, Sunshine Market has never, ever been entirely empty of customers since the day it opened. Grocery stores can be badly managed or poorly situated or undercut by the competition, but as a general rule they are popular places. Of course, rules are made to be broken. Angel Ruiz once quit his job at Sunshine and moved to Pompano Beach, Florida, and bought a supermarket there. Everything about the place suggested clover. What happened instead was, and remains, a mystery. Day after day, no one came into the store. Angel couldn't even get anyone to come in and buy a pack of cigarettes. Eventually, he lost all his money. Then he returned to New York and got his job back at Sunshine.

All kinds of people from all over the world come to live in Jackson Heights. Most of them have jobs and homes and regular lives. Some of them move here and get into trouble. One day, coming back to my car after a day at Sunshine, I saw a twenty-dollar bill stuck on my windshield. When I picked it up, I saw that it wasn't money at all. It was a little leaflet that was printed on one side to look like a twenty; the other side had a photograph of a woman with a big rump jutting out of a little pair of underpants, and underneath the photograph was a message about how unsuccessful she'd been in satisfying her prodigious sexual desires and how anyone who empathized and wanted to address the problem with her could call a number printed at the bottom of the page. A few days before, the *Times* had run a story saying that Roosevelt Avenue had become the city's largest prostitution center outside Manhattan and that brothels staffed with South American and Asian girls were operating all along it.

In the mid-eighties, police noted that thousands of Chinese immigrants, many of them illegal, were moving into neighborhoods in Queens, including Jackson Heights, and were establishing criminal organizations, known as "tongs," whose roots could be traced back to the 1850s. Around the same time, members of the Shining

Path, the Peruvian Maoist terrorist group, were rumored to have established their North American headquarters in Jackson Heights. Also in the eighties, it became widely known that Jackson Heights was one of the most important centers for Colombian cocaine traffic in this country; called "the colony" by Colombians in the drug business, Jackson Heights has since had an enormous volume of drug trade and drug-related crimes. In August 1990, a thirty-six-year-old woman was killed and her two companions were injured in a gangland shooting at the corner of Roosevelt Avenue and Seventy-ninth Street, a corner that local police called "a known drug location." And in March 1992, a journalist named Manuel de Dios Unanue — the Cuban-born former editor of *El Diario–La Prensa*, who often reported on drug cartels, many of them operating out of Jackson Heights, and on political corruption — was shot twice in the back of the head and killed while eating dinner at Mesón Asturias, one of a dozen Argentine restaurants in the neighborhood.

Jackson Heights used to be a region of productive farms, part of an area known as Newtown. In 1909, Edward A. MacDougall, a real estate developer, began buying land in the area and later renamed it in honor of John Jackson, president of the Hunters Point and Flushing Turnpike Company. The apartment houses MacDougall developed were innovative. Many were built European style, with a square block of apartments enclosing a garden courtyard. And many of the buildings had automatic elevators, which meant that they could be six stories high, instead of the five then standard in Queens. Also, MacDougall offered the apartments for collective ownership; they were among the first co-op apartments in America. Between 1920 and 1930, Jackson Heights was said to be the fastest-growing community in the country. Charlie Chaplin once lived in Jackson Heights, and so did Douglas Fairbanks Sr., but by and large the neighborhood consisted of middle-class Italians, Irish, and Jews until 1965, when immigration quotas were loosened and thousands of South and Central Americans, Koreans, Indians, Chinese, and Southeast Asians came to the United States. Jackson Heights, which was generally quieter, cleaner, safer, and prettier than similarly inexpensive neighborhoods in Manhattan, Brooklyn, or the Bronx, held great appeal.

Jackson Heights now has a hundred and

twenty-nine thousand residents. Twenty-eight percent are white; forty-three percent are Hispanic; fifteen and a half percent are black; eleven and a half percent are Asian. More than half of the ninety-four thousand Indians in New York City live in Queens — mainly in Jackson Heights and Flushing. Soviet immigrants are forming a settlement in the neighborhood. There is a chain of Uruguayan bakeries on Thirty-seventh Avenue. Jackson Heights is the de facto capital of the Argentine community in the United States. In some ways, the various nationalities have blended together, but in other ways, even in this small, crowded space, they have managed to remain clearly articulated. A sari shop and a Dominican diner side by side on the same block can still manage to feel ten thousand miles apart.

One morning, I was riding in a taxi and struck up a conversation with the driver. He was a black man, native to New York, and it turned out that he had recently moved to Jackson Heights from another section of Queens. I asked him how he liked it, and he said he liked it just fine, except that every once in a while he felt like a stranger there.

"Everyone's nice," he said. "But there's

hardly anyone like me."

Telling you where the employees of Sunshine Market are from will sound like the beginning of one of those jokes about an airplane, some parachutes, a priest, a rabbi, and a minister. The day shift of cashiers: Nohora is from Colombia, Marta is from Guatemala, Ruthie is from Venezuela, Ashima is from India, Rose Mary is from Bolivia. In the grocery department: José Aguilar is from El Salvador, and Neptali Chavez, who handles the dairy and frozen foods, is from Ecuador. Josie Andaya, the bookkeeper, has an Indian father and a Chinese mother and grew up in the Philippines. Many of the high school kids who work at the store in the afternoon are first-generation mixtures of the sort that results when a variety of new immigrants from all over the world end up in the same New York neighborhood: half Greek and half Bolivian; half French and half Ecuadoran; half Irish and half Romanian. The produce guys (Jerry Goldberg and Bruce Mitchnick), the grocery manager (Bruce Reed), the butchers (Richard Schindler, Bill Getty, and Alfonce Spicciatie), Toney, and Herb were born and raised in America.

Many of the people who work at Sunshine

live near the store, in Queens or Brooklyn. The immigrants among them all moved to this country expecting to spend their time with Americans, and they have ended up spending most of their time with other people who came here from somewhere else expecting to hang around with Americans. Many of them have described the ethnic makeup of Sunshine's employees as "all mixed up." They use this description when discussing Sunshine's customers, too. "Some of the shoppers are American," Ashima once said. "The rest of them are all mixed up."

Working together, the employees of Sunshine Market have learned a lot about people from other lands. "Indians are very emotional," Rose Mary Cervantes, the head cashier, once told me. "It's their culture." Angel Ruiz, the former assistant manager, whose family is Puerto Rican, is married to a former cashier who is Argentine. "They're very wild people, Argentines," he once said to me. "They love to eat. They'll eat anything. Meat. Meat stuffed with eggs. Meat stuffed with pizza. They'll even eat rocks. When I'm at my in-laws', I check on the cats once in a while, just to make sure no one in the kitchen got carried away." Toney is often mistaken for Spanish. "I'm not Spanish at all," he says. "One thing about Spanish people, they're crazy about meat. I'm not." Richard, a high school student of Romanian heritage who bags groceries in the afternoon, says, "The biggest thieves in the store are the Russians." One day, I noticed that Marta, the Guatemalan cashier, had been crying, and I mentioned it to José, who said, "Guatemalans are like that. They're always crying all the time." Herb says, "We have assembled an extremely varied group of people here, and we work together well. We're like a family. We have our ups and downs like a family, but we really are close-knit, the way a family is."

Angel's nickname for Toney is Sleeping Beauty, because he sometimes takes naps on his breaks. His nickname for José is Eagle Eye, because José's last name, Aguilar, means "eagle" in Spanish. Angel calls Jim McCague, a regular customer, Mr. OTB. Mr. McCague recently bet on a horse named Call Me Angel in Angel's honor; the horse and Mr. McCague both lost. Angel calls Richard, the afternoon bagger, Lover Boy, because he's always hitting on the cashiers; among the afternoon cashiers are girls he calls Hot Lips, Bambi, Sweet Pea, and Grouchy. It was Angel who came up with the name Peruvian Army for the group of shy, mild men who pack out the groceries twice a week. The soldiers of the Peruvian Army talk very little, and then only among themselves, so I never had any idea of what they thought about the market, or the neighborhood, or living in America. To me they seemed self-contained and somewhat detached from the modern world, but someone told me that they call Bruce the grocery manager Cabezón, which is Spanish for "big head," because he has a large forehead, and Bruce the produce man Spuds, after the dog in the beer commercial, and they call Jerry Goldberg, the produce manager, Oscar, after Oscar from *Sesame Street*.

Most of the time, Frank Sinatra provides the soundtrack for the life and times of Sunshine Market. This is because Herb is a huge fan. One of the privileges of being an independent retail food merchant is that if you want to play "My Kind of Town" rather loudly several times a day in your store — well, it's your business. "Strangers in the Night" is also your business. Also "Saturday Night (Is the Loneliest Night of the Week)" and, for that matter, Frank's entire Capitol catalog, plus his recordings for Columbia and Reprise. Several years ago, the cashiers submitted a petition to Herb requesting equal time for rock music. "It was very nicely written," Herb says. "I thanked them for it, and then pointed out that there was a Key Food around the corner that was accepting applications."

A few weeks ago, Marta the cashier turned her radio at home to an unfamiliar station and half listened to it for about an hour, humming along, without giving any thought to what it was. Then she realized. "It was Frank, from the store!" she said. "I couldn't believe! I didn't know him in Guatemala, but I knew him from the store. I used to hate him, but now it was — I don't know, okay."

One day, Rose Mary Cervantes was up in Herb's office, and I saw her looking at some of his Sinatra tapes. The expression on her face was partly one of distaste and partly one of semi-scientific curiosity. She caught me looking at her and quickly put down the tapes and then said, "Really, I'm not crazy about Frank, but I'm getting used to him. If I had my pick, I'd pick soft rock or maybe the sixties, but really what I'd pick would be Julio Iglesias, because when I hear him" — she began fluttering her hands and rolling her eyes back — "my heart starts beating and it fills me up. Oh, yes, Julio. Ju-lee-oh." Actually, Herb does have a few Julio tapes, and I pointed this out. "Yeah," Rose Mary said gloomily, "but just Julio's English ones."

One Tuesday, which happened to be the day of the store's tenth birthday party, the first truck to arrive was Pepperidge Farm. It was delivering four bunches of yellow and blue balloons, to decorate the cash registers (yellow and blue are the official colors of Sunshine Market); half a dozen yellow and blue carnation corsages, for the cashiers; and Rose Mary, whose boyfriend, the Pepperidge Farm man, was giving her a lift so she could get all the birthday supplies to the store.

Rose Mary has worked at Sunshine Market since the store opened. Once in a while, she takes a vacation, but for most of the past seven years she has worked every single day, seven days a week. Last year, she didn't take any vacation at all, because she forgot to make any plans. There are times when she looks as if she wished she had remembered. Before taking off her coat on the birthday, she began lashing the bunches of balloons to the cash registers. She stopped for a moment to ring up a grapefruit, a jar of honey, and a half carton of eggs for a skinny man with a mustache who had followed her in the front door. Someone practicing to be a psychic might enjoy working as a supermarket cashier. Ring up people's orders and you develop quite a hunch about their next meal. This one gave a premonition of breakfast. It was not yet eight, but everyone in the neighborhood knows that if you want to get your shopping in a little early, no one at Sunshine is going to hold you to the clock.

Ashima arrived a few minutes later, carrying a big sheet cake, frosted in blue and yellow, with white letters saying "Happy Tenth Anniversary Sunshine Market." Robert Felder arrived next. He is the utility infielder at the market: He bags, he crushes boxes, he tidies up. Usually, he loves to clown around. Today, he was in an uncharacteristic bad mood, because the previous night a transit cop had issued him a summons for playing his radio too loud on the subway. Hanging up his coat, he told Rose Mary the story and said, "It couldn't have been too loud. I was sleeping while it was playing." The butchers came in next and went straight to the back of the store and started cutting up meat. Then Toney came. Ordinarily, Tuesday is his only day off, but he decided to come in so he'd be on hand for the party. Immediately behind him was the Arnold's Bread guy. As Toney was taking off his coat, he said, "Hey, it's Mr. Arnold's! It's the pushiest guy in the business. You want to stick around for the birthday party?" The Arnold's guy elbowed his way past him, pushing a hand truck stacked with loaves, and said, "Toney, don't mess with me today. I'm un-believably late. Give me my money and let me get out of here."

At a few minutes before eight, Frank Sinatra was singing about Chicago, Herb was in the office reviewing orders, Jerry and Bruce were out front checking the day's produce delivery, José was counting cases of groceries, and Neptali was price-labeling egg cartons that had come in from Lancaster County, Pennsylvania. Neptali, who is known as Nick because no one at the store can pronounce his name, is the store's best labeler. He has smooth, slender, long-fingered hands and a loose wrist. He grew up in Ecuador, and though he worked in a food store there, nothing he did fore-told his labeling facility. In Ecuador, prices were handwritten. After moving to America, he got a job at Key Food at the suggestion of a friend, and there he met up with a label gun. He got so good at labeling that the Key Food managers consulted him when they were buying new guns. He fired a round of price stickers onto the egg cartons. The pile of cartons was as high and wide as a chicken coop. Another customer who had slipped in early, an elegant old man, stepped up to him, motioned with his cane, and said, "Do you have any eggs for me, my friend?"

The first customer when the store officially opened was a bald man in a green T-shirt. He disappeared down one of the aisles, then reemerged at the cash register with a box of Entenmann's chocolate-covered doughnuts, two tubs of Philadelphia cream cheese, and a head of iceberg lettuce. At the last moment, he backed out of the line and jettisoned the lettuce in the Pepsi display at the head of Aisle 5. An elderly man in a tweed blazer came up behind him, picked up the lettuce, carried it over to Toney, and said, "Is it possible for a person to get a tender piece of meat around here?" As he spoke, he was gesturing with the lettuce. A moment later, he turned, took a few steps, put down the lettuce, and headed toward the dairy case. The lettuce was now in the Frookie All Natural cookies display. An Asian woman was passing the

Frookie display. In her shopping cart were a box of Birds Eye Frozen Mixed Vegetables and two pumpernickel bagels she had just fished out of the roll bin. She picked up the lettuce, put it in her cart, and headed for the cashiers.

The cashiers had pinned on their corsages. A woman with a sleek silver pageboy walked over to Ashima's line, looked at her corsage, and said, "Who's getting married?"

Ashima said, "It's the birthday of the store. No one's getting married."

The woman said, "Rose Mary? Is Rose Mary getting married?"

Rose Mary was one checkout line over, ringing up the groceries of three Indians — mother, daughter, and granddaughter. The mother had a caste mark on her forehead and was wearing a turquoise sari shot through with gold threads. Her daughter was in black slacks and a red turtleneck. The little girl was in a plaid jumpsuit. There are seventeen sari stores in Jackson Heights. There are a dozen Indian grocery stores, where you can buy red and green lentils, garam masala, and puri mix. These women were buying Eggo Homestyle waffles, frozen corn on the cob, a loaf of Italian bread, and two containers of La Yogurt, strawberry flavored. Rose Mary said, "I'm not getting married. My boyfriend isn't part of this. That's not why we have the flowers."

The woman with the pageboy said, "Rose Mary, if your boyfriend won't help out, then get rid of him."

A heavyset man entered the line behind her. He was wearing a gingham shirt and a baseball cap that said HBO on the crown. In one hand he was holding some Internal Revenue Service forms. Wrapped around his other wrist was a cinnamon-colored Chihuahua. Rose Mary said, "Hi, Eddie. Hi, Pancho."

Pancho trembled. Eddie patted him on the head with one finger and said, "Hey, what's with the flowers?"

The lines at the cash registers began to build. A freckle-faced teenage boy wearing an Orlando Magic hat: a bag of Doritos, a box of Strawberry Pop-Tarts, a can of Spam, a box of Kraft Macaroni & Cheese, a gallon of milk, a box of Teddy Grahams. A glamorous blonde, wearing gold mules: a Sara Lee cheesecake, four packages of veal. A man and woman speaking Russian: a box of Post Shredded Wheat 'N Bran, a box of Grape-Nuts, a box of Honey Bunches of Oats. A woman in a pink cape:

a pound of Hershey's Kisses and a steak. A youngish man wearing a Yankees cap: one hero roll, two six-packs of Meister Bräu. An ample-looking middle-aged woman in purple stretch pants and spike heels: a package of Ore-Ida frozen French fries, a bunch of bananas, a one-pound package of Oscar Mayer wieners. A rotund, rosy-faced old man: a frozen piecrust, two packages of Brussels sprouts, a can of Campbell's Chicken Broth, and a pound of butter.

It was impossible for me to watch this cavalcade of products and not either picture them being eaten together or try to imagine the circumstances that led this particular person to need this particular, random-looking assortment of things at this particular moment. A good cashier, on the other hand, appears to notice nothing. Ashima, who everyone concedes is the best cashier, likes to chatter while she's ringing orders; this makes her seem both totally focused and completely distracted, as if she were putting on mascara while driving sixty miles an hour. A skinny man with a crew cut, his glasses held together over his nose with electrical tape, unloaded three cans of Budweiser, a can of Krasdale apricots, a ham steak, a can of Blue Diamond walnuts, two kaiser rolls, and a box of

Haviland chocolates from his shopping cart. "My son is at Pennsylvania State, in premed," Ashima said, punching in the prices. "He's a very good boy. I don't know how I got so good at this. To me, it's easy. Everyone loves me, because I am the best."

The party was supposed to start at ten, then at eleven, then at twelve. Then people started taking their breaks. At one, word filtered down from the office that Herb had a dentist appointment and had to leave immediately. Finally, at two o'clock, Robert said he was going to eat the cake if someone else didn't start it, so a skeleton crew was left at their posts and everyone else came up to Herb's office.

Upstairs, Rose Mary pulled the cake out of the box and said, "I think we should cut the cake, and leave a piece for Herb to have tomorrow, and take a picture, and that's it, because it's too busy out there." Sometime long ago, Rose Mary had ascended to the role of den mother here. There were eight people clustered in the corner of the office: Ashima, Marta, Rose Mary, Jerry, Robert, Toney, and Richard and Bill, who had taken a break from carving a side of beef. Someone was drinking a Coke. I took the picture, and then Robert had me take another, so that the Coke bottle would be turned the right way in the picture — with the label pointed toward the camera, so you could read it clearly.

My favorite thing at Sunshine was a small sign in the back of the produce department that said:

MELLOW, VERSATILE BANANAS — FOR A DIFFERENT TREAT, FRY OR BAKE AND SERVE HOT.

Some supermarkets post recipes above certain products, or have their aisles choked with dump displays, or have music playing at subliminal levels to encourage acquisitive urges. Sunshine, by comparison, is an aloof selling environment. Herb likes a clean-looking store and Frank Sinatra, who has no track record as a sales tool. Toney hates having the aisles cluttered. One of Sunshine's few concessions to conventional sales psychology was the banana sign. Many people left the store with a bunch of bananas. Either the sign worked or it was a case of restating the obvious. People seem to love bananas, and also green bananas and plantains, which were added to Sunshine's produce department a few years ago, when the neighborhood was reconfigured ethnically. Also calabaza, fresh yautia, red *batata,* and coconuts. Also yucca, which are laid out like big costume jewelry on green liner paper, beside the avocados and the honeydews and the navel oranges and the Granny Smiths.

Long ago, Jerry Goldberg, the produce manager at Sunshine, ran a green market on Allerton Avenue in the Bronx. Eventually, he got tired of standing outside in the cold. He has worked indoors at Sunshine for ten years, but he always looks dressed for Allerton Avenue. Jerry is in charge of ordering and displaying and tending to the produce. It is not a desk job. Mornings, he starts by prepping the vegetables to put on display. He has huge hands, with fingers as gnarled as parsnips. It is quite a sight to wander back to his worktable and catch him hacking at the lettuce heads, cutting off the ugly leaves and tossing them away. A few heads into it, he's ankle deep in greenery. One day when I was hanging around with him, he had a dozen cases of heads to sculpt. "Look at these," he said, motioning to the cases. "Half of them, the outer leaves, all get thrown away."

A husky man in a blue jumpsuit came up to the worktable and said, "Yo, Jerry, I've got something with your name on it." Jerry kicked his way through the lettuce leaves, and the two men walked past the dairy case to the produce section.

The man in the jumpsuit was Michael Singleton, and he was delivering from Loi Banana/Global Tropicals of Brooklyn. Most of the produce at Sunshine Market, and at most supermarkets in New York, comes from Hunts Point Market in the Bronx, where the wholesalers gather every morning before dawn. Loi Banana/Global Tropicals brings citrus, specialty items, and a few things that Jerry doesn't find to his liking at Hunts Point. Michael had deposited thirty cases of fruits in the aisle beside the produce section — Ruby Red grapefruits, Don Antonio's Delight Quality Cantaloupes, Seald Sweet Oranges, Qual-A-Key Limes, and Bonita's Pride Tomatoes. One stack was strictly bananas and tropicals.

Michael handed Jerry an order form. Jerry wiped his hands on his pants and took the papers. He had lettuce leaves on his shoes, strawberry stains on his jeans, and something green on the front of his shirt. When he read the order form, he groaned and said, "Twenty-three dollars for apples?"

"That's what it says."

"Twenty-three? You got no heart."

"I don't make the rules. I just collect the money."

Bruce Mitchnick, the assistant produce manager, was walking past, advising a woman on how to peel a beet. Toney was following behind him, checking the seal on a bottle of Deer Park water for a nervous woman who wanted him to assure her it was safe. Bruce Mitchnick is small and solid and sometimes wears a weight lifter's leather belt while he works, which when he is hoisting a melon or a case of tomatoes gives him the aspect of a gladiator confronting vegetables. For twelve years, Bruce owned a produce market in Kew Gardens. He started in the business as a kid growing up in Brooklyn. He loves fruits and vegetables. He is a fountain of produce lore. Once he told me, "Don't wash anything before you eat it. That's where all the vitamins are. If you wash the produce, you wash the vitamins away." Another time he said, "People are afraid of broccoli rabe, but I know for a fact it's delicious."

Jerry was saying, "Hey, Mike, what I need from you is five *platanos*, ten bananas, one calabaza, three avocados, one wax yucca, one coconut, two apples, and three oranges." He meant cases.

Michael pointed at the stacks and said, "Right here."

Bruce stopped his beet discourse and said, "Jerry, take a look at these gorgeous strawberries."

Jerry said, "I can't look at strawberries. I'm too heartsick about these apples for twenty-three."

The woman with Bruce grabbed his elbow and said, "Don't leave me now. I've got the beets out of the water, and so now what?"

One unwritten law in supermarkets is that whatever is just being unloaded and is not yet marked and not ready to sell is exactly the thing that people want. Being boxed and waiting to be unpacked makes all products irresistibly attractive to shoppers. Within seconds, four or five people were circling the stack that Michael had deposited. A woman with glittering eyeglasses got hold of half a banana sticking out of the top of the crate. Jerry shooed her away. A moment later, a pear-shaped man in a peacoat grabbed it. It did not budge.

Michael said, "Jerry, sign off for me, because I got to get back to Brooklyn."

The pear-shaped man let go of the banana, looked at Jerry, and said, "I have to tell you, I have a problem with this."

Jerry said, "Mister, there are plenty of bananas out. There are bananas out you can get to."

The man said, "No, I don't want any bananas. I was just thinking to myself, Why doesn't he ever play any Al Jolson here? Sinatra I hear plenty, but I don't think there's as much Jolson as I'd like, and I'm here every day."

Jerry signed the produce order form, and Michael wiggled his hand truck out from under the boxes and rolled it away.

A weather map of Sunshine Market would show considerable variety. In the big walk-in dairy refrigerator, which is called "the dairy box," the temperature is thirty-eight degrees. In the produce box, it is about forty and slightly damp. In the frozen box, in the basement, where the frozen food is stored, it is below zero and breezy. In the meat box, it is thirty-seven degrees. In the cutting room, where the butchers and wrappers work, it is exactly the temperature you would like it to be if you were going to a college football game in the Midwest and were wearing a sweater, corduroy pants, a muffler, mittens, and a hat. To the meat crew it feels absolutely normal. In fact, most of them can no longer stand ordinary room temperature; within a few minutes, they break into a sweat.

The butchers at Sunshine Market are Bill Getty, Richard Schindler, and Alfonce Spicciatie. Mariana Rivera is the meat wrapper. Bill, Alfonce, and Mariana started working at the store the day it opened; Richard joined them a few months later. The four of them have been working cheek by jowl in the cutting room, which measures twenty feet by forty, for a decade — a fact that, when I pointed it out to them, evoked this response from Richard: "I guess that's true. Hey, whaddya know?"

Lack of sentimentality may actually be an advantage when you're spending eight hours a day around carcasses. Once, Bill, who is the meat manager, was telling me what I thought was going to be a sweet story about a little old lady who approached him one Thanksgiving for advice on cooking her bird. His summation: "I said to her, 'Hey, lady, you're seventy-two bleeping years old. I'm sure this isn't your first turkey.'"

The beef at Sunshine Market is from Iowa. The chicken is from Maryland. The pork, according to Bill, is from wherever you can find a dead pig. Richard is from Ozone Park, Queens. Alfonce is from Brooklyn. Bill is from Astoria. Mariana is from Ecuador. All of them came to their positions by the ordinary route — that is, they learned meat cutting right out of high school, because it was a good, solid trade — except for Mariana, who had been a housewife and a mother until one day when she was out shopping and someone at her butcher shop offered her a job. Mariana is trim and has a high-fashion rooster-style haircut and a taste for snug jeans and tiny, fragile-looking spiky-heeled shoes. At work, she is always dressed as if she could be ready to go to a disco at a moment's notice. She told me once about how she got started: "When the butcher said this to me about a job, I said, 'What, me work?' He said, 'Yes, you.' I said, 'Me? You're kidding.' It was really just an accident." It was a pretty major accident: She has now been a meat wrapper for nineteen years. "I didn't want any job. It was all just an accident," she said again. As she was talking, she was flipping a plastic-foam platter of gooey pink veal cutlets onto the wrapping machine, pulling plastic wrap around it, and then pressing the package onto a flat plate at the front of the machine, which melts the wrap shut. The plate was the warmest thing in the room. She flipped another foam package onto the warm plate and said, "Then I joined the union, and now I'm in it for good."

The meat people spend most of their time in the cutting room, which is in the left rear corner of the store. On occasion, they will step out to take care of some meat-related or personal concern, and when they do they rarely bother to take off their cutting coats, which are calf-length white smocks that snap up the front and are splattered and smeared with blood. Bill attended the store's anniversary party in his bloodied coat. He is a big, tall man with considerable presence. In every snapshot taken at the party, Bill and his bloody coat loom. In some of the pictures, it almost looks as if a homicidal maniac had dropped in for cake and ice cream.

The meat people are separated from the rest of the market by their body temperatures, by their union (Amalgamated Meat Cutters), and by a swinging door leading into the cutting room. The door has a small oblong window. The butchers can look out on the market as they work, but the window's shape and size and glassiness make the store look as if it were a show on television. Describing what they see going on in the store, the butchers sound as if they were discussing a sitcom. One day, they watched a shoplifter load five pounds of shrimp into a plastic bag and then vanish. "In my life, I never saw a person pick through shrimp in a more meticulous way," Richard says. The next day, the man came back four or five times, neatly palming packages of boneless shell steak on each visit. The butchers marveled at his switch from surf to turf. Then they passed along their observations to Angel, who chased the guy out and lost him on the avenue but found the shell steak stockpiled in the Dumpster behind the store. The shrimp were never recovered.

One Thursday morning, Stephen C. Costa, who is the district sales manager of the Best Foods Baking Group, which is a unit of Best Foods, which is a wholly owned subsidiary of CPC International, which is a multinational grocery products corporation, had a new chocolate-chip toaster cake he wanted to bring to Herb Spitzer's attention. Thursday morning is salesmen's time at Sunshine Market. It used to be almost a ritual: On Thursday, the salesmen would stack up outside

Herb's office door, shuffling brochures and presentation folders praising New Liquid Tide, or Cycle Lite dog food with real chicken, or Redpack canned tomatoes, and he would usher each man in and sit through the pitch. When Herb was younger, he got a kick out of Thursday mornings, but ever since he turned sixty he has had a greedy feeling about time. More often than not these days, Herb has Toney tell the salesmen to send in their material and he will call them back if he's interested. "I could spend my life up here with the salesmen, if I let them," he says. "And who needs it?"

Stephen Costa, therefore, had got lucky, and he knew it. He is youngish, curly haired, bespectacled, beefy, and on the shy side when it comes to salesmanship. His district is Queens, and he oversees fourteen delivery routes. All told, each week he peddles forty-five thousand pounds of Thomas' products — including Thomas' English muffins and Toast 'R Cakes and Sahara pita breads. Forty-five thousand pounds sounds like a lot of dough to me, but Stephen Costa would like to sell more.

Herb tapped his pencil on a pad of paper and said, "Okay, tell me about it. You're a pretty good guy, I've heard."

Costa said, "You can discount the chocolate-chip toaster cakes if you want." He swung his chair around. Shoulder to shoulder, he and Herb faced the little window that affords a view of the whole store. The lines at the register were three deep. Someone had just broken a ketchup bottle in Aisle 4.

"We'll go regular price. Next."

"Next, uh," Costa said, stumbling. "Okay, next, uh, the following week we have Toast 'R Cakes on sale. The regular retail is one twenty-nine."

Herb said, "Fine. We'll come out at ninety-nine, and we'll do an ad in our circular. Arrange for your route man to get it. Next?"

"We have a two-week window on Sahara pita breads again. White and wheat. We'd like it in the circular also."

"We're a small little operation here," Herb said. "We can't do a circular every single time. Is that it? You don't have much ammunition for your presentation here, do you?"

"I'm kind of new. Let's see, I do want to talk to you about another English muffin. The Thomas' twin-pack."

"What can you do for me?"

"Twenty cents off, plus another dime if

you do a coupon. I'm not able to offer much more. I'm the new kid on the block."

"I'd like to go at one ninety-nine, but if your price is one ninety-seven and a half, I'll have to go at two oh-nine. At the lower price, you can have a dump display and move a lot of product."

The intercom rang, and while Herb was answering it, Costa flipped through his papers for another muffin to flog. The call was from Toney, telling Herb that another sales representative was downstairs and eager to meet with him. "Tell him he'd be wasting his time," Herb said into the phone.

There was a knock on the door, and someone called out, "Herb, it's Ronnie from Pepsi. Key Food is going ninety-nine on liters."

"Then so will I. Have your guy mark them."

He didn't bother opening the door. The transaction was completed through drywall.

Costa signed his paperwork on the muffins and stood up to leave. Herb glanced at him and said, "Nice job."

Herb's office is a narrow second-floor wedge in the back of the store, above the trash compactor and the dairy and produce boxes. The wall separating it from the trash compactor isn't totally sealed, so the loud growl and crunch of the compactor is as audible as if it were in the office. The compactor runs, on and off, all day long. Conversations in the office that begin in a normal speaking tone often shift into a shout at some point. "Nice job" was a shout.

As Costa was going down the stairs, a man named Don Vitale was coming up. Don Vitale is the Mazola man. He is also the Skippy man and the Hellmann's man. He and Costa don't know each other, but, as it happens, both of them work for CPC International, which owns Mazola as well as Thomas'.

Vitale is a strapping fellow, and he was wearing a loose raincoat. He and his coat seemed to take up most of the office. The coat was brushing along the top of the desk. His head was brushing the ceiling. Taking his files out of his briefcase, he knocked a chair backward. As he picked up the chair, he said, "Herb, we've got a Mazola promotion to the Hispanic market. We've got these ballot boxes, and you put them with an aisle display, and we're giving away bicycles and twenty-five-dollar grocery coupons and whatever. It's a tie-in with the Spanish television show that Mazola helps sponsor, called *Sábado Gigante*."

"This thing was dreadful last time you did it," Herb said, and he began riffling through papers on his desk.

Vitale said, "The show is a huge hit, Herb. The girls on the show are models, or whatever, and they're incredibly popular. They're cute girls." He paused and looked at Herb for a reaction.

Herb had turned slightly away from him and was scanning some paperwork on his desk. He once told me that he was now quite inured to being pitched, even by someone of Vitale's gusto. "At this point, I know exactly what I want for the store," Herb had explained to me. "Someone else isn't likely to present me with something I haven't already decided I want. I've been in this business long enough that I know my style."

Vitale tried again, adding, "Herb, the girls are appearing at some of the stores in combination with the promotion."

"I used to do this sort of thing more often," Herb said, mostly to himself. "We used to give away samples of new products and so forth. Maybe we should start it again, although I'm inclined to think that good service matters to people more than this sort of hoopla."

Vitale said, "Herb, this has been a major success in other places. The girls were just in a store on Roosevelt, and it was a mob scene."

Without looking up, Herb said, "That's why you'll never see them here."

At the end of the day, you close down a supermarket by first putting the more tender vegetables in the cooler and the money in the safe. At Sunshine Market, at the end of every day, the afternoon cashiers — mostly high school girls from Jackson Heights who are saving for college or for a solid start in life — go around the store and collect the abandoned things and put them back where they are supposed to be. Then they go up and down each aisle and tidy up all the merchandise. Bruce Reed told me that in grocery language this is known as "leveling the shelves" or "touching the shelves." If you take the time to do this, then every morning, when the store opens, it looks fresh and full and ready for business, brimming with everything anyone might need, instead of looking like a place where hundreds of people had been racing through all day, pulling things off the shelves and carrying them away faster than they could be replaced.

One Sunday I spent at the store had been a big shopping day, so the shelves were particularly empty and somewhat disordered. There was a Reynolds Wrap and a four-pack of Charmin in the magazine rack, some Scooter Pies in the Ding Dongs, a Cadbury chocolate bar on top of the Schaefer beer display, a five-pound bag of Heckers All Purpose Flour on the Maxwell House shelf, a can of Carnation Leche Evaporada with the Sanka, and a can of Krasdale Fancy Small Whole Beets in with the Calimyrna figs. A basket with Downy fabric softener, two cucumbers, a head of lettuce, and a roll of ScotTowels was abandoned on the Pepsi display: Maybe someone had left his wallet in his other pair of pants. A box of Duncan Hines Devil's Food Cake Mix, a half pint of whipping cream, and a package of Joseph Woo's slivered almonds had been abandoned in the canned tomatoes: maybe the sudden onset of a diet or the decision to hold off baking for a cooler day. It took the girls a good half hour just to round up the stray groceries. I watched them put those things back where they belonged and then start touching each shelf in each aisle. By the time I headed out the door that night, they had just begun touching Aisle 3.

The Lady and the Tigers

On January 27, 1999, a tiger went walking through the township of Jackson, New Jersey. According to the Tiger Information Center, a tiger's natural requirements are "some form of dense vegetative cover, sufficient large ungulate prey, and access to water." By those measures, Jackson is really not a bad place to be a tiger. The town is halfway between Manhattan and Philadelphia, in a corner of Ocean County — an easy commute to Trenton and Newark, but still a green respite from the silvery sweep of electric towers and petroleum tanks to the north, and the bricked-in cities and mills farther south. Only forty-three thousand people live in Jackson, but it is a huge town, a bit more than a hundred square miles, all of it as flat as a tabletop and splattered with ponds and little lakes. A lot of Jackson is built up with subdivisions and Wawa food markets, or soon will be, but the rest is still primordial New Jersey pinelands of broom sedge and pitch pine and sheep laurel and peewee white oaks, as dense a vegetative cover as you could find anywhere. The local ungulates may not be up to what a tiger would find in more typical habitats like Siberia or Madhya Pradesh — there are just the usual ornery and overfed pet ponies, panhandling herds of white-tailed deer, and a milk cow or two — unless you include Jackson's Six Flags Wild Safari, which is stocked with zebras and giraffes and antelopes and gazelles and the beloved but inedible animal characters from Looney Tunes.

Nevertheless, the Jackson tiger wasn't long for this world. A local woman preparing lunch saw him out her kitchen window, announced the sighting to her husband, and then called the police. The tiger slipped into the woods. At around five that afternoon, a workman at the Dawson Corporation complained about a tiger in the company parking lot. By seven, the tiger had circled the nearby houses. When he later returned to the Dawson property, he was being followed by the Jackson police, wildlife officials, and an airplane with an infrared scope. He picked his way through a few more backyards and the scrubby fields near Interstate 195, and then, unfazed by tranquilizer darts fired at him by a veterinarian, headed in the general direction of a middle school; one witness described seeing an "orange blur." At around nine that night, the tiger was shot dead by a wildlife official, after the authorities had given up on capturing him alive. A pathologist determined that he was a young Bengal tiger, nine feet long and more than four hundred pounds. Nothing on the tiger indicated where it had come from, however, and there were no callers to the Jackson police reporting a tiger that had left home. Everyone in town knew that there were tigers in Jackson — that is, everyone knew about the fifteen tigers at Six Flags Wild Safari. But not everyone knew that there were other tigers in Jackson, as many as two dozen of them, belonging to a woman named Joan Byron-Marasek. In fact, Jackson has one of the highest concentrations of tigers per square mile of anywhere in the world.

Byron-Marasek is famously and purposely mysterious. She rarely leaves the compound where she lives with her tigers; her husband, Jan Marasek; and scores of dogs, except to go to court. On videotapes made of her by the New Jersey Department of Environmental Protection, she looks petite and unnaturally blond, with a snub nose and a small mouth and a startled expression. She is either an oldish-looking young person or a youngish-looking old person; evidently, she has no Social Security number, which makes her actual age difficult to establish. She has testified that she was born in 1955 and was enrolled in New York University in 1968; when it was once pointed out that this would have made her a thirteen-year-old college freshman, she allowed as how she wasn't very good with dates. She worked for a while as an actress and was rumored to have appeared on Broadway in Tom Stoppard's play *Jumpers*, swinging naked from a chandelier. A brochure for her tiger preserve shows her wearing silver boots and holding a long whip and feeding one of her tigers, Jaipur, from a baby bottle. On an application for a wildlife permit, Byron-Marasek stated that she had been an assistant tiger trainer and a trapeze artist with Ringling Brothers and L. N. Fleckles; had trained with Doc Henderson, the illustrious circus veterinarian; and had read, among other books, *The Manchurian Tiger*, *The World of the Tiger*, *Wild Beasts and Their Ways*, *My Wild Life*, *They Never Talk Back*, and *Thank You, I Prefer Lions*.

The Maraseks moved to Jackson in 1976, with Bombay, Chinta, Iman, Jaipur, and

Maya, the five tigers they had gotten from an animal trainer named David McMillan. They bought land in a featureless and barely populated part of town near Holmeson's Corner, where Monmouth Road and Millstone Road intersect. It was a good place to raise tigers. There was not much nearby except for a church and a few houses. One neighbor was a Russian Orthodox priest who ran a Christmas-tree farm next to his house; another lived in a gloomy bungalow with a rotting cabin cruiser on cement blocks in the front yard.

For a long time, there were no restrictions in New Jersey on owning wildlife. But beginning in 1971, after regular reports of monkey bites and tiger maulings, exotic-animal owners had to register with the state. Dangerous exotic animals were permitted only if it could be shown that they were needed for education or performance or research. Byron-Marasek held both the necessary New Jersey permit and an exhibitor's license from the United States Department of Agriculture, which supervises animal welfare nationally.

After arriving in Jackson, Byron-Marasek got six more tigers — Bengal, Hassan, Madras, Marco, Royal, and Kizmet — from McMillan and from Ringling

Brothers. The next batch — Kirin, Kopan, Bali, Brunei, Brahma, and Burma — were born in the backyard after Byron-Marasek allowed her male and female tigers to commingle. More cubs were born, and more tigers were obtained, and the tiger population of Holmeson's Corner steadily increased. Byron-Marasek called her operation the Tigers Only Preservation Society. Its stated mission was, among other things, to conserve all tiger species, to return captive tigers to the wild, and "to resolve the human/tiger conflict and create a resolution."

"I eat, sleep, and breathe tigers," Byron-Marasek told a local reporter. "I never take vacations. This is my love, my passion." A friend of hers told another reporter, "She walks among her tigers just like Tarzan. She told me, 'I have scratches all along the sides of my rib cage and both my arms have been cut open, but they're just playing.' Now that's love."

You know how it is — you start with one tiger, then you get another and another, then a few are born and a few die, and you start to lose track of details like exactly how many tigers you actually have. As soon as reports of the loose tiger came in, the police asked everyone in Jackson who had tigers to make sure that all of them were accounted for. Six Flags Wild Safari had a permit for fifteen and could account for all fifteen. At the Maraseks', the counting was done by a group of police and state wildlife officers, who spent more than nine hours peering around tumble-down fences, crates, and sheds in the back-yard. Byron-Marasek's permit was for twenty-three tigers, but the wildlife officers could find only seventeen.

Over the years, some of her tigers had died. A few had succumbed to old age. Muji had an allergic reaction to an injection. Diamond had to be euthanized after Marco tore off one of his legs. Marco also killed Hassan in a fight in 1997, on Christmas Eve. Two other tigers died after eating road-killed deer that Byron-Marasek now thinks might have been con-taminated with antifreeze. But that still left a handful of tigers unaccounted for.

The officers filmed the visit:

"Joan, I have to entertain the notion that there are five cats loose in town, not just one," an officer says on the videotape.

Byron-Marasek's lawyer, Valter Must, explains to the group that there was some sloppy math when she filed for the most recent permit.

The officers shift impatiently and make a few notes.

"For instance, I don't always count my kids, but I know when they're all home," Must says.

"You don't have twenty-three of them," one of the officers says.

"Exactly," Must says.

"You'd probably know if there were six missing," the officer adds.

"I would agree," Must says.

On the tape, Byron-Marasek insists that no matter how suspicious the discrepancy between her permit and the tiger count appears, the loose tiger was not hers. No, she does not know whom it might have belonged to, either. And, gentlemen, don't stick your fingers into anything, please: I'm not going to tell you again.

The officers ask to see Byron-Marasek's paperwork. She tells them that she is embarrassed to take them into her house because it is a mess. The tiger quarters look cheerless and bare, with dirt floors and chain-link fences and blue plastic tarps flapping in the January wind, as forlorn as a bankrupt construction site. During the inspection, a ruckus starts up in one of the tiger pens. Byron-Marasek, who represents herself as one of the world's foremost tiger authorities, runs to see what it is and re-appears, wild-eyed and frantic, yelling, "Help me! Help! They're going to . . . they're going to kill each other!" The officers head toward the tiger fight, but then Byron-Marasek waves to stop them and screams, "No, just Larry! Just Larry!" — meaning Larry Herrighty, the head of the permit division, about whom she will later say, in an interview, "The tigers hate him."

The day of the tiger count was the first time that the state had inspected the Maraseks' property in years. New Jersey pays some attention to animal welfare — for instance, it closed the Scotch Plains Zoo in 1997 because of substandard conditions — but it doesn't have the resources to monitor all its permit holders. There had been a few complaints about the tigers: In 1983, someone reported that the Maraseks played recordings of jungle drums over a public-address system between four and six a.m., inciting their tigers to roar. The New Jersey State Office of Noise Control responded by measuring the noise level outside the compound one night, and Byron-Marasek was warned that there would be monitoring in the future, al-though it doesn't appear that anyone ever came back. Other complaints, about strange odors, were never investigated. Her permit was renewed annually, even as the number of animals increased.

Anyone with the type of permit Byron-Marasek had must file information about the animals' work schedule, but the state discovered that it had no records indicating that her tigers had ever performed, or that anyone had attended an educational program at Tigers Only. The one tiger with a public profile was Jaipur, who weighed more than a thousand pounds, and who, according to his owner, was listed in the *Guinness Book of World Records* as the largest Siberian tiger in captivity. Later, in court, Byron-Marasek also described Marco as "a great exhibit cat" — this was by way of explaining why she doted on him, even though he had killed Diamond and Hassan — but, as far as anyone could tell, Marco had never been exhibited.

Now the state was paying attention to the Tigers Only Preservation Society, and it wasn't happy with what it found. In court papers, DEP investigators noted, "The applicant's tiger facility was a ramshackle arrangement with yards (compounds), chutes, runs, and shift cages . . .

some of which were covered by deteriorating plywood, stockade fencing and tarps, etc. . . . The periphery fence (along the border of the property), intended to keep out troublemakers, was down in several places. There was standing water and mud in the compound. There was mud on the applicant's tigers." There were deer carcasses scattered around the property, rat burrows, and a lot of large, angry dogs in separate pens near the tigers. Suddenly, one wandering tiger seemed relatively inconsequential; the inspectors were much more concerned about the fact that Byron-Marasek had at least seventeen tigers living in what they considered sorry conditions, and that the animals were being kept not for theatrical or educational purposes, but as illegal pets. Byron-Marasek, for her part, was furious about the state's inspections. "The humiliation we were forced to suffer is beyond description," she said later, reading from a prepared statement at a press conference outside her compound. "Not only did they seriously endanger the lives of our tigers — they also intentionally attempted to cut off their food supply."

The one suspicion that the state couldn't confirm was that the loose tiger had belonged to Joan Byron-Marasek. DNA tests and an autopsy were inconclusive. Maybe he had been a drug dealer's guard animal, or a pet that had gotten out of hand and was dropped off in Jackson in the hope that the Tiger Lady would take him in. And then there were the conspiracy theorists in town who believed that the tiger had belonged to Six Flags, and that his escape was covered up because the park is the biggest employer and the primary attraction in town. In the end, however, the tiger was simply relegated to the annals of suburban oddities — a lost soul, doomed to an unhappy end, whose provenance will never be known.

It is not hard to buy a tiger. Only eight states prohibit the ownership of wild animals; three states have no restrictions whatsoever; and the rest have regulations that range from trivial to modest and are barely enforced. Exotic-animal auction houses and animal markets thrive in the Midwest and the Southeast, where wildlife laws are the most relaxed. In the last few years, dealers have also begun using the Internet. One recent afternoon, I browsed the Hunts Exotics website, where I could have placed an order for baby spider monkeys ($6,500 each, including delivery); an adult female two-toed sloth ($2,200); a northern cougar female with blue eyes, who was advertised as "tame on bottle"; a black-capped capuchin monkey, needing dental work ($1,500); an agouti paca; a porcupine; or two baby tigers "with white genes" ($1,800 each). From there I was linked to more tiger sites — Mainely Felids and Wildcat Hideaway and NOAH Feline Conservation Center — and to pages for prospective owners titled "I Want a Cougar!" and "Are You Sure You Want a Monkey?" It is so easy to get a tiger, in fact, that wildlife experts estimate that there are at least fifteen thousand pet tigers in the country — more than seven times the number of registered Irish setters or Dalmatians.

One reason that tigers are readily available is that they breed easily in captivity. There are only about six thousand wild tigers left in the world, and three subspecies have become extinct just in the last sixty years. In zoos, though, tigers have babies all the time. The result is thousands of "surplus tigers" — in the zoo economy, these are animals no longer worth keeping, because there are too many of them, or because they're old and zoo visitors prefer baby animals to mature ones. In fact, many zoos began breeding excessively during the seventies and eighties when they realized that baby animals drew big crowds. The trade in exotic pets expanded as animals were sold to dealers and game ranches and unaccredited zoos once they were no longer cute. In 1999, the *San Jose Mercury News* reported that many of the best zoos in the country, including the San Diego Zoo and the Denver Zoological Gardens, regularly disposed of their surplus animals through dealers. Some zoo directors were so disturbed by the practice that they euthanized their surplus animals: According to the *Mercury News*, the director of the Detroit Zoo put two healthy Siberian tigers to sleep, rather than risk their ending up as mistreated pets or on hunting ranches. Sometimes dealers buy surplus animals just for butchering. An adult tiger, alive, costs between two hundred and three hundred dollars. A tiger pelt sells for two thousand dollars, and body parts from a large animal, which are commonly used in aphrodisiacs, can bring five times as much.

Between 1990 and 2000, Jackson's population increased by almost a third, and cranberry farms and chicken farms began yielding to condominiums and center-hall Colonials. It was probably inevitable that something would come to limn the town's changing character, its passage from a rural place to something different — a bedroom community attached to nowhere in particular, with clots of crowdedness amid a sort of essential emptiness; a place practically exploding with new people and new roads that didn't connect to anything, and fresh, clean sidewalks of cement that still looked damp; the kind of place made possible by highways and telecommuting, and made necessary by the high cost of living in bigger cities, and made desirable, ironically, by the area's quickly vanishing rural character. A tiger in town had, in a roundabout way, made all of this clear.

In 1997, a model house was built on the land immediately east of the Maraseks' compound, and in the next two years thirty more houses went up. The land had been dense, brambly woods. It was wiped clean before the building started, so the new landscaping trees were barely toothpicks, held in place with rubber collars and guy wires, and the houses looked as if they'd just been unwrapped and set out, like lawn ornaments. The development was named the Preserve. The houses were airy and tall and had showy entrances and double-car garages and fancy amenities like Jacuzzis and wet bars and recessed lighting and cost around three hundred thousand dollars. They were the kinds of houses that betokened a certain amount of achievement — promotion to company vice president, say — and they were owned by people who were disconcerted to note that on certain mornings, as they stood outside playing catch with their kids or pampering their lawns, there were dozens of buzzards lined up on their roofs, staring hungrily at the Maraseks' backyard.

"If someone had told me there were tigers here, I would have never bought the house," one neighbor said not long ago. His name is Kevin Wingler, and where his lawn ends, the Maraseks' property begins. He is a car collector, and he was in his garage at the time, tinkering with a classic red Corvette he had just bought. "I love animals," he said. "We get season passes every year for the Six Flags safari, and whenever I'm out I always pet all the cows and all the pigs, and I think tigers are majestic and beautiful and everything. But we broke our ass to build this house, and it's just not right. I could have bought in any development! I even had a contract elsewhere, but the builder coaxed me into buying this." He licked his finger and dabbed at a spot on the dashboard and laughed. "This is just so weird," he said. "You'd think this would be happening in Arkansas, or something."

I drove through the Preserve and then out to a road on the other side of the Maraseks' land. This was an old road, one of the few that had been there when the Maraseks moved in, and the houses were forty or fifty years old and weathered. The one near the corner belonged to the owner of a small trucking company. He said that he had helped Joan Byron-Marasek clean up her facilities after the state inspection. "I knew she was here when I moved here fifteen years ago," he said. "Tigers nearby? I don't care. You hear a roar here and there. It's not a big concern of mine to hear a roar now and then. The stench in the summer was unbearable, though." He said he didn't think that the wandering tiger was one of Byron-Marasek's, because her tigers were so dirty and the tiger that was shot looked clean and fit. He said that a few years before, Byron-Marasek had come by his house with a petition to stop the housing development. He didn't sign it. "The new neighbors, they're not very neighborly," he said. "They're over there in their fancy houses. She's been here a lot longer than they have." Still, he didn't want to get involved. "Those are Joan's own private kitty cats," he said, lighting a cigarette. "That's her business. I've got my life to worry about."

The tiger that had walked through Jackson for less than eight hours had been an inscrutable and unaccountable visitor, and, like many such visitors, he disturbed things. A meeting was held at City Hall soon after he was shot. More than a hundred people showed up. A number of them came dressed in tiger costumes. They demanded to know why the roving tiger had been killed rather than captured, and what the fate of Byron-Marasek's tigers would be. Somehow the meeting devolved into a shouting match between people from the new Jackson, who insisted that Byron-Marasek's tigers be removed immediately, and the Old Guard, who suggested that anyone who knew the town — by implication, the only people who really deserved to be living there — knew that there were tigers in Holmeson's Corner. If the tigers bothered the residents in the Preserve so much, why had they been stupid enough to move in? Soon after the meeting, the state refused to renew Byron-Marasek's wildlife permit, citing inadequate animal husbandry, failure to show theatrical or educational grounds for possessing potentially dangerous wildlife, and grievously flawed record-keeping. The township invoked its domestic-animals ordinances, demanding that Byron-Marasek get rid of some of her thirty-odd dogs or else apply for a formal kennel license. The home owners in the Preserve banded together and sued the developer for consumer fraud, claiming that he had withheld information about the tigers in his off-site disclosure statement, which notifies prospective buyers of things like toxic-waste dumps and prisons, which might affect the resale value of a house. The neighborhood group also sued Byron-Marasek for creating a nuisance with both her tigers and her dogs.

Here was where the circus began — not the circus where Joan Byron-Marasek had worked and where she had developed the recipe for "Joan's Circus Secret," which is what she feeds her tigers, but the legal circus, the amazing three-ring spectacle that has been going on now for several years. Once the state denied Byron-Marasek's request to renew her permit, she could no longer legally keep her tigers. She requested an administrative review, but the permit denial was upheld. She appealed to a higher court. She was ordered to get rid of the animals while awaiting the results of her appeal of the permit case. She appealed that order. "Tigers are extremely fragile animals," she said at a press conference. "Tigers will die if removed by someone else. If they are allowed to take our tigers, this will be a tiger holocaust." Byron-Marasek won that argument, which allowed her to keep the tigers during her permit appeal, as long as she agreed to certain conditions, including preventing the tigers from breeding. During the next couple of years, two of her tigers had cubs, which she hid from state inspectors for several weeks. She declared that the state was trying to destroy her life's work. Through her Tigers Only website, she supplied form letters for her supporters to send to state officials and to the DEP:

Dear Senator:

I am a supporter of the Tigers Only Preservation Society and Ms. Joan Byron-Marasek in her fight to keep her beautiful tigers in their safe haven in Jackson, New Jersey. . . . We should all be delighted with the fact that these tigers live together in

*peaceful harmony with their environment
and one another right here in New Jersey.
If anything, the T.O.P.S. tigers should be
revered as a State treasure, and as such, we
citizens of New Jersey should all proudly
and enthusiastically participate in this
State-wide endeavor to keep the T.O.P.S.
tigers in New Jersey.*

*If we are successful . . . future genera-
tions of constituents will be eternally
grateful for your efforts in keeping these
magnificent creatures living happily in our
midst for all to enjoy.*

In the meantime, legal proceedings
dragged on while she changed attorneys five
times. Her case moved up the legal chain
until it reached the state's appellate court.
There, in December 2001, the original ver-
dict was finally and conclusively upheld —
in other words, Byron-Marasek was denied,
once and for all, the right to keep tigers in
New Jersey.

The Byron-Marasek case reminded some
people of the 1995 landmark lawsuit in Oregon against Vickie Kittles, who had a hundred and fifteen dogs living with her in a
school bus. Wherever Kittles stopped with
her wretched menagerie, she was given a

tank of gas and directions to get out of town. She ended up in Oregon, where she was finally arrested. There she faced a district attorney named Joshua Marquis, who had made his name prosecuting the killer of Victor the Lobster, the twenty-five-pound mascot of Oregon's Seaside Aquarium who had been abducted from his tank. When the thief was apprehended, he threw Victor to the ground, breaking his shell; no lobster veterinarian could be found and Victor died three days later. Marquis was able to persuade a jury that the man was guilty of theft and criminal mischief. He decided to prosecute Kittles on grounds of animal neglect. Kittles contended that she had the right to live with her dogs in any way she chose. Marquis argued that the dogs, which got no exercise and no veterinary care and were evidently miserable, did not choose to live in a school bus. Vickie Kittles was convicted, and her dogs were sent to foster homes around the country.

The Kittles case was the first prominent suit against an "animal hoarder" — a person who engages in the pathological collecting of animals. Tiger Ladies are somewhat rare, but there are Cat Ladies and Bird Men all over the country, and often they end up in headlines like 201 CATS PULLED

FROM HOME and PETS SAVED FROM HORROR HOME and CAT LOVER'S NEIGHBORS TIRED OF FELINE FIASCO. A study published by the Hoarding of Animals Research Consortium says that more than two-thirds of hoarders are females, and most often they hoard cats, although dogs, birds, farm animals, and, in one case, beavers, are hoarded as well. The median number of animals is thirty-nine, but many hoarders have more than a hundred. Hoarders, according to the consortium, "may have problems concentrating and staying on track with any management plan."

On the other hand, animal hoarders may have boundless energy and focus when it comes to fighting in court. Even after Byron-Marasek lost her final appeal, she devised another way to frustrate the state's efforts to remove her tigers. The Department of Environmental Protection had found homes for the tigers at the Wild Animal Orphanage in San Antonio, Texas, and come up with a plan for moving the tigers there on the orphanage's Humane Train. In early January, the superior-court judge Eugene Serpentelli held a hearing on the matter. The Tiger Lady came to court wearing a dark-green pantsuit and square-toed shoes and carrying a heavy black briefcase. She was edgy and preoccupied and waved off anyone who approached her except for a local radio host who had trumpeted her cause on his show and a slim young man who huddled with her during breaks. The young man was as circumspect as she was, politely declining to say whether he was a contributor to the Tigers Only Preservation Society or a fellow tiger owner or perhaps someone with his own beef with the DEP.

Throughout the hearing, Byron-Marasek dipped into her briefcase and pulled out sheets of paper and handwritten notes and pages downloaded from the Internet, and passed them to her latest lawyer, who had been retained the day before. The material documented infractions for which the Wild Animal Orphanage had been cited by the USDA over the years — storing outdated bags of Monkey Chow in an unair-conditioned shed, for instance, and placing the carcass of a tiger in a meat freezer until its eventual necropsy and disposal. None of the infractions were serious and none remained unresolved, but they raised enough questions to delay the inevitable once again, and Judge Serpentelli adjourned to allow Byron-Marasek more time to present an alternate plan. "Throughout this period of time, I've made it clear that the court had no desire to inflict on Mrs. Marasek or the tigers any hardship," the judge announced. "But the tigers must be removed. I have no discretion on the question of whether they should be removed, just how."

Before the state acts, however, there is a good chance that the Tiger Lady will have taken matters into her own hands. Last fall, in an interview with the *Asbury Park Press*, she said that she was in the process of "buying land elsewhere" — she seemed to think it unwise to name the state — and suggested that she and her dogs and her tigers might be leaving New Jersey for good. Typically, people who have disputes with the authorities about their animal collections move from one jurisdiction to another as they run into legal difficulties. If they do eventually lose their animals, they almost always resurface somewhere else with new ones: Recidivism among hoarders is close to a hundred percent. In the not-too-distant future, in some other still-rural corner of America, people may begin to wonder what smells so strange when the wind blows from a certain direction, and whether they actually could have heard a roar in the middle of the night, and whether there could be any truth to the rumors about a lady with a bunch of tigers in town.

I had been to Jackson countless times, circled the Maraseks' property, and walked up and down the sidewalks in the Preserve, but I had never seen a single tiger. I had even driven up to the Maraseks' front gate a couple of times and peered through it, and I could see some woolly white dogs scuffling behind a wire fence, and I could see tarps and building materials scattered around the house, but no tigers, no flash of orange fur, nothing. I wanted to see one of the animals, to assure myself that they really existed.

One afternoon, I parked across from the Winglers' and walked past their garage, where Kevin was still monkeying around with his Corvette, and then across their backyard and beyond where their lawn ended, where the woods thickened and the ground was springy from all the decades' worth of pine needles that have rained down, and I followed the tangy, slightly sour smell that I guessed was tiger, although I don't think I'd ever smelled tigers before. There was a chain-link fence up ahead. I stopped and waited. A minute passed and nothing happened. A minute more, and then a tiger walked past on the other side of the fence, its huge head lowered and its tail barely twitching, the black stripes of its coat crisscrossed with late-day light, its slow, heavy tread making no sound at all. It reached the end of the fence and paused, and turned back the other way, and then it was gone.

Super-Duper

I learned a lot by spending a week in Miami just before Super Bowl XXIX. For instance, I learned the superlative degree of the word *nude* just by reading the ads in the *Miami Herald*. Throughout Super Bowl week, dozens of nightclubs declared that they would be throwing the Super Bowl party of the year; as the competition heated up, one club went to a hurry-up offense, changing its ad from "Wide Screen TVs — Nude Girls" to "W-i-d-e Screen TVs — Nudest Girls in Miami." At a press conference heralding the resurrection of the World Football League, I learned from former 49ers coach Bill Walsh how the new league would redefine football. "I can tell you this," Walsh said with emotion. "You will see the ball thrown and caught." Excellent. I learned that even cops call bad guys bad guys. This came up at the Stolen Ticket Press Conference, held after some smart aleck conned a Federal Express office into giving him packages containing two hundred and sixty-two Super Bowl tickets intended for the Miami Dolphins. "We don't want to say much more than that," the police spokesman declared. "It would be unfortunate if the bad guys found out what we know."

I learned that some American men still haven't heard of Lycra. The hostesses at the Bud Bowl party, on the Tuesday before the game, were a half-dozen young women with large breasts and collapsing mountains of hair, wearing really tight tube dresses that were meant to look like Budweiser labels. The dresses provoked spirited but ignorant conjecture at the party regarding how a girl could get into one of them. Oh, Dan Marino was there, too. I thought this was kind of exciting — after all, Marino is the Miami Dolphins' quarterback, we were in Miami, we were getting ready for the year's climactic football game, and spotting NFL players seemed to be the pregame sport of the week — so I mentioned it to a football fan as I was leaving the party. He had a plate of stone-crab claws in one hand and a Polaroid of himself discussing the merits of a nickel-back defense with some of the Bud Girls in the other. "He was?" the fan said. "Marino? Oh. I didn't notice."

I learned that the Super Bowl and the week of revelry leading up to it feels exactly like prom week — if you had happened to go to a high school with seventy-four thousand in the graduating class and your prom had been televised to seven hundred and fifty million people worldwide and your parents had been liberal about your curfew and you had accessorized your prom outfit by wearing on your head a piece of polyurethane foam shaped like a thunderbolt (if you were a Chargers fan) or a miner's pickax (if you were for the 49ers). The only difference — which in the case of most Super Bowls turns out to be a minor one — is that most proms don't feature a football game.

If football is a metaphor for war, then Super Bowl week is a metaphor for football. Throughout the week, everything had a sort of battlefield urgency and martial precision. Posted at the Media Center: "Following is a press release regarding the Super Bowl Sod. It is from Bermuda Dunes (near Palm Springs), California, not Las Vegas. . . . It is very important for it to be known that the sod is from Palm Springs . . . and not Las Vegas, as has previously been reported." Over the PA at an outdoor souvenir fair: "Attention, personnel! We need mini-helmets at the autograph booth! Mini-helmets! ASAP!" At the

Commissioners' Party, an enormous gala at the Miami Beach Convention Center, the league owners were penned in a corner apart from the crowd and were guarded by wiry tough guys with walkie-talkies. One tough guy had collared a small, tan man with luminous white hair who was heading into the pen. "Station to command base," the guard said into his walkie-talkie. "I have a certain individual here asserting he is one of the owners of the Seattle Seahawks. Can you clear me?" He was, and they did.

The Super Bowl is billed as the ultimate American sporting event and the ultimate athletic battle: No other television broadcast attracts a larger audience, and the money and effort that people spend to attend it is stupendous. But during my week in Miami, I didn't feel that I was on the brink of a singular, decisive battle: I felt that I was bouncing from one little skirmish to another — the mini-helmet crisis, the heavy-duty credentials checkpoints at the parties, the elbowing through crowds to get near one of the players, the press briefings about which Charger had a case of the gout and whether the 49ers practiced in full pads or just in sweatclothes. Very few Super Bowls ever turn out to be exciting games. This is blamed, variously, on the misalignment in the two football conferences, which means the matchup always has one clearly superior team; on the fact that you can never guarantee that any single game in any sport will be suspenseful (as opposed to a playoff series, which builds momentum); or on the simple fact that nothing, no matter how thrilling, could ever live up to the hype that precedes every Super Bowl. Still, everyone runs around all week in a state of high excitation. There is a real contest at the Super Bowl, but it's not on the field — it's a battle for tickets and hotel rooms and invitations and autographs and access and souvenirs, and it requires both an offensive and a defensive strategy.

The Merchandise Bowl was decided early in the first quarter of Super Bowl week, with victory going to the mini-footballs, which are about the size of a hand grenade and are totally adorable. Other contenders were Super Bowl hats, pins, earrings, coffee mugs, ashtrays, key chains, and diaper bags, and, of course, the Super Bowl sweatshirt, with appliquéd lettering, which cost $79.98. This seemed expensive, especially since Hosty the Super Bear, the mascot of the South Florida Super Bowl

XXIX Host Committee, had taken an Official Super Bowl Superhost Pledge, assuring visitors that Miami merchants would be offering fair prices and quality service, despite the powerful temptation to gouge the seventy-four thousand fans in town for the game. I expressed surprise at the sweatshirt price to one vendor, and he explained, with special Super Bowl Superhost logic, that it cost that much because it had "authentic stitching."

Autographs were going for free, at least at the NFL Experience, which is a big football-themed carnival set up each year next to the Super Bowl stadium, with displays and games where you can test your football skills. Ken Stabler, the former quarterback of the Oakland Raiders, was there, signing stuff, one afternoon. The place was mobbed: A sign posted near the autograph table warned, in English and Spanish, DUE TO PLAYERS' TIME CONSTRAINTS, NO AUTOGRAPHS GUARANTEED. I gave up on getting Stabler's autograph and wandered around the on-site Foot Locker store; the sand sculpture busts of television commentators Dan Dierdorf, Frank Gifford, and Al Michaels; and booths for face painting, quarterback challenges, football cards, lost children, and a game called the Emmitt

Zone, in which you dive for a pass over gigantic air mattresses shaped like Dallas Cowboys running back Emmitt Smith.

The underground economy typical of mega-events was in play early in the week: Miami was dotted with guys scalping tickets to get into the game (fifteen hundred dollars by midweek); guys scalping tickets to get into the NFL Experience (twenty-five dollars for tickets that legitimately cost twelve dollars); guys with sandwich boards advertising for tickets ("True Fan Needs Tickets. Top Dollar Paid. Please Help"); guys offering to buy your press credentials, your tickets to any of the pregame parties, and even, the minute you stepped out of Joe Robbie Stadium after the game, your ticket stub (twenty dollars, any seat). Mega-events tend to inflame beyond reason — everyone wants to be part of them and to take a piece of them home for possible future resale. At a souvenir booth at the game, an agitated fellow wearing a Chargers shirt pushed his way to the front of the line and tried to buy the Stadium Staff hat that the cashier was wearing. The cashier stared at him in amazement. "Don't you understand me?" the man barked at the cashier. "This is a major kind of day!" It is so major that many people come to the Super Bowl city without tickets, just to soak up the Super Bowl vibe. Some people don't seem to care whether they actually get into the game, but others hang on to the hope that they will eventually stumble on tickets. Except for the brokers and the scalpers, only a few opportunities present themselves. One Miami radio station offered a pair of tickets to the individual who could come up with the most disgusting stunt. Sadly, only one person could win; in this case, it was a young man who ate another young man's vomit. I was sorry the radio station didn't release the location of the winner's seats: I had wanted to be sure he wasn't seated anywhere near me.

Everything about the Super Bowl is extra-large — the parties, the prices, the buildup, the letdown. Even things you don't expect to be huge are huge. For instance, the average size of the man on the street in Miami during Super Bowl week was at an all-time high, because so many football players from other teams were in town for the game and because so many fans had cultivated at least the form, if not the function, of an offensive lineman. There were times when it looked as if Miami were holding a big and tall men's convention. At an outdoor café on South Beach on Saturday, I passed a table of seven giants wearing straw cowboy hats and gold chains as thick as cobras; they looked like football players and acted as cocky as football players and eventually drew a crowd of autograph seekers, whom they cheerfully obliged. They were not, in fact, football players. At that point it didn't seem to matter: They were big, enormous, cool-looking guys, and it was the day before the big game.

On Thursday, I had gone to the fashion show for the World Football League, which aspires to become the NFL's European counterpart, because I expected the models to be real football players; after all, it would look pretty weird to have a waif drift down the runway in a helmet and pads. The event did not pack them in, and that meant that I was among the few who saw the uniforms for the Barcelona Dragons, the London Monarchs, and the Düsseldorf!Fire. When a model named Tim came out wearing the Amsterdam Admirals' uniform ("Tim's wearing an away jersey. . . . There's the insert in the pants for an aggressive-type look"), I remarked to a reporter sitting near me that I thought Tim was pretty cute and perhaps a little slight for a football player. The reporter snorted and turned to me. "That's no player," he said, shaking his head. "That's just some surfer."

The real players — the 49ers and the Chargers, that is — were scarce, except on Friday, when 49ers Ricky Watters, William Floyd, Todd Kelly, and Toi Cook, along with Tim Irwin of the Dolphins, showed up at a press conference announcing a joint venture between Tommy Boy Music and Gridiron Records that will give football stars the opportunity to become recording stars. Then Watters, Floyd, and Kelly performed a rap song, and Irwin sang a few bars of a wistful country paean to his GMC truck. The female rappers Salt-N-Pepa had come to give the singers moral support. When someone in the audience asked them what an athlete needed to succeed as a rapper, Salt — or maybe it was Pepa — chuckled and said, "A nice butt."

At last, it was time for what had been described at one press briefing as "the on-the-field part of the product" — the ultra-big event that 49er Bart Oates had said early in the week he considered "better than a poke in the eye with a sharp stick." On game day, the parking lots were filled with tailgate parties and with people still trying to buy tickets. Dozens of white tents had been set up beside the stadium: This was the Corporate Hospitality Village, where companies like Ford and Budweiser and Reebok were holding lavish private parties for their guests. The tents made the place look like a refugee camp, except that the VIP parking lot beside the Corporate Hospitality Village was packed with long white stretch limos — almost a hundred of them, idling in endless rows. Overhead, planes hauling banners buzzed back and forth: FLORIDA PEST CONTROL WORKS FOR YOU, followed by PRES. CLINTON: PUNISH CASTRO NOT OUR KIDS AT GITMO AND PANAMA, then LET US CUBANS SACK CASTRO, and then THE REAL WINNER IS JESUS.

The real winners, of course, were the 49ers. It happened in a flash: Steve Young passed to Jerry Rice for a touchdown one minute and twenty-four seconds into the first quarter, and half the people around me threw up their hands and said, "Well, that's the game." It was, and three and a half unsuspenseful hours later, the final score was 49–26. In their locker room after the game, the San Francisco players looked sweaty and happy but not the least bit surprised. I talked for a while with Chris Dalman, an offensive lineman with pink cheeks and upper arms the size of turkeys. I had never seen upper arms like that in my life. He was telling me that it really hurts to play football and that after a game you feel lousy for a couple of days. I finally interrupted him and asked him if he had any idea of the circumference of his arms, and he said he didn't. "I don't even know exactly how tall I am," he said. "The one size I need to know is my ring size, and that's a Super Bowl size fourteen."

THERE
Part Two

The Homesick Restaurant

In Havana, the restaurant called Centro Vasco is on a street that Fidel Castro likes to drive down on his way home from the office. In Little Havana, in Miami, there is another Centro Vasco, on Southwest Eighth — a street that starts east of the Blue Lagoon and runs straight to the bay. The exterior of Miami's Centro Vasco is a hodgepodge of wind-scoured limestone chunks and flat tablets of Perma-Stone set in arches and at angles, all topped with a scalloped red shingle roof. Out front are a gigantic round fountain, a fence made from a ship's anchor chain, and a snarl of hibiscus bushes and lacy palm trees. The building has had a few past lives. It was a speakeasy in the twenties, and for years afterward it was an Austrian restaurant called the Garden. The owners of the Garden were nostalgic Austrians, who in 1965 finally got so nostalgic that they sold the place to a Cuban refugee named Juan Saizarbitoria and went back to Austria. Saizarbitoria had grown up in the Basque region of Spain, and he had made his way to

Cuba in the late thirties by sneaking onto a boat and stowing away inside a barrel of sardines. When he first arrived in Havana, he pretended to be a world-famous jai alai player, and then he became a cook at the jai alai club. In 1940, he opened Centro Vasco, and he made it into one of the most popular restaurants in Havana. Having lost the restaurant to Castro, in 1962, Juan Saizarbitoria moved to Miami and set up Centro Vasco in exile. Along with a couple of funeral homes, it was one of the few big Cuban businesses to come to the United States virtually unchanged. The first Centro Vasco in America was in a small building on the edge of Miami. After a year or so, Saizarbitoria bought the Garden from the departing Austrians. He didn't have enough money to redecorate, so he just hung a few paintings of his Basque homeland and of the Centro Vasco he'd left behind in Havana; otherwise, the walls remained covered with murals of the Black Forest and rustic alpine scenes. The restaurant prospered: It became a home away from home for Miami's Cubans in exile. Soon there was money to spend, so a room was added, the parking lot was expanded, awnings were replaced. Inside, the walls were redone in a dappled buttery yellow, and the memories of Austria were lost forever under a thick coat of paint. Until then, there might have been no other place in the world so layered with different people's pinings — no other place where you could have had a Basque dinner in a restaurant from Havana in a Cuban neighborhood of a city in Florida in a dining room decorated with yodeling hikers and little deer.

These days, Centro Vasco is an eventful place. During a week I spent there recently, I would sometimes leaf back and forth through the reservation book, which was kept on a desk in the restaurant's foyer. The pages were rumpled and blobbed with ink. Los Hombres Empresa, luncheon for twelve. Beatriz Barron, bridal shower. The Velgaras, the Torreses, and the Delgados, baby showers. A birthday party for Carmen Bravo and an anniversary party for Mr. and Mrs. Gerardo Capo. A paella party for an association of Cuban dentists. A fund-raiser for Manny Crespo, a candidate for judge. Southern Bell, a luncheon for twenty-eight people; someone had written next to the reservation, in giant letters and underlined, "NO SANGRIA." The Little Havana Kiwanis Club cooking contest had been held in the Granada Room; the finals for Miss Cuba en Exilio had taken place on the patio. There were dinner reservations for people who wanted a bowl of *caldo Gallego,* the white-bean soup they used to eat at Centro Vasco in Havana; lunches for executives of Bacardi rum and for an adventurous group of Pizza Hut executives from Wisconsin; hundreds of reservations for people coming on Friday and Saturday nights to hear the popular Cuban singer Albita; a twice-annual reservation for the Centauros, 1941 alumni of a medical school in Havana; a daily reservation for a group of ladies who used to play canasta together in Cuba and relocated their game to Miami thirty years ago.

Juan Saizarbitoria goes through the book with me. This is not the Juan of the sardine barrel; he died four years ago, at the age of eighty-two. This is one of his sons — Juan Jr., who now runs the restaurant with his brother, Iñaki. The Saizarbitorias are a great-looking family. Juan Jr., who is near sixty, is pewter haired and big nosed and pink cheeked; his forehead is as wide as a billboard, and he holds his eyebrows high, so he always looks a little amazed. Iñaki, fifteen years younger, is rounder and darker, with an arching smile and small, bright eyes. Juan Jr.'s son, Juan III, is now an international fashion model and is nicknamed Sal. He is said to be the spitting image of sardine-barrel Juan, whom everyone called Juanito. Before Sal became a model, he used to work in the restaurant now and then. Old ladies who had had crushes on Juanito in Havana would swoon at the sight of Sal, because he looked so much like Juanito in his youth. Everyone in the family talks a million miles a minute — the blood relatives, the spouses, the kids. Juan Jr.'s wife, Totty, who helps to manage the place, once left a message on my answering machine that sounded a lot like someone running a Mixmaster. She knows everybody, talks to everybody, and seems to have things to say about the things she has to say. Once, she told me she was so tired that she could hardly speak, but I didn't believe her. Juanito was not known as a talker; in fact, he spoke only Basque, could barely get along in Spanish, and never knew English at all. In Miami, he occasionally played golf with Jackie Gleason, to whom he had nothing to say. Some people remember Juanito as tough and grave but also surprisingly sentimental. He put a drawing of the Havana Centro Vasco on his Miami restaurant's business card, and he built a twenty-foot-wide scale model of it, furnished with miniature tables and chairs. It hangs over the bar in the Miami restaurant to this day.

On a Friday, I come to the restaurant early. The morning is hot and bright, but inside the restaurant it's dark and still. The rooms are a little old-fashioned: There are iron chandeliers and big, high-backed chairs; amber table lamps and white linen; black cables snaking from amplifiers across a small stage. Pictures of the many presidential candidates who have come here trolling for the Cuban vote are clustered on a wall by the door.

Now the heavy door of the restaurant opens, releasing a flat slab of light. Two, three, then a dozen men stroll into the foyer — elegant old lions, with slick gray hair and movie mogul glasses and shirt-sleeves shooting out of navy blue blazer sleeves. Juan comes over to greet them, and then they saunter into the far room and prop their elbows on the end of the bar that is across from Juanito's model of the old Centro Vasco.

These are members of the Vedado Tennis Club, which had been one of five exclusive clubs in Havana. Immediately after the revolution, the government took over the clubs and declared that from now on all Cuban citizens could use them, and just as immediately the club members left the country. Now the Vedado members meet for lunch on the first Friday of every month at Centro Vasco. Meanwhile, back in Havana, the old Vedado clubhouse is out of business — a stately wreck on a palm-shaded street.

The Vedado members order Scotch and martinis and highballs. The bartender serving them left Cuba just three months ago. They themselves left the Vedado behind in 1959, and they are as embittered as if they'd left it yesterday. A television over the bar is tuned to CNN, and news about the easing of the Cuban embargo makes a blue flash on the screen.

A buoy-shaped man with a droopy face is standing at the other end of the bar. He is Santiago Reyes, who had been a minister in the Batista regime, the bartender tells me. Santiago Reyes winks as I approach him, then kisses my hand and says, "My sincere pleasure, my dear." He bobs onto a bar stool. Four men quickly surround him, their faces turned and opened, like sunflowers. Santiago Reyes's words pour forth. It's Spanish, which I don't understand, but I hear a familiar word here and there: "embargo," "United States," "Miami," "Castro," "yesterday," "government,"

"Cuba," "Cuba," "Cuba." Across the room, the Vedado members chat in marbled voices. There are perhaps thirty-five of them here now, out of a total of a few hundred, and there will never be more. There has never been anything in my life that I couldn't go back to if I really wanted to. I ask if Little Havana is anything like the real Havana.

One gray head swivels. "Absolutely not at all," he says. "Miami was a shock when we got here. It was like a big farm. Plants. Bushes. It was quite something to see."

I say that I want to go to Havana.

"While you're there, shoot Fidel for me," the man says, smoothing the lapels of his blazer.

I say that I think I would be too busy.

He tips his head back and peers over the top of his glasses, measuring me. Then he says, "Find the time."

The tennis club sits down to *filete de mero Centro Vasco.* The food here is mostly Basque, not Cuban: *porrusalda* (Basque chicken-potato-and-leek soup), and *rabo encendido* (simmered oxtail), and *callos a la Vasca* (Basque tripe). Juanito made up the menu in Havana and brought it with him to Miami. It has hardly changed; the main exception is the addition of a vegetarian paella that the cook concocted for Madonna one night when she came here for a late dinner after performing in Miami.

I wander into the other dining room. At one table, Dr. Salvador Lew, of radio station WRHC, is having lunch with a couple who have recently recorded a collection of Latin American children's music. They are talking and eating on the air — as Dr. Lew does with one or more different political or cultural guests every weekday. The live microphone is passed around the table, followed by the garlic bread. From one to two every day, at 1550 AM on the radio dial, you can experience hunger pangs.

Iñaki and Totty sit at a round table near Dr. Lew, having a lunch meeting with two Colombians. The four are discussing a plan to market the restaurant to Colombians, who are moving into the neighborhood in droves. More and more, the Cubans who left Havana after Castro's arrival are now leaving Little Havana, with its pink dollhouses guarded by plaster lions and its old shoebox-shaped apartment buildings hemmed in by sagging cyclone fences — Little Havana, which is nothing like big Havana. The prosperous Cubans are moving to the pretty streets off Ponce de Leon Boulevard in Coral Gables, which looks like the elegant Miramar section of Havana; or to Kendall, near the newest, biggest Miami malls; or to breezy golf course houses on Key Biscayne. Centro Vasco, which had been an amble from their front doors and a home away from home, is now a fifteen-minute drive on a six-lane freeway — a home away from home away from home.

Totty and Iñaki think a lot about how to keep Centro Vasco going in the present. They have plans to open a Little Havana theme park behind the restaurant: There would be cigar and rum concessions and a huge map of Cuba, made out of Cuban soil, and a mural showing the names of American companies that want to do business in Cuba as soon as the embargo is lifted and Castro leaves. Totty and Iñaki have already added more live music on weekends in order to draw young people who were probably sick of hearing their parents talk about old Havana and who otherwise might not want to spend time somewhere so sentimental and old-fashioned, so much part of another generation. Now performers like Albita and Malena Burke, another popular singer, draw them in. And even that has its ironies, because the music that Malena Burke and Albita perform here and have made so popular with young Cuban Americans is *son* and *guajira* and bolero — the sentimental, old-fashioned music of the prerevolutionary Cuban countryside.

Totty and Iñaki have also come up with the idea that Centro Vasco ought to have a special Colombian day. As I sit down at their table, they and the Colombians are talking about something that ends with Iñaki saying, "Barbra Streisand, okay, she has a great, great, great voice, but she doesn't dance! She just stands there!"

The Colombians nod.

"Anyway," Totty says, "for the special Colombian day we'll have a Colombian menu, we'll decorate, it'll be so wonderful."

One of the Colombians clears his throat. He is as tanned as toast and has the kind of muscles you could bounce coins off. He says to Totty, "The perfect thing would be to do it on Cartagena Independence Day. We'll do a satellite feed of the finals from the Miss Colombia beauty pageant." He lifts his fork and pushes a clam around on his plate. "I think this will be very, very, very important to the community."

"Perfect," Totty says.

"We'll decorate," Iñaki says.

Totty says, "We'll make it so it will be just like home."

★ ★ ★

I told everyone that I wanted to go to Havana. The place had hung over my shoulder ever since I got to Miami. What kind of place was it, that it could persist so long in memory, make people murderous, make them hungry, make them cry?

"If you go, then you should go to the restaurant and look at the murals," Iñaki said. "If they're still there. There's one of a little boy dressed up in a Basque costume. White shirt, black beret, little lace-up shoes. If it's still there. Who knows? Anyway, the little Basque boy was me."

Juan laughed when I said I was going. I asked what it had been like on the day Castro's people took the restaurant away, and he said, "I was working that day, and two guys came in. With briefcases. They said they were running the restaurant now. They wanted the keys to the safe, and then they gave me a receipt for the cash and said they'd call me. They didn't call."

Was he shocked?

"About them taking the restaurant? No. Not really. It was like dying. You know it's going to happen to you eventually — you just don't know exactly what day."

One night at dinner, I tried to persuade Jauretsi, Juan's youngest daughter, to go with me, and she said, "It would be a scandal, the daughter of Centro Vasco going to Cuba. Seriously, a scandal. No way." I was eating *zarzuela de mariscos,* a thick seafood stew, with Jauretsi, Totty, and Sara Ruiz, a friend of mine who left Cuba fifteen years ago. Juan came over to our table for a moment, between seating guests. All the tables were full now, and grave-faced, gray-haired, black-vested waiters were crashing through the kitchen doors backward, bearing their big trays. Five guys at the table beside us were eating paella and talking on cellular phones; a father was celebrating his son's having passed the bar exam; a thirtyish man was murmuring to his date. In the next room, the Capos' anniversary party was under way. There was a cake in the foyer depicting the anniversary couple in frosting — a huge sheet cake, as flat as a flounder except for the sugary mounds of the woman's bust and the man's frosting cigar. The guests were the next generation, whose fathers had been at the Bay of Pigs and who had never seen Cuba themselves. The women had fashionable haircuts and were carrying black quilted handbags with bright gold chains. The young men swarmed together in the hall, getting party favors — fat cigars, rolled by a silent man whose hands were mottled and tobacco stained.

"If you go to Havana, see if the food is any good now," Juan said to me.

"I heard that there is only one dish on the menu each night," Totty said.

Sara, my émigré friend, said she used to go to Centro Vasco all the time after Castro took it over. Now she was eating a bowl of *caldo Gallego*, which she said she had hankered for ever since the Saizarbitorias' restaurant was taken away.

"In the Havana Centro Vasco, the food isn't good anymore," she said. "It's no good. It's all changed." You have to pay for the food in United States dollars, not Cuban pesos, she said, but you don't have to leave a tip, because doing so is considered counterrevolutionary.

The basque boy is still there, in Havana. His white shirt is now the color of lemonade, though, because after the revolution the murals on the walls of Centro Vasco were covered with a layer of yellowish varnish to preserve the old paint.

My waiter in Havana remembered Juanito. "He left on a Thursday," the waiter said. "He told me about it on a

Wednesday. I was at the restaurant working that day." I was at Centro Vasco, sitting at a huge round table with a Cuban friend of Sara's, eating the *caldo Gallego* that made everybody so homesick, but, just as I'd been warned, it wasn't the same. The waiter whispered, "We need a Basque in the kitchen, but we don't have any Basques left," and then he took the soup away.

The restaurant looks exactly like Juanito's model — a barnlike Moorish-style building, with an atrium entryway. The government has had it for thirty-five years now and has left it just as Juanito left it, with a fish tank and a waterfall in the foyer, and, inside, thronelike brown chairs, and cool tile floors, and the murals — Basques playing jai alai and rowing sculls and hoisting boulders and herding sheep — wrapping the room. As I had been told, business is done in dollars. People with dollars in Cuba are either tourists or Cubans who have some business on the black market or abroad. When my new Cuban friend and I came in, a Bruce Willis movie was blaring from the television in the bar. At a table on one side of ours, a lone Nicaraguan businessman with clunky black eyeglasses was poking his spoon into a flan, and at the table on our other side, a family of eight were singing and knocking their wine goblets together to celebrate the arrival of one of them from Miami that very day.

I myself had been in Havana for two days. On the first, I went to the old Centro Vasco, where Juanito had started: not the place where he had moved the restaurant when it became prosperous, the one he'd built a model of to hang over the Miami bar, but the original one — a wedge-shaped white building on the wide road that runs along Havana's waterfront. The wedge building had been Havana's Basque center — the *centro Vasco* — and it had had jai alai courts and lodgings and a dining room, and Juanito, the pretend world-famous jai alai player, had started his cooking career by making meals for the Basques who came.

That was years ago now, and the place is not the same. My new friend drove me there, and we parked and walked along the building's long, blank eastern side. It was once an elegant, filigreed building. Now its ivory paint was peeling off in big, plate-size pieces, exposing one or two or three other colors of paint. Near the door, I saw something on the sidewalk that looked like a soggy paper bag. Close up, I saw that it was a puddle of brown blood and a goat's head, with a white striped muzzle and tiny, pearly teeth. My friend gasped and said that it was probably a Santería ritual offering, common in the countryside but hardly ever seen on a city street. We looked at it for a moment. A few cars muttered by. I felt a little woozy. The heat was pressing on my head like a foot on a gas pedal, and the goat was pretty well cooked.

Inside the building, there were burst-open bags of cement mix, two-by-fours, bricks, rubble. An old barber chair. A fat, friendly, shirtless man shoring up a doorway. On the wall beside him was a mural of Castro wearing a big hat and, above that, a mural from the first day of the revolution, showing Castro and his comrades wading ashore from a cabin cruiser. This room had been the old Centro Vasco's kitchen, and its dining room had been upstairs. Now the whole building is a commissary, where food is prepared and then sent on to a thousand people working for the government's Construction Ministry.

After a minute, a subdirector in the ministry stepped through the rubble — a big, bearish man with shaggy blond hair and an angelic face. He said the workers' lunch today had been fish with tomato sauce, bologna, boiled bananas, and rice and black beans. He wanted us to come upstairs to see where the old Centro Vasco dining room had been, and as we made our way there he told us that it had been divided into a room for his office and a room where the workers' gloves are made and their shoes are repaired. He had eaten there when it was the old Centro Vasco, he added. It had had a great view, and now, standing at his desk, we could see the swooping edge of the Gulf of Mexico, the hulking crenellated Morro Castle, the narrow neck of the Bay of Havana, the wide coastal road, the orange-haired hookers who loll on the low gray breakwater, and then acres and acres of smooth blue water shining like chrome in the afternoon light. The prettiness of the sight made us all quiet, and then the subdirector said he had heard that some Spanish investors were thinking of buying the building and turning it back into a restaurant. "It's a pity the way it is now," he said. "It was a wonderful place."

That night, my friend and I ate dinner at a *paladar*, a kind of private café that Cubans are now permitted to own and operate, provided it has no more than twelve chairs and four tables and is in their home. This one was in a narrow house in Old Havana, and the kitchen was the kitchen of the house, and the tables and the chairs were set in the middle of the living room. The owner was a stained-glass artist by trade, and he sat on a sofa near our table and chatted while we ate. He said that he loved the restaurant business and that he and his wife were doing so well that they could hardly wait until the government permitted more chairs, because they were ready to buy them.

I went back to Centro Vasco one more time before leaving Cuba — not the old place, in the wedge building, but the new, Moorish one, in a section of Havana called Vedado, which is now a jumble of houses and ugly new hotels but for decades had been a military installation. I wanted to go once more to be sure I'd remember it, because I didn't know if I'd ever be back again. I went with my new friend and her husband, who was sentimental about the restaurant in the Vedado, because during the revolution he had fought just down the street from it. While he was driving us to Centro Vasco, he pointed to where he'd been stationed, saying, "Right there! Oh, it was wonderful! I was preparing a wonderful catapult mechanism to launch hand grenades." In front of the restaurant someone had parked a milky white 1957 Ford Fairlane, and some little boys were horsing around near it. On the sidewalk, four men were playing dominoes at a bow-legged table, and the clack, clack of the tiles sounded like the tapping of footsteps on the street. The same apologetic waiter was in the dining room, and he brought us plates of *gambas a la plancha* and *pollo frito con mojo criollo* and *tortilla Centro Vasco*. The restaurant was nearly empty. The manager came and stood proudly by our table, and so did the busboys and the other waiters and a heavy woman in a kitchen uniform who had been folding a huge stack of napkins while watching us eat. Toward the end of the meal, someone came in and warned us that our car was going to be lifted and carried away. I thought he meant that it was being stolen, but he meant that it was being relocated: Castro would be driving by soon, and because he was worried about car bombs, he became nervous if he saw cars parked on the street.

As we were leaving, the waiter stopped us at the door. He had a glossy eight-by-ten he wanted to show me — a glamorous-looking photograph of Juan Jr.'s wedding.

He said that it was his favorite keepsake. The Saizarbitorias had left nearly everything behind when they left Cuba. Juan was allowed to take only a little bit of money and three changes of clothes. In Miami, Juan's daughter Mirentxu had remarked to me on how strange it was to have so few family mementos and scrapbooks and pictures — it was almost as if the past had never taken place. I admired the wedding picture for a minute. Then the waiter and I talked a little about old Juanito. I couldn't tell whether the waiter knew that Juanito had died, so I didn't say anything. Meanwhile, he told me that a friend of his had once sent him a napkin from Centro Vasco in Miami, and he had saved it. He said, "I've had so many feelings over these years, but I never imagined that Juanito would never come back."

There had been one other Centro Vasco, but it wasn't possible for me to visit it. It had been the first Centro Vasco that Juanito opened in the United States, on the corner of Ponce de Leon and Douglas Road, in a building that straddled the border between Miami and Coral Gables — a place that might have been satisfactory except that the two cities had different liquor laws. If you wanted a drink, you had to be sure to get a table on the Miami side. The border had come to be too much trouble, so Juanito moved to Southwest Eighth Street, and eventually the old building was torn down.

But I did go back to the Centro Vasco on Southwest Eighth one more time after I came back from Cuba. It was a Saturday night, and it was busy: People were coming for dinner and to hear Malena Burke sing. I wanted to tell the Saizarbitorias about my trip, to tell them that the Basque boy was still there and that the food wasn't very good, but that the restaurant was just as they had left it and, in spite of the thirty-three years that had passed, was still in fine shape. Then I realized that I didn't know whether they would be glad or sorry about what I would tell them. In Havana, everyone I met talked constantly about the future, about what might happen when the United States lifted its embargo and when Castro retired, both of which events they expected soon. To the people I met in Cuba, the present seemed provisional and the past nearly forgotten, and their yearning was keen — charged with anticipation. In Miami, the present moment is satisfying, and thought is given to the future, but the past seems like the richest place — frequently visited and as familiar and real and comforting as an old family home.

The music wasn't to start until after midnight, so for a long time I stood in the foyer and watched people parade in: the executive of a Latin American television network, in a tight white suit and high white shoes; an editor from a Spanish soap opera magazine; a Puerto Rican singer who had just performed at Dade County Auditorium, followed by her entourage; another singer, named Franco, who called out to someone while he and I were talking, "Hey, man, you look great! I thought you were dead!"; and dozens of good-looking couples speaking in bubbly Spanish and all wearing something that glistened or sparkled or had a satiny shine. Toward midnight, Sherman Hemsley of *The Jeffersons* came in with a television producer, and Iñaki wrote "Cherman Jemsli Del Show Los Jeffersons" on a little slip of paper for Malena, so that when she pointed him out in the audience, she'd know what to say.

Malena came onstage at one in the morning. She began with a ballad that had been made famous in Cuba in the fifties by a singer called La Lupe, who used to get so emotional when she reached the crescendo that she hurled things at the audience — usually her shoes and her wig. The room had been roaring before Malena came out, but now it was hushed. Malena had left Cuba just a few months earlier. Someone told me that the tears she sheds when she's singing about lost love are real. By then, I was sitting at a table in the back of the room with Totty. I had some snapshots with me that I had taken in Havana for the family, because I'd thought they might like to see the old home again. Just as I was about to slide the pictures across the table to Totty, the singer sobbed to her crescendo, so I decided to wait until another day.

Rough Diamonds

Most of the time, the boys in *categoría pequeña* — the Cuban equivalent of Little League baseball — play on days when there hasn't been a coup in Latin America, or at least not in a country that supplies a lot of oil to Cuba. Unfortunately, the Ligeritos, a team made up of kids from the Plaza de la Revolución neighborhood of Havana, had a practice scheduled for the Sunday in April after the president of Venezuela was deposed. The uprising evaporated in a matter of days, but when I went to watch the Ligeritos play, it was still fresh news, and many people were staying home and watching television reports on the crisis. Kids who wanted a ride to the practice had to wait out the developing story of the coup.

The practice was supposed to start at nine, but when I arrived there were only a few boys at the ball field. The Ligeritos play at a big and fitfully grassy park called El Bosque, at the end of a narrow neighborhood road. The park is flat and open, bracketed by tall, weary trees, and it has an unevenly paved basketball court at one end and enough room for a few baseball games at the other. That day, a loud game between two government ministries was already under way on the best diamond, and a couple of military police officers were on the basketball court taking foul shots with a flabby orange ball. The handful of boys who'd managed to get to the field had gathered on an overgrown area near the basketball court. One had a ball, one had a bat, and another had the most important equipment for playing baseball in Cuba — some sixteen-inch-long machetes, for grooming the field. While the boys played catch, a few of their fathers stripped to the waist and started slicing through the tall grass.

I had obtained an introduction to Juan Cruz, the Ligeritos' shortstop, through a friend in Havana. Juan is a slip of a kid, eleven years old, with dark, dreamy eyes, long arms, big feet, and the musculature of a grasshopper. His thirteen-year-old brother, Carlos, plays for the Ligeritos, too, but it is Juan who woke up at four every morning during the 2000 Olympics to watch the baseball games and who cradles his glove as if it were a newborn and who always wears a baseball cap, indoors or out. When his stepfather, Víctor, is asked about Juan, he says, "Oh my God, this one dreams in baseball." In spite of the morning's news, Juan had persuaded Víctor to drive Carlos and him to the ball field at nine. He popped out of the car almost before Víctor had finished parking and ran onto the field.

The morning was soft and wet, just on the verge of summer. In Havana's Parque Central, a daily assembly of old men were arguing fine points of Yankee and Red Sox history and the likelihood of Havana's Industriales sweeping the upstarts from Camagüey in the national series. The Havana baseball mascot — a fat, placid dachshund wearing a baseball shirt, sunglasses, and a Greek fisherman's hat — was brought to a spot near the trinket market every afternoon for souvenir snapshots. And everywhere boys were playing baseball. They were playing in the parking lot of Estadio Latinoamericano, home of Havana's two teams, the Industriales and the Metropolitanos; and alongside the Malecón seawall, observed by the snobby young hookers who like to line up there and smoke; and in the dense downtown of Old Havana, wherever some building had finally completed its gradual and melodramatic collapse, opening up just enough room to field a pickup game. Every time I came in or out of my hotel, a group of boys were in the street, dodging potholes as big as washtubs, and, whether it was the bright start of the morning or the half darkness at the end of the day, they were always in the middle of a game.

There has been baseball in Cuba almost as long as there has been baseball anywhere. Introduced in the 1860s, it has been the dominant sport in the country ever since; volleyball and basketball are distant seconds, and soccer, the prevailing sport in the rest of Latin America, is hardly played. From the start, baseball has been strangely tangled up with politics. Cubans embraced it as a statement of rebellion because it was a modern and sophisticated export from democratic America, rather than an imposition of imperial Spanish culture on the island. It was also played by people of all races, not just the white elite, which added to its political allure, and Cubans fleeing Spanish oppression took it with them to Venezuela, Puerto Rico, and the Dominican Republic.

In 1911, the Cincinnati Reds drafted two Cuban players, the first of more than a hundred to be recruited to the American major leagues over the next fifty years. In the 1940s and 1950s, some teams even had full-time scouts in Cuba. It has long been rumored that, in 1942, a scout working for the Washington Senators met with a promising teenage pitcher named Fidel Castro, a rangy right-hander with velocity but no technique. Castro claims that the team gave him a contract, which he turned down; baseball historians say the Senators never made him an offer. It has also been rumored that he passed on a five-thousand-dollar signing bonus from the New York Giants in order to go to law school. There is no dispute, however, that he remained passionate about the game.

After the revolution, Castro banned most aspects of American popular culture, but baseball was so embedded in Cuba and in his own life — he sometimes pitched for an exhibition team called the Bearded Ones — that it persisted and even expanded, although Castro remade it in the revolutionary spirit. In 1961, he enacted National Decree 83A, which outlawed professional sports in Cuba. Henceforth, all competitive sports would be played by amateurs, the best of whom would receive a small government stipend equivalent to a worker's salary. This would end, as Castro took care to point out, American-style "slave baseball," in which players were bought and sold like property and in which players and owners — especially owners — were enriched at the expense of the public. Cuban players would represent their home provinces, would never be traded, and would never get rich. The first Cuban national series, in 1962, was, according to Castro, *el triunfo de la pelota libre sobre la pelota esclava*— the triumph of free baseball over slave baseball. Cuba's gold medals in the 1992 and 1996 Olympics were celebrated as vindication of revolutionary baseball, and the loss to the United States in Sydney was regarded as a calamity. Castro has said he would like two major league franchises in the country, so that Cuban teams can regularly prove themselves against Americans. "One day, when the Yankees accept peaceful coexistence with our own country, we shall beat them at baseball, too," he said in a 1974 speech. "Then the advantages of revolutionary over capitalist sport will be shown."

Baseball, with its runs to home, its timeless innings, its harmony between the lone endeavor and the collaboration of a team, has always implied more than athletics. In Cuba, it has also come to describe a social history: The version of baseball you are part of is also the version of Cuba you are part of. There are still scores of retired ballplayers in Cuba who remember the game before the revolution, who hosted American players in the Cuban winter leagues, who might have played a few seasons in Texas or Florida, and whose superstar teammates were scooped up, legally, by American teams. There is a middle generation, players in their twenties and thirties, who were born after Decree 83A and grew up knowing only *la pelota libre,* who saw friends defect to play up north, and who have Castro as an occasional pitching coach and de facto commissioner of the game. Finally, there are the kids like Juan, in *categoría pequeña,* who are now learning to play. Unless Castro lives to be a hundred, these kids will reach their prime without him — the first generation in three who will have baseball without having Castro telling them how to play the game.

Juan dreams about both Cuban and American baseball. It is illegal to watch American games in Cuba — that is, it is illegal to have satellite television on which you could see the games. But for years Cubans have been sneaking small satellite dishes into the country by painting them to look like decorative platters, and those people who haven't managed to get their own dish often barter for tapes of the major leagues at *categoría pequeña* games. As a result, Juan is now equally loyal to the Yankees and to the Industriales. "My favorites are, for the Cubans, Omar Linares, Germán Mesa, and Javier Méndez," he says, "and, for the Americans, Derek Jeter, Tino Martinez, and Baby Ruth." When I asked him whom he had rooted for during the Olympics, he just grinned and said, "My team."

That morning, he was wearing the Ligeritos' uniform, a white jersey with purple raglan sleeves and the team's name in jazzy blue letters across the front, and his favorite hat, an old Albert Belle Cleveland Indians cap that he had got from a friend. I asked him if he was an Albert Belle partisan. "No, I don't really even know him. I just like the picture on the hat," Juan said, referring to the Indians' Chief Wahoo logo. The Ligeritos' neighborhood rivals are the suspiciously counterrevolutionary-sounding Coca-Colas, and the Brigada Especiales, a team sponsored in part by the Special

Brigade police, whose barracks are across the street from El Bosque. Even teams with sponsors just squeak by when it comes to equipment. You rarely see wooden bats in Cuba, because of their cost — until two years ago, even the major league teams used aluminum ones — and new leather gloves are a luxury. Many of the kids I saw playing on the street were bare-handed or had gloves that were so limp and splayed that they looked like leather pancakes. The most popular street game in Cuba, four corners (or its variant, three corners), is super-economy baseball — you play it without gloves, and it involves whacking a round thing (rock, bottle cap, ball, wad of tape) with a long thing (tree branch, broom handle, two-by-four) over the heads of your opponents.

While Juan and Carlos took turns swatting at pitches and fielding grounders, Víctor and I sat on a concrete beam lying at the edge of the field. "When I was a kid, I always played four corners," Víctor said. "We had some sewers on our street, and they had those round metal covers, and we just used them as our bases. With us, it was always baseball, baseball, baseball, all the time." He smiled and shook his head. "With these guys, with Juan especially, it's the same. I can't wait to get him a bike so he can take himself to his games."

For some boys in Cuba, it really is baseball all the time: Every child in the country is evaluated at the age of five and steered toward a particular sport, and boys favoring baseball begin playing interschool tournaments and join a *categoría pequeña* team. The talented kids are usually well-known to the national scouts by the time they're ten. (Currently, there is no baseball program for girls, although a *categoría pequeña* is planned for next year.) At thirteen, the outstanding athletes are admitted to one of fifteen Sports Initiation Schools, the first rung in the Soviet-model athletic program that Castro established in 1961. The very best of those are sent to an Advanced School for Athletic Perfection when they turn sixteen. Castro is especially proud of the system. A billboard in the Havana stadium carries one of his favorite declarations: "Cuba has developed a real and healthy sports culture."

The Ligeritos' coach, Máximo García Cárdenas, was at El Bosque when I arrived, and, after greeting the parents, he called the boys together for some drills. Cárdenas is sixty-five years old. He played professional baseball in Cuba from 1955 to

1960 — the last five years that pro ball existed in the country. In 1961, he left for the United States and pitched in the Double-A Texas League; he spent the next fourteen years with various teams in Mexico. When he returned to Cuba, he went to work for the National Commission of Baseball as a pitching coach for the Cuban national team. He has been coaching the Ligeritos for four years. He has known baseball before and during Castro and likes to keep his hand in the baseball that will come after him. "Some of these boys are very, very good," he said during a break. "Watch Héctor, this one." He gestured toward a wiry boy wearing the team jersey, Snoopy socks, and black Nike sneakers. The boy noticed Cárdenas pointing toward him, so he crouched and put out his glove and got a tough look on his face. "That one might really be something," Cárdenas went on, keeping his eyes on the boy as he spoke. "He could really be something."

By ten, the news from Venezuela must have been drying up, because a dozen more boys appeared, fanned out, and started throwing to one another, ducking around the men who were still clearing the field with machetes. The kids were dressed in an international array of T-shirts advertising Mexican rock groups, Korean cars, Canadian concert tours, and American baseball teams; all of them were slight and tan and excited, too earnest to horse around much yet old enough to affect a little bluster.

Now that most of the team was in place, Cárdenas started another series of drills, hollering at the boys to move quickly and watch the ball. They practiced for ten minutes or so, and then Cárdenas called them together near the scrap of cardboard that was marking third base. He divided them into two squads for the practice game and then turned to Héctor, who was the captain of the team. Héctor stood at attention in front of him, and the rest of the boys lined up to the side. "Are you and your colleagues ready?" Cárdenas asked him.

"My colleagues and I are ready," Héctor said.

The boys yelled, "Ready!"

"Are you ready to play for the good of the team?" Cárdenas asked.

"We are ready," Héctor said.

The boys again yelled, "Ready!" They jostled one another and crowded closer to Cárdenas.

"Who owns the right to sports?" Cárdenas asked.

The boys chanted, *"El deporte es un derecho del pueblo!"* ("Sport is the right of the people" — one of Castro's trademark slogans.)

"Tell me again?"

"Sport is the right of the people!"

"Once more?"

"Sport is the right of the people!" they yelled, and then scrambled to their positions on the field.

Juan says that if he doesn't get to play baseball professionally, he would like to be an investigator, a policeman, a doctor, or a hero. "Those would be okay," he says, "but I would like to be a baseball player." He says he would be happy to have his career either in Cuba or in the United States, although he likes Cuban baseball more than American. "The Cubans play for fun, not for money," he explained to me between innings. I asked him what he thought of American athletes, and he said, "They play only for the millions. A real player plays because he likes baseball and doesn't need that much money to live a normal life."

At the top of the second inning, Javier Méndez, an outfielder for the Industriales and one of Juan's heroes, stopped by El Bosque with his four-year-old son, Javier

Jr. Méndez is broad chested and sturdy, with meaty arms and legs, and he has a goatee and a buzz cut and big dimples. That morning, he was wearing Oakley sunglasses, an Olympic website T-shirt, and a cast on his right hand. Méndez is thirty-seven years old and a huge star in Cuba. He had been on pace to tie the Cuban record for lifetime doubles and to get his two thousandth hit — something only ten other Cuban players have managed — when he was struck by a pitch and had to end his season. He had hoped to retire this year, but he wants to polish off those records. "Next season," he said, flexing the fingers of his injured hand, "if all goes well."

Méndez had come by to visit a friend whose son played for the Ligeritos, but it was also a chance to let little Javier take a few swings. The boy was dressed in a tiny, spotless Industriales uniform and an oversize batting helmet. When he swung, the bat nearly toppled him. When he finally hit a pitch, he toddled straight to second base. "Javi, tag first! Tag first!" Méndez shouted. He yelled something to Cárdenas, and they both started laughing. "Oh my God, look at him," Méndez said. "Well, I wasn't any good when I was young. I was weak and really small. I just practiced and persevered. I grew up in a fishing village, but I didn't know how to fish, so I played baseball. But I wasn't any good until I was sixteen."

Méndez has been on one Olympic team and won a slew of national championships. The Cuban government allowed its players to take sabbaticals in Japan in the early nineties, and Méndez and a few other Cubans played there for two seasons, but he subsequently returned to his team, at around the time that the pitcher Liván Hernández defected to play in the United States. Just a few years later, Méndez's teammate (and Liván's older brother) Orlando Hernández also defected and signed a multimillion-dollar contract with the Yankees. Star athletes in Cuba often receive gifts from the government, houses, equipment — but most of the time their compensation is measly.

A few days after the Ligeritos' practice, when I took Juan and Carlos to a major league game between Havana's Metropolitanos and Camagüey, a vendor offered to sell me not only coffee, cigars, and potato croquettes, but, for fifteen dollars, any of the players' hats or shirts — as soon as they were done using them in the game.

Méndez has played one game in the United States. On May 3, 1999, the Cuban national team played the Baltimore Orioles at Camden Yards, as part of a cultural exchange that had begun in March, when the Orioles played the national team in Havana. The Cubans won the game in Baltimore, 12–6, suffered an interruption during the fifth inning when an anti-Castro protester ran onto the field, and lost one pitching coach, who defected afterward. The game was nevertheless considered a success — the beginning of what was being called "baseball diplomacy." Méndez loved playing in Baltimore and said it was a shame about the defection, especially since it might interfere with any future games. "You know, it's hard when anyone on the team leaves for other countries," he said. "It's hard on the team. It's hard on the fans. It makes people very depressed."

I asked him if it was a good life, to be a Cuban baseball star. He watched the next boy come up to the plate and slap at a pitch. "It's a good life," he said, "in a sense."

The boys drifted over to see Méndez, most of them too shy to get close or say anything when he asked them how they were doing. He watched the game intently, applauding the good hits and the good catches, shouting encouragement and corrections along with Cárdenas, as if this were the most important game in the world, a big-league game, a game he might play in now or one that Cárdenas starred in forty years ago, rather than a matchup between gawky boys on a ragged field on a quiet street in Havana.

It was now midday and the game was over. Juan had had a great morning: Not only had he hit a single and a double and made one flashy catch — a hard-hit bad-hopping shot from Héctor — but he had got up the nerve to ask Méndez to pose with him for a photograph. Even after the other boys had headed off, Juan wanted to keep hitting, but his father said it was time to go home.

Carbonaro and Primavera

One thing will never change: Carbonaro must always be on the right. Five years from now, ten years, even twenty, if all goes well, Carbonaro will still be on the right and Primavera on the left, the two of them yoked together, pulling a spindly plow across the loamy fields in the hills outside Cienfuegos. Oxen are like that: absolutely rigid in their habits, intractable once they have learned their ways. Even when a working pair is out of harness and is being led to water or to a fresh spot to graze, the two animals must be aligned just as they are accustomed or they will bolt, or at the very least dig and refuse to go any farther until order is restored, each ox in his place.

Carbonaro and Primavera were not always a pair. Twenty years ago, Primavera was matched up and trained with an ox named Cimarrón. They worked side by side for two decades. But Cimarrón was a glutton, and he broke into the feed one day and ate himself sick, dying happy with incurable colic. It was an enormous loss. An ox costs thousands of pesos and must be babied along until the age of two and then requires at least a year of training before he can be put to work. It is especially difficult to lose half of a working pair: You have to find a new partner who fits the temperament and strength of your animal, and above all, you have to find an ox who can work on the now vacant side. Primavera would work only on the left. He could be matched only with a partner who was used to working on the right. It was a lucky thing to find Carbonaro, a right-sider and a pretty good match in terms of size, although to this day he is a little afraid of Primavera and hangs back just a bit.

Anyway, it was a lucky thing to find an ox at all. For a while, oxen had seemed part of the Cuban landscape — huge, heavy-bodied creatures, with necks rising in a lump of muscle, their gigantic heads tapering into teacup-size muzzles; homely animals with improbably slim legs and a light tread, their whip-thin tails flicking in a kind of staccato rhythm, the rest of their being unmoving, imperturbable, still. But then cheap Soviet oil came to Cuba, and chemical fertilizers, and, most important, tractors. In fact, during the 1960s and 1970s, so many tractors were being sent to

Cuba that there were more than the farmers could use. Sometimes when the Agriculture Ministry called the cooperatives to announce the arrival of more tractors, no one even bothered to go to the port to pick them up. During that time, hardly anyone wanted oxen. With a heavy tractor a farmer could rip through a field at five or six times the speed he could with a team. It was, or so it seemed, so much more modern, and so much simpler, than dealing with the complicated politics of a flesh-and-blood team. Hardly anyone was raising or training oxen. With such a windfall of tractors, no one imagined that oxen would ever again be anything other than a quaint anachronism.

Even during the time of abounding tractors, Humberto Quesada preferred using Primavera and Cimarrón — and then, of course, Carbonaro — but Humberto is an independent sort of man. His grandfather was brought to Cuba as a slave and was put to work on a sugar plantation of seventy thousand rich acres owned by a Massachusetts family. Humberto's father was a slave there, too, and Humberto as a child worked beside him in the fields, so that he could learn how to do what he assumed he's grown up to do. Although the

Quesadas were slaves, they were mavericks. Humberto's sister Ramona, a tiny woman with tight curls and a dry laugh, married the son of a white farmer down the road — a scandal at the time, but one that yielded a happy fifty-year marriage that became the warm center of the joined families. And, of course, Humberto went his own way. After the Castro revolution he became a truck driver, but he kept a hand in farming. It was different, because he was farming on his own land, a piece of the old plantation. "The land is the foundation of everything," he told me not long ago. "If you have land, you always have something." He was encouraged to join a cooperative, but like many Cuban farmers, he chose to work alone. "There's always a lazy person in a group, so I don't like being a part of groups," he explained. Moreover, he resisted each time the government tried to cut back a little bit of his land. Recently the government wanted to build a health clinic on a piece of his property, but once the official in charge of the appropriation realized that the magnificent sweet potatoes he regularly enjoyed were from Humberto's farm, he changed his mind and said Humberto should have *more* land, not less.

Once or twice, Humberto rented a tractor, but he didn't like it. "It presses too hard," he explained. "The land ends up flattened, like a Cuban sandwich." Even when everyone else was using tractors, using chemicals, growing only sugar, Humberto plowed with oxen; fertilized naturally, the way his father had taught him; cultivated tomatoes and corn and lettuce and beans — and sweet potatoes. Humberto never actually owned the oxen. He borrowed them from his neighbor, whose father had fought beside Humberto's father in the War of Independence.

When the Soviet money ran out, the battalions of tractors, now out of gas, rattled to a standstill, and oxen — quaint, anachronistic oxen — were once again worth their weight in gold. It was a lucky farmer who had never given them up, who still had a working team, who could still plow and plant even in the worst moments after the Soviet collapse. Luckier still was a farmer who had such with crops such as corn and tomatoes rather than being seduced by the money that had seemed as if it would flow forever from sugar. In such a moment, a man like Humberto no longer seemed a throwback. Now in his eighties, slightly lame, wizened, Humberto is everything the new Cuban farmer needs to be: small-scale, efficient, diversified, organic — and, more important, invulnerable to the ups and downs of Cuba's gasoline economy, which once depended entirely on Soviet goodwill and has since come to rest precariously on Venezuelan. Most of the imported oil in Cuba these days comes from Venezuela, and because of the good relationship between Fidel Castro and Hugo Chávez, Venezuela's president, the price had, until recently, been especially favorable. But Chávez was nearly overthrown in April of last year, and when he regained his footing he suspended the shipments. Across Cuba, gasoline prices rose by as much as twenty percent. It was a very good time to have an ox.

One recent morning, Humberto stopped by to say hello to his sister, who lives with her extended family on another piece of the old plantation property. It was a brilliant breezy day. Outside Ramona's little cottage, a couple of chickens were worrying the dirt, and a litter of piglets was chasing around in a pile of hay. The cottage is tidy, old, and unadorned; there is something timeless about it, as if nothing here, or nearby, had changed in twenty or thirty or fifty years. And, of course, nothing much has changed in the countryside; the elemental facts, the worries over sun and water, whether the seeds have germinated and the eggs have hatched, don't ever change. In Cuba right now there is a sense of the moment, a sense that the country is on the brink of newness and change, a sense that the future is unfurling right now — but the countryside has a constancy, a permanence. And these days Humberto feels like a rich man. He said that everyone he knows is going crazy looking for oxen, and that you have to barter for them or apply to the government, and that anyone who still knows how to train a team — a skill that was of course considered obsolete when the tractors prevailed — is being offered a premium for his talents. He grinned as he said this, pantomiming the frantic gestures of a desperate man looking high and low for a trained plowing team.

Someday, no doubt, the tractors will start up again, and the hills beyond Cienfuegos and the fields outside Havana and the meadows in Camagüey and Trinidad and Santiago de Cuba will be plowed faster than the fastest team could dream of. Then, once again, oxen won't be golden anymore. They will be relics, curiosities. But this is their moment, when being slow and shrewd and tough is paying off.

After we'd talked awhile, Humberto got up and headed down the drive and over to his neighbor's, and a few minutes later he reappeared, leading the two oxen, who were walking side by side. He stopped in the yard near the cottage and brought the animals to a halt and stood beside them, one hand laid lightly on Primavera's neck. The oxen had shuffled their feet a little and looked sidelong at the cottage, the chickens, a curtain ruffling in the breeze in Ramona's entryway. Humberto's straw hat was tipped back, and it cast a lacy shadow across his face; he leaned a little against the animal's warm gray shoulder and he smiled.

The Congo Sound

Hervé Halfon, a French person who hates French people, owns a record store on the rue des Plantes in Montparnasse, just a few Métro stops from the Eiffel Tower but spiritually closer to avenue Gambela in Congo or to the Mokolo district in Yaoundé, Cameroon. The store is called Afric' Music. It has a small sign and an unremarkable window display, and it's about the size and shape of a Parisian parking space. Inside, Hervé has spared all expense on the décor. Besides the floor and ceiling and one long counter, the store is nothing but rows and rows of CDs in racks and on shelves and in piles, all of them devoted to African music, except for a section reserved for the music of the Caribbean. A sound system sits somewhere behind the counter, out of view and, more important, out of reach of any customer who might want to, perhaps, switch the new N'Dombolo recording for something by M'Pongo Love. The sound system is on, loud, all the time. If you walk down the rue des Plantes, you will at first hear just the usual rumbling and tootling and clattering sounds of a Paris street, and then, as you pass the open door of Afric' Music, you will be blasted by a few bars of a Congolese ballad, and as soon as you step past the door, the ballad will suddenly be out of earshot and the Paris street sounds will resume, as if you had walked through a harmonic cloudburst.

As is the custom in record stores all over the world, a song rarely gets played in its entirety at Afric' Music. What happens is that Hervé and a customer will be listening to a song — let's say, something by Wenge Tonya Tonya — and a certain guitar line will make Hervé think of a cut on an old Franco and O.K. Jazz album, which he will put on, and then the Franco song will remind the customer of a song by Les Youles that he heard the other day on the world music show on Radio Nova, so Hervé will turn off the Franco and put on Les Youles, and then another customer will wander in and suggest that the Les Youles song is a pitiful imitation of a much better song recorded twenty years ago by Tabu Ley Rochereau. Hervé will have that recording, too, so he will play it, and then the two customers will start arguing about it, and then Hervé, in his role as a peacekeeping force, will take off the Tabu Ley record and put on something uncontroversial, like the new album *Bang Bang*, by Carimi, whose members are Haitian but grew up in Miami.

Afric' Music opened twenty-six years ago. The store was founded by Hervé's cousin David Halfon, who had picked up a taste for African music at clubs around town. At the time, David was working as a salesclerk in a musical instrument shop in the Paris neighborhood of Saint-Michel. On a gamble, he asked the owners of the shop to let him sell African records and tapes out of the back corner of the store. There was no store in France devoted to African music in 1976, even though there were already more than a million Africans living in the country, many of whom came from the French-speaking nations of Gabon, Benin, Togo, Mali, Chad, Ivory Coast, and Senegal, as well as from Zaire — the country now known as Congo — whose music, called "soukous," or just *la musique moderne,* was the least parochial and most widely embraced throughout Africa. Moreover, a number of the Congolese expatriates living in Paris happened to be that country's greatest musicians. And even though there was nowhere to buy African music in France in the mid-seventies, much of it was actually being recorded in studios in Paris and in Brussels and shipped back to Africa for release.

This peculiar cross-continental journey was actually in keeping with the history of soukous — and of all African music, which, in the words of the Cameroonian saxophonist Manu Dibango, was essentially "a music of encounters." To begin with, soukous was a mélange of indigenous village music and Cuban rumba, which had become popular in Congo through a series of records released there in the 1930s. Rumba was in fact finding its way back to its origins, since it, too, was a mélange — in this case, a combination of Spanish music and the sounds brought to the Caribbean by African slaves. In other words, soukous had left home, absorbed a new culture, returned home, and was being absorbed and reinterpreted once again. The music that resulted was especially elastic. Its lyrics were almost always sung in Lingala, a trading language of the Congo region and a distinct African dialect, but one that is generic and unprovincial — a sort of lingua franca with no fractious history attached. But what made soukous the preeminent music in Africa was its sound, the voluptuous interplay of three or four or even five guitars, swirling around keening melodies and a dreamy, compelling beat. It is emotional, complex music, with the brightness and propulsion and hot guitars of popular music but with a less hurried, mounting intensity. It sounds neither contemporary nor old; it is melodic and highly structured, even orchestral, but also powerfully rhythmic and cyclic, like a chant. You can dance for hours and hours to soukous music; it has that kind of drive. But it is also strangely, ineffably poignant. Even the biggest, brassiest soukous songs have a wistful undercurrent, the sound of something longed for or lost.

Kinshasa, the capital of the Democratic Republic of the Congo, was once the home of Africa's most energetic recording industry. Gary Stewart, in his authoritative history, *Rumba on the River*, recounts how, in 1948, a Greek merchant named Nicolas Jeronimidis opened the Ngoma studio in downtown Kinshasa. Eventually, there were a score of studios, including many owned and operated by Congolese, and soukous's most successful musicians ran studios of their own. Soukous was the sound on every street, in clubs, on the airwaves, even on public address systems, which blared the music for anyone who didn't have a radio. It became so entwined in the country's sense of identity that in 1960, when its delegates went to Brussels for a conference on independence, the leading soukous orchestra at the time, Joseph Kabasele and African Jazz, accompanied them.

Mobutu Sese Seko, the dictator who ruled the country for thirty-two years, was aware of how directly music communicated to the Congolese. When he took power in 1965, he demanded that the country's musicians write songs to celebrate his achievement and then arranged for them to receive generous state sponsorship as a sort of insurance policy against future songs that might question his actions. When he introduced his Authenticité campaign in 1971, with the aim of ridding the country of foreign influence, he designated the great soukous orchestra O.K. Jazz the official musical medium for conveying his doctrine. He traveled throughout Zaire with the orchestra; after each of his speeches, O.K. Jazz performed, both to sweeten the medicine of Authenticité and to use its lyrics to lecture the crowds, however gorgeously, about Mobutu's programs. It would be like George W. Bush giving a series of speeches about why he wanted to go to war with Iraq, accompanied by foreign policy songs by Bruce Springsteen.

Official intimacy did have its tribulations. Songs that Mobutu considered controversial or disparaging were banned; musicians who were too mouthy were subtly — or overtly — run out of the country. Even the greatest soukous master of all, Franco Luambo Makiadi, who led O.K. Jazz for thirty-three years, was jailed once, had his songs censored, and several times left for Europe when he felt an official chill. Franco was a huge man with a husky voice and a chiming, lacy style on guitar. His playing was so hypnotizing that throughout his life he was quite seriously accused of being a sorcerer. It is said that Mobutu loved Franco's music so much that each time Franco left, the dictator would eventually send word that he would be pardoned if he was willing to come home and perform. When Franco died, in Brussels, in 1989, Mobutu declared four days of national mourning and gave him a state funeral.

But Mobutu was responsible for the

music business's eventual exodus from the country. By the mid-1970s, the price of copper, Zaire's chief export, had fallen dramatically, and the president's totalitarianism and his move toward Mao-inspired nationalization of industry had chased away investors and set off terrible inflation. Before long, almost all of Kinshasa's studios had gone out of business or relocated to Paris or Brussels, and the few that remained had little money for equipment, engineers, or even vinyl. Record sales were also flagging. It wasn't that the passion for soukous was fading; it was that people in Zaire were broke. Meanwhile, as the domestic economy worsened throughout the decade, Mobutu and his family skimmed at least five billion dollars from the treasury and from international aid.

One by one, all of soukous's biggest stars made their débuts in Paris: Tabu Ley Rochereau, in 1970; Joseph Kabasele, also in 1970; Franco and O.K. Jazz, in 1978. In Paris you could sing about anything you wanted, you could record in the best studios, you could play to the ever growing population of Africans and West Indians. It was safe; there was money. Nightclubs catering to the African community were opening — Keur Samba, a swanky place near the Place de la Concorde, was the first, in 1975, followed by the Black and White Club, the Atlantis, Timmy's, L'Alizé, Au Petit Tam-Tam. By the late seventies, more and more of Zaire's most prominent musicians were leaving Africa to tour Europe and weren't coming back. In 1980 came the most symbolic move of all: While touring with O.K. Jazz, Franco bought a house in Brussels and an apartment in Paris and started spending more time far from home.

David Halfon's back corner of the instrument shop in Saint-Michel quickly became one of the most famous back corners in Paris. Most Africans in Paris lived in other neighborhoods — in the north, in Barbès and Saint-Denis, or to the east, in the "red" suburb of Montreuil, which is said to have the largest community of Malians outside Mali and as a municipality has financed public works projects in Mali's villages. But the goods to be found in Saint-Michel were worth traveling for — it was the sound of the familiar, of the life that had been left behind. Before long, David had rented a storefront and set up a proper store.

Hervé worked in Afric' Music after

school. He was then a teenager, mildly disgusted by French pop treacle like Plastic Bertrand and only occasionally moved by French crooners like Charles Aznavour. His musical interests were black soul, black reggae, black blues. Hanging around David, he became fluent in the music of Congo, Senegal, Nigeria, and Antilles. Fourteen years ago, David decided to sell Afric' Music and open a chain of fast-food restaurants, so Hervé and a partner bought him out. They also began producing a number of African bands, including the renowned Congolese guitarist Diblo Dibala and his band, Matchatcha; Les Coeurs Brisés; Branché; and Flaisha Mani, known as the Diamond of Zaire.

Hervé is now thirty-six years old, with a sinewy build, receding dark hair, and the chic, messy look of a tragic intellectual. It has never struck him as weird or incongruous that he is a white guy, and a Jewish one at that, selling African music to expatriates. His parents both grew up in Tunisia and imparted something of an outsider's perspective to him; as a result, Hervé's outlook on the archetypal French persona is somewhat negative. One recent morning, as he was shelving new CDs, he said, "I don't like the narrow-mindedness of French people. I'm more comfortable with Africans. They have a different attitude — more open to the world." He is tempted to leave France altogether. Five years ago, a customer of his who had moved back to Ivory Coast asked him to come to Abidjan and help him open a record store. Hervé and his wife visited for two weeks. They were put up in the best hotel in the country and had a car and driver at their disposal, but, ultimately, they decided that they felt too out of place. Hervé now says he is considering moving to Canada or Israel but isn't sure how or when he will ever really leave.

Hervé's role in the store is all-inclusive. He orders new music, arranges it on the shelves, writes the Afric' Music bestseller lists — African and Caribbean — that hang on the back wall, answers the phone, writes up sales, and takes out the trash. He also dispenses opinions and directives to anyone willing to hear them. He has a generous policy regarding test drives: He is willing to open any CD to let you have a listen; as a result, about half the CDs in the store no longer have their plastic wrappers. Hervé likes to steer customers toward what he calls "hot music." By hot he means sexy, intense, and exciting rather than trendy. Only a small amount of dancing occurs in the store, though; the customers, who are overwhelmingly male, usually just lean up against the counter and move only one part of their body — a foot, a hand, a chin — in time with the song. Hervé is less inhibited and often pounds out the beat on his thighs or on the counter, sometimes using the plastic cover of a CD. When he's not at the store, he plays drums as a hobby, but the fact that he lives in an apartment with his wife and their two small kids cuts into his rehearsal opportunities.

Hervé is a cheerful person, although he says that being in the record store business is a living nightmare. For one thing, Afric' Music no longer enjoys the primacy it had when it opened in 1976. African music has become a real commodity in Paris: A number of competing specialty shops have cropped up in the past two decades, and FNAC, the large French music-and-bookstore chain, now features an African section. The specialty record store mortality rate is high — Blue Moon Musique, Anvers Musique, and Kim Music, among others, have gone out of business — but new ones open all the time. In the past year or so, five or six tiny stores have opened in Saint-Denis.

One morning in early September, I headed over to Afric' Music. There was a pinch in the air, a scrim over the sun, and smoke gray clouds scudding across the horizon. Placards advertising Ray Charles's upcoming concert were pasted on every light pole and bus shelter in Paris. When I arrived at Afric' Music, Hervé was chatting with two young men from Benin, who were taken with an album called *Hot Zouk Love*. Hervé knows almost all his customers by sight and most by name; some are even second-generation shoppers. One of the young men from Benin was the son of a longtime customer. After a moment, a short, bubbly guy carrying two cellphones and a set of car keys came in, gave Hervé a hug, and started scanning the CD section marked "Nigeria." We started to talk, and I asked him what he did for a living.

"I was a student in economics," he said, "but now I drive a taxi, madame." He chuckled and added that he was from Nigeria but was looking for a record by a Haitian band called Digital Express. "These days, you have to go to London to find really good Nigerian music," he said. He winked at me and then said in a loud voice, "Hervé, he doesn't like Nigerians."

Hervé broke off his conversation with the men from Benin and started hollering in agitated French. He grabbed an album by King Sunny Ade, who is from Nigeria, and poked the taxi driver with it. "And what about Tilda?" Hervé said. "I have Tilda albums, too."

"She's not Nigerian!" the man said.

"Yes, she is," Hervé said.

"No! She isn't!" the man said excitedly. "Her father is Nigerian, but her mother is from Cameroon!"

"Well, she's Nigerian, then," Hervé said, pleased with himself.

"No," the cabdriver said. "Half of her is not Nigerian. She sings Nigerian songs, but she's only half."

The men from Benin paid for their copy of *Hot Zouk Love* and quietly edged out of the store.

A young lawyer from Cameroon came in. He shook hands with Hervé and explained that he was going to DJ at a party that night — the wedding of a French friend and an African friend — so he wanted the best dance music he could find. Hervé put on a singer named Sandra Melody doing a reggae version of the American group T.L.C.'s song "No Scrubs." I mentioned to the lawyer that it was an American song, and he gasped.

"No way is this an American song!" he exclaimed. "Listen!" He rested his right hand on his right hip, held up his left hand as if he were holding a partner, and then started to shimmy back and forth. Everyone in the store paused as he completed his turn around the floor. When the song ended, he turned to me and said, "See? You couldn't dance to it like this if it were an American song!"

There was a moment when it seemed as if Congo would once again be the home of the Congo sound. In 1997, Laurent Kabila, the leader of the People's Revolutionary Party, marched with his troops into Kinshasa, and the aging Mobutu, who was suffering from terminal cancer, fled the country. Kabila's takeover was celebrated everywhere, including in Paris, where Tabu Ley Rochereau, one of the last members of the generation that had invented soukous, was quoted as saying that it was time for the diaspora to end, for Congo's musicians to go home. Kabila offered him a deputy post in his transitional parliament, and Tabu Ley accepted. A few others followed, most notably Sam Mangwana and the singer Kanda Bongo Man, but soon they returned to Europe: Even with Mobutu gone, the country's political and economic turmoil continued. (Kabila was assassinated in 2001; his son, Joseph, is now in power.) And, for their part, the musicians who had lived in Europe had grown used to being able to sing about whatever they wanted, used to forty-eight-track studios and the most advanced synthesizers and drum machines and to an audience that had spread from the rue des Plantes all over the world.

While I was in Paris, I visited the guitarist Diblo Dibala, who had moved to Europe in 1989. He said that he was a supporter of both Kabilas but that he still couldn't imagine going back. "When you've been away for fifteen or twenty years, the reality of the place is different from what you remember," he said. "We're much more popular here than in Congo. The people there forget you when you leave for so long." He hasn't performed in Kinshasa since 1995. He said that he finds his inspiration in Paris, because it is where most African musicians are, and he doesn't think that will change. "Everyone comes to Paris," he said.

Soukous has become, then, the music of Africa once removed; it has absorbed yet another new culture, and when you listen to what is being recorded now, you hear a briskness and shimmer, as if the clamor and sleekness of modern Paris were a constant underscore. You might miss the pensive majesty of Franco's orchestra, but it is the nature of Congolese music to reach out, react, and remake itself each time it encounters a different world. One afternoon, Dany Engobo, the leader of Les Coeurs Brisés, stopped by my hotel to bring me the group's latest CD. I was staying in a smart new place in Montparnasse that I had chosen because of its proximity to the record store but that also happened to be decorated in Africa chic; it had animal-print wallpaper and ethnic knickknacks, and African music — mostly Senegalese and Nigerian — was piped into the lobby all day long, recreating in this bourgeois arrondissement of Paris a mythic version of pre–French colonial Africa. Engobo has lived in Paris since 1976 and started Les Coeurs Brisés after he arrived. The group — which includes musicians from Algeria, France, and Israel — has played throughout the United States and Europe and in a few African countries, but never in Kinshasa or Brazzaville, where Engobo is from. He doesn't expect that they will play there anytime soon. "It's too dangerous to go," Engobo said, shrugging. "I'd like to go sometime, but . . ."

He paused, and the music whirled around us, a King Sunny Ade melody with tinkling thumb piano and the singer's reedy alto spelling out the tune. "I am a citizen of the world," Engobo said. "I don't think I'll ever go back. But in life, you never know."

At Afric' Music, while the Cameroonian lawyer was dancing, a tall man with a hospital employee ID around his neck walked in. "Hervé," he said, "I'm dying for the new Gilberto Santa Rosa. Do you have it?" Hervé pulled several Santa Rosa CDs out of a stack. The man shuffled through them and said he wasn't sure if any of these was the one he wanted. He pulled his cellphone out of a holster, called one of Hervé's competitors, who was unhelpful, and then briefly contemplated calling friends in Martinique for a consultation.

While he was thinking, a heavyset blind man from Guadeloupe eased his way through the doorway, folded up his cane, leaned on the counter, and asked Hervé to put on something by the popular young band Zouk Station. Hervé found the album, split the shrink-wrap with a two-euro coin, and put it on. The blind man smiled and said he would buy it. Two elderly women walking past with groceries, their baguettes sticking up like exclamation points, glanced in anxiously as they moved through the blast of Zouk Station. A red-cheeked drunk zigzagged across the rue des Plantes toward the music, rolled through the door, and came to rest against the counter. Just then, the man who was thinking about calling Martinique realized that it was four in the morning in the Caribbean, so he told Hervé he would take two Santa Rosa albums. As he was paying, a cab pulled onto the sidewalk in front of Afric' Music, and a compact old man from Togo wearing a newsboy cap and a bomber jacket got out of the driver's seat, walked into the store, headed for the rack marked "Congo," ran his hands up and down the CDs, and said, "Franco! Oh, oh, Franco!" After a moment, he walked back out of the store, got into his cab, and drove away.

"He likes Franco," Hervé said.

The Cameroonian lawyer had chosen five albums and wanted more. Hervé removed the previous selection and blasted Fara Fara. The lawyer did a two-step, a tango move, and then shook his head. Off with Fara Fara. On with the new CD by Wenge Musica. The song had a galloping bass line and a bright, chattering guitar, and soon the lawyer was doing a modified cha-cha and Hervé was smiling, beating a tattoo on the counter. The sound was huge, pushing out of the little store and ballooning onto the Paris sidewalk, where the businesspeople and the shop clerks of Montparnasse were striding by in the dull autumn sunlight, smoking and talking on their way to lunch. As the song reached its crescendo, a man from Ivory Coast stepped into the store, slapped Hervé on the back, pulled out his cellphone, called a friend, and, when his friend answered, said simply, "Hey. I'm here."

Like Waters and Chocolate Pancakes

The lame and the halt come to Héviz. The arthritic, the rheumatoid, and the spinally challenged come, too, and those with gout, with sore gums, and with the nonspecific but acute craving to be young. They come to the little round lake in the middle of Hungary and strap on inflatable water wings or squeeze an inner tube under their arms and then float for hours, as motionless as lily pads, waiting for Héviz to work. The water in the lake is warm and glassy blue. It comes from a spring deep in the earth and supposedly contains minerals and radioactivity with healing powers. Nothing happens when you touch it, except that you start to smell a little like an egg-salad sandwich.

When my mother and I went to Héviz recently, I told her that I wasn't sure I believed the thermal waters there could do anything, and a man overhearing me poked my mother in the ribs and said, "Wait and see, madam! You'll look younger than your daughter when you get out!" This got me thinking. If my mother was going to end up looking younger than me, I wondered what I would end up looking like. What if my mother went in and I didn't, and then we ended up looking the same age, like those indistinguishable mothers and daughters in the old Breck commercials? Nobody at the lake looked young or perky, but maybe they were, like, two hundred years old, in which case they looked great!

But that made me think of something else: Exactly how many years would the lake take off your age? I wanted to know this because I'm not *that* old, and I didn't want the Héviz waters to send me back to my teenage years, because they weren't that enjoyable. Unfortunately, no one at the lake could tell me how long to stay in the lake in order to rejuvenate myself to a specific age that I liked a lot. It's probably more like cooking a turkey, where you have guidelines, but in the end you have to rely on instinct and touch and what time you need to get dinner on the table. I also think you aren't supposed to come here worrying about such things. You come to Héviz to bob around in the hot pond and luxuriate in knowing that whatever ails you will be cured.

If you are Hungarian and have a note from your doctor, you can come to Héviz and stay in the square brick hostels in the park that surrounds the lake. Everybody else stays in hotels and guesthouses on the hills that rise up beyond the park. The visitors appear to be approximately one hundred percent German or Austrian, with the occasional Swiss. The parking lot of our hotel, the Danubius Thermal Hotel Aqua, was filled with late-model white Mercedeses lined up in a long, shiny row like a mouthful of molars. The new houses nearby are painted cocoa brown and have projecting eaves and window boxes and pierced woodwork along their balconies, in the style of an alpine chalet. In Héviz, there are German sausage stands and prices posted in German denominations. There are even a few teenage German greasers with pierced ears and round-toed leather boots and Metallica T-shirts. Perhaps they were actually middle-aged businessmen from Frankfurt who had spent a lot of time in the lake. The number of Germans here caught me by surprise, although I'd heard that families scattered in East and West Germany used to reunite during vacations in this part of Hungary, because it was almost neutral ground.

The Thermal Hotel Aqua is on one of those hills above the lake; it is a newish building with clean lines that could house an insurance company in a Midwest office park. The big indoor pool is filled with water pumped out of the lake. Everyone walks around in fluffy white robes and rubber thongs. People at the Thermal Hotel Aqua look a little glossy all the time, which might be from soaking in the radioactive water or from starting their days at the breakfast buffet, which includes two kinds of hot dogs and chocolate cake. Health, of course, is a relative thing.

"What is your problem?" the doctor asked me when I went in for my required initial consultation. I said I had come just to relax at the spa and see if there was something special about the Héviz water. "I understand," he said, tapping his mustache with the end of his pencil. "I'll put down 'recreation' for your diagnosis."

He wrote for a moment on a little chart on his desk and then handed it to me. On the front was a list of the baths he recommended — two twenty-minute sessions each day in the thermal pool, one electric compartment bath, one underwater massage. On the back of the chart there were printed outlines of bodies; he had scribbled wiggly lines on them to indicate where he wanted me massaged and mud packed. I liked the sound of the carbonic acid bath and the infrared treatment, but he shook his head and said those were for people with joint and bone problems. We then talked for a moment about the Gundel's nut-and-chocolate-filled pancakes I'd had at dinner the night before.

I realized then that the Héviz canon is that you come and get cured of your aches and pains and then get younger and younger; once you plateau at whatever age you're going to regress to, you go and eat a lot of hot dogs and chocolate cake and loll around. Exercise here is something you sign up and pay for; it's called "gymnastic," it's listed as a therapy on the hotel price list, and unless the doctor prescribed it for you, you don't have to do it.

I was thinking about this one afternoon, while I dangled from a sort of traction device at the deep end of the thermal pool. I had huge lead weights around my ankles that made my legs hang heavily, pulling my torso down while I was suspended from a contraption with bars and hooks that was wedged under my arms. This is called "subaquale traction" and is recommended for, among other things, "congenital or acquired disturbances of motion." I felt really tall while I was hanging there, but once the trainer fished me out and unbuckled the weights, I shrank back to my normal height. Then I went and got massaged by a Hungarian valley girl, who was snapping her gum and listening to a radio station playing Tom Jones singing "Delilah" while she worked on me. At the same time, she was carrying on a conversation with another masseuse, who was on the other side of a muslin curtain and slapping around another pasty tourist. I rather liked the no-nonsense style of the massage: nothing mystical, nothing spiritual, no need to gaze up at the masseuse when she finished and mutter something about how in touch I felt with my energy, which is what I usually feel obligated to do whenever I get a massage from a post-hippie body works expert here in the United States.

So, does the water work? The Romans were the first to come to Héviz and float around in the pond, and then the Hungarians, and then, apparently, the Germans and Austrians and Swiss. My mother, after a few soaks, still looked like my mother, but I confess I felt younger every day I stayed around the lake. If you walk at even a decent clip, you fly by everyone who is shuffling toward Lake Héviz. When I went running, I felt Olympian. One afternoon, I ran through town, past those cocoa-colored alpine cottages and the tour buses from Munich, and a little girl scampered after me and then smacked me on the butt. I guess if I looked spankable to a four-year-old, something must have happened. It was our last day in Héviz. I cut my run short, went back to the hotel, ate more chocolate pancakes, and jumped into the pool.

Shooting Party

When I went to Scotland for a friend's wedding last summer, I didn't plan on firing a gun. Getting into a fistfight, maybe; hurling insults about badly dressed bridesmaids, of course; but I didn't expect to shoot or get shot at. The wedding was taking place in a medieval castle in a speck of a village called Biggar. There was not a lot to do in Biggar, but the caretaker of the castle had skeet-shooting gear, and the male guests announced that before the rehearsal dinner they were going to give it a go. The women were advised to knit or shop or something. I don't know if any of us women actually wanted to join them, but we didn't want to be left out, so we insisted on coming along.

We were not outfitted like an Edwardian shooting party. One woman was in a denim minidress with red, white, and blue platform shoes. Another was wearing pedal pushers and wobbly pumps. I was in something lightweight and was tripping around in rubber flip-flops. The caretaker must have been horrified by the sight of us. He had small dark eyes and a tragic manner and was wearing a proper field jacket with suede patches in the right places. He handled his gun with a wary tenderness, as if it were a baby alligator; it was about the size of one, with a double barrel and a thick wooden stock. None of us had ever done this before. We were gunless, gun-fearing city people, writers and filmmakers and art historians — sissies, in fact, who cringed when the caretaker raised the shotgun, wordlessly indicating that it was time to begin. He muttered a few instructions, then held out the gun, waiting. No one stepped up. After a moment, we turned on the bridegroom and shoved him forward.

It was just one of those things — dumb luck, probably — but the bridegroom had perfect aim, and he exploded the clay pigeon into a million pieces. The caretaker nodded and released another pigeon, and again the groom hit the target. It was inspiring. We all crowded up to take our turns. The guest in platform shoes went next and missed by a mile. An usher in Ray-Bans winged a few. One bridesmaid had perfect form but a hot finger on the trigger. Finally, it was my turn. I hadn't expected to like the feel of the gun, but I did: It was warm and smooth and knee-bucklingly heavy, with two triggers that were set so far apart that they might have been fitted for a giant's hand span. The caretaker sized me up and then spoke quietly. "You want to hold it as tight against your shoulder as you can," he said. "It has a very powerful recoil."

I squeezed the gun against my body.

"Tighter," he said.

"That's as tight as I can get it."

"A little tighter."

I have never been kicked by a mule, so I can only imagine that it would feel a little like the gun slamming into me after I fired. My teeth rattled, and my head rang like a school bell. I was hysterically excited, as breathless and thrilled as if I'd just robbed a bank. Having missed, I begged for another shot. The caretaker released another pigeon, and I followed it, my arm aching from the weight of the gun and the shock of the recoil. I missed again, but I was close. The second recoil was just as bad as the first. I shot again and again and again, sending not a single clay pigeon to its reward but each time getting closer. Me! Firing a double-barreled shotgun! And I couldn't stop! The caretaker was egging me on, murmuring that if I had a gun that fit me properly, I'd be hitting everything.

I didn't stop until the groom pointed out that we were being charged about a pound sterling per shot and that at the rate I was going he wouldn't be able to afford a honeymoon. Shooting enchanted me; this is my sport, I thought. I wondered where in Manhattan I could go to fire a gun. The next morning — the day of the wedding — I woke up nearly unable to lift my arm. The bruise extended from my armpit to my elbow, and it was black and green and a deep imperial purple. I was wearing a sleeveless dress, as all the women in the wedding were, and they were all bruised to varying colors, depending on how enthusiastic they'd been about the sport. We considered covering our injuries with undereye concealer, but there was not enough to go around. Fortunately, single-malt Scotch was available in huge quantities, and by the end of the night we were showing off our bruises like tattoos.

Fertile Ground

The penises in Bhutan amazed me, there were so many of them. I didn't see them right away when I arrived in the kingdom of Bhutan's one airport, a narrow drive shaved into the Paro Valley's shaggy green grass. I might not have noticed them anyway, because I was so woozy from the flight — the scariest one in regularly scheduled commercial aviation, mastered by fewer than a dozen pilots in the world, which requires a right-hand turn at Mount Everest and then a sort of swooning, tree-trimming slide through the high Himalayas to the airstrip. I was so preoccupied with making landfall that I didn't take note of anything about the airport, really, not even the paintings of curly-tailed dragons and birds, whose beaks are curved like meat hooks, and blue poppies and auspicious Buddhist symbols — conch shells and endless knots and golden fish.

It wasn't until my second day, when I was some distance from the airport, that I first saw the penises. I was driving through a ten-thousand-foot mountain pass called

Dochu La when I came to a big farm-house, broad hipped and white walled, with a traditional Tibetan-style beamed roof and a huge wooden doorway twice as tall as anyone who might ever walk through it. In the rocky front yard, a thousand or so chili peppers were spread out to dry in the sun. On either side of the door, someone had painted a huge phallus — peachy pink, with a matte finish, poised in a salutatory arc with little wisps of whatever curling from the bottom and the top. I happened to be in Bhutan with a group of American women who were hoping to get pregnant by being blessed at Bhutanese fertility ceremonies, so the penises were a big hit — a particularly auspicious symbol for those who were looking for that particular kind of good fortune. The owner of the house stepped out as we were taking photographs. He was a wiry and windburned little man, wearing blue knickers, a woven jacket, a red skullcap, and rubber boots. At first, he seemed puzzled by our attention, but after studying us for a moment, he nodded knowingly, then arranged himself by the doorway and puffed up with pride for our cameras. Whether it was pride in his house or his red hot chilies or his fertile mural, we would never know.

From then on, the penises were everywhere: sketched on houses in Wangduephodrang and in Punakha, on walls in Trongsa, and on a storefront in Jakar, where they were painted above muslin sacks printed with the Bhutanese population control slogan: SMALL FAMILY HAPPY FAMILY. At the monastery at Chime Lhakhang, which is the most auspicious of auspicious places to be blessed for fertility in Bhutan, the monk performing the ceremony had two penises on the altar. One was of hand-carved ivory, and the other was a piece of wood that was anatomically credible and is said to have grown into its shape naturally in a forest in Tibet, where it was found in the fifteenth century by Drukpa Kunley, the most popular saint in Bhutan.

Eventually, we began seeing penises that weren't really there at all or were only vaguely suggested — the result, I'm sure, of that first, startling, two-pronged annunciation at Dochu La and also of the self-referential nature of the human mind. Any woman trying to get pregnant will swear that everyone she passes on the street is pregnant, just as anyone driving a new red Ford will swear that everyone in the world is driving a red Ford these days. At an immigration checkpoint on the way to Trongsa, we clambered out of the bus and took a turn around the village. In front of a café, there was a concrete piling or stone column, or something like that — an erect object about knee-high and rock hard, which might have insinuated a little of the silhouette, proportion, and character of the male organ. In any case, it was enough insinuation to make it, for this group, exciting. Within a minute, the Americans had gathered around the stone, examined it, discussed it, and shot off a few rolls of film. After the photo session, we killed time by visiting a shop in the village. The proprietor was a stout woman, and she had a half-dozen children of different sizes on her and around her and beside her. A couple of feckless-looking men loitered at the back of the store. We ordered tea and surveyed the place while she heated water on an electric burner. The children were unusually beautiful — dark haired and dark eyed, with skin like polished oak. We admired them and made gestures and signs to the woman: Were these her children? Yes, she indicated, all of them were hers. So the stone phallus works? one of our group asked, pointing outside. You have lots of children if you pray to the stone? The woman giggled and shook her head, and soon the men at the back of the store were giggling, too, and then the children started in, and the woman laughed even harder, and the men poked one another in the ribs and howled. It was a riot. When the woman finally caught her breath, she peered over the counter and waved her hands: That stone? No, that has nothing to do with having children. That's where we clean the mud off our shoes.

There was a baby at the center of this particular trip — a ten-month-old seventeen-pounder from California, with ash blond hair and blue green eyes, named Rachelle (for her maternal great-grandmother, Ruchel, and her paternal great-grandmother, Ruggia) Tashi (at the bidding of the Bhutanese monk who had conjured her) McKellop (her father's last name). For the few weeks we were in Bhutan, she was the most famous baby there. This was because she was the first American baby — actually, the first western hemisphere baby — to be born after her mother was blessed, in 1996, at the temple at Chime Lhakhang and the following year at a festival in Jakar. The efficacy of Chime Lhakhang and Jakar for getting people pregnant is old news in Bhutan — nice old news, of course, but not remarkable beyond the usual gladness that attaches to good but unastonishing news, like finding out that you've been approved for a mortgage. It would be bigger news outside Bhutan, because most people have never even heard of the place, and because many people are curious about anything that helps someone get pregnant, and especially because most people don't associate Himalayan Buddhism — austere, solemn, anticorporeal Himalayan Buddhism — with issues like fecundity and sex.

In Bhutan, the real news was that a Westerner had been blessed. Bhutan wasn't formally opened to tourists until 1974. Even then, the opening was more theoretical than actual. The airport wasn't built until 1983, and the sole Bhutanese airline services only Bangkok and Kathmandu and Delhi, but only on a rotating schedule, and only when the weather in the Paro Valley is flawless, and only during daylight, and only when one of the scary-landing-qualified pilots is scheduled for the trip. You can't just pop over to Bhutan when the spirit moves you. The

Bhutanese airline has no competition, and flights are expensive. Tourists have to travel with a licensed guide, and they also have to pay a daily fee, which is now two hundred and forty dollars per person. The fee covers hotel and food costs but is intentionally steep, to discourage the sorts of aimless backpackers who tramp through India and Nepal on a nickel and with an open-ended itinerary.

Even though it sits in the gorgeous saddle of the Himalayas and has a charmed and intriguing culture, Bhutan has had few foreign visitors. In 1997, twenty-three years after opening to tourists, Bhutan had a total of only 5,363 tourists. That same year, Nepal had 421,857 visitors. Tourism was viewed by most Bhutanese as an interesting, mildly significant development, but possibly a troublesome one. There was a certain dread of Westerners in hot pants and bush shirts traipsing through the ancient monasteries and a question of whether they would contribute to the king's stated goal of increasing Gross National Happiness rather than Gross National Product.

Chime Lhakhang is situated on a round hill above patches of rice fields and a thread of a river, about fifty miles from Thimphu, the capital of Bhutan. The temple was built in 1499, after Drukpa Kunley blessed the site. It is fitting that a site hallowed by Drukpa Kunley should be associated with fertility, because he was a hypersexed kook and a libertine. He was born in Tibet in 1455 and was given a traditional ecclesiastical education, but he veered away from it because he considered the Buddhist orthodoxy too stiff. He is said to have drunk a lot, is rumored to have had sex with his mother, to have spoken lines like "My meditation practice is girls and wine/I do whatever I feel like, strolling around in the Void," to have once tied a special "blessing string" around his penis, and to have refused to travel anywhere without his little dog, Shachi. He was an obscene and shocking show-off, but only, it is said, in order to bring attention to himself and, consequently, to Buddhist teachings. People in Bhutan really like him. They refer to him fondly as the Divine Madman. His favorite sport, archery, has been adopted as the Bhutanese national game and is the kingdom's only entry in the Olympics.

All over Bhutan, there are images of Drukpa Kunley — a chesty man in a predatory crouch with a bad-landlord mustache and wild black eyes, a kind of meat-eating leer on his face, and a little white dog by his side. His disembodied penis — usually a muted pink and energetically arched — is honored in paintings and sculptures and front-yard murals all over the country. Bhutan is a chaste society in which bare legs and shoulders are never seen, eyes are cast down in modesty, affection is never displayed in public, and propriety and simplicity and dignified shyness are cherished. To find the country adorned in such a way was as astounding as it might be if the Amish decided to decorate their barns with enormous breasts.

Chime Lhakhang is popular because of its connection to Drukpa Kunley and also because it is a beautiful old temple with a broad view of the valley and the spiky mountains beyond. It is one of the few temples in Bhutan whose grounds tourists are allowed to visit, although only people wearing traditional Bhutanese clothing are allowed to approach the altar inside. A few years ago, a Japanese woman stopped at Chime Lhakhang and asked a monk to give her the fertility blessing. The request was unusual, but somehow she prevailed — the first time, as far as anyone could remember, that a non-Bhutanese had been blessed. The woman became pregnant soon afterward. She was sure that it had been due to the Divine Madman, so in appreciation she visits Chime Lhakhang regularly and donates a hundred thousand butter lamps to the fertility festival in Jakar each year. Everyone in the kingdom knew about the Divine Madman's Japanese baby. Actually, in a country with a population of only six hundred thousand, everyone always seems to know everything about everything, and in this case everyone talked about the baby because of its novelty and because of the lifting of the long-standing embargo on foreigners in the sacred rooms of the temple.

The first westerners to visit Bhutan were two Portuguese Jesuits, who came in 1627, though not, undoubtedly, on a fertility mission. Quite possibly they were on a Christian mission, and they almost certainly left disappointed, since Bhutan is fully subscribed to Tantric Mahayana Buddhism, in particular the Drukpa sect of the Kagyupa school. Mahayana Buddhism preaches enlightenment for the welfare of all beings over the search for individual enlightenment; Kagyupa, one of its four major schools, emphasizes intense meditation and the relationship between teacher and disciple. The Drukpa sect is a Bhutanese variety of Kagyupa, which reveres certain favorite local saints like Drukpa Kunley. Bhutan is, in fact, the only sovereign Buddhist kingdom in the world now that the neighboring Buddhist states of Ladakh, Sikkim, and Tibet have been absorbed into India or China. Buddhism was introduced to Bhutan in the seventh century and then revitalized in the eighth century by Guru Rinpoche, the Tantric Buddhist saint whose teachings also galvanized Tibet. Since then, Buddhism has been as elemental as air in Bhutanese life. All ceremonies and most holidays are religious. All art is anonymous and sacred and follows the exacting rules of Buddhist iconography. The legal system is based on seventeenth-century Buddhist moral doctrine. Until 1907, when the absolute monarchy was established, a theocracy ruled the country.

For centuries, Bhutan was more or less left alone, a pinpoint in the eastern Himalayas, encircled by India and Tibet but essentially untouched by them. It is a little country, no bigger than Switzerland — a fretwork of rhododendron stands and pine forests and rice fields and cattle farms. Its southern tier is flat and warm, an extension of the fertile northern Indian plains. From there, the land rises up like an escalator until it reaches the top floor of Tibet. Bananas and oranges grow in the south; in the north, yaks ramble across the snowy mountains. Bhutan's tiny population is not surprising when you consider the ruggedness of the landscape, but it is very surprising when you consider that it is flanked by the two most populous nations on earth.

Most of what the Bhutanese need is grown or harvested or handmade locally. Until 1974, the chief source of foreign exchange was the sale of commemorative postage stamps honoring all manner of things: the seventy-fifth anniversary of Boy Scouting, the dogs of Bhutan, the birth of the Royal British Baby, Donald Duck, World Population Year, the Mask Dance of the Judgment of Death. Until 1962, Bhutan had no paved roads, no electricity, no hospitals, no central education system, no newspaper, no television, no modern postal service, no airport, no diplomatic contact with the West, no industry. There are still no stoplights.

When Jawaharlal Nehru visited in 1958,

he had to go overland from Delhi. The trip from the Indian border to Thimphu is only a hundred and twenty-seven miles, but it required six days of travel on foot and by mule. In the early fifties, after Tibet was seized by China, King Jigme Dorje Wangchuck began modernizing Bhutan. For one of the first major development projects, the Indian government sent crews to Bhutan on two-year assignments to pave their way through the valleys and hills. When they were done, Bhutan had two thousand miles of new ribbon roads.

The ceremonies of Kagyupa Buddhism are as methodical as knitting. In addition to wearing the traditional dress, supplicants at Chime Lhakhang must bring specific offerings: a kilo of butter, a bottle of locally made wine, cookies, sticks of incense, bags of candy, and a modest amount of money in small denominations. Tovya Wager, the mother of the famous blond baby, did the shopping for the American group. This was Tovya's third trip to Bhutan. The first, three years earlier, was a reconnaissance mission for her travel company, which specializes in adventure vacations in Asia and was considering adding Bhutan to its roster. Around the same time, Tovya and her husband, Harry, had been trying to have a baby. Tovya has blond hair and watery green eyes and dainty features and the strong back of a baggage handler. At the time of her first trip to Bhutan, she was forty-four years old and had traveled everywhere in the world. Her sentences often begin with phrases like "The first time I was in a lean-to in northern Laos" and "When I was staying with former headhunters in Borneo." She was an old hand at infertility treatments and had grown so discouraged that she had applied to adopt a baby from China. She was not, however, thinking about babies when she went to Bhutan. It was really just happenstance — a Bhutanese friend who knew that Tovya wanted a child introduced her to Pem Dorji, then the governor of the Bumthang district, and he offered to petition the clergy at Chime Lhakhang, using the blessing of the Japanese woman as a precedent. I met the governor when Tovya went to his house to introduce Rachelle. As he was giving her his baby gifts — a roll of cloth and a prayer scarf — he recalled his work on behalf of Tovya's fertility. Our visit took place moments after he had finished a meeting with the Indian ambassador and right before he began work on a speech celebrating Bhutan's rare black-necked crane. I mentioned that this lineup of tasks — conception, international politics, birds — seemed interesting. "I have a lot of responsibilities," he said in formal, British-inflected English. "Being a governor in Bhutan is an all-around job."

Tovya didn't get pregnant after her first blessing, so she put it out of her mind and continued to work on a Chinese adoption. A year later, she needed to return to Bhutan on business. This time, both Governor Pem Dorji and her friend urged her to get a fertility blessing at Jampa Lhakhang Drub, an annual festival in the town of Jakar. By then, Tovya was forty-six. She was blessed at the festival in Jakar and went home without any great expectations. Four months later, she was pregnant. When she found out, she faxed her friend and Governor Pem Dorji and promised to bring the baby to Bhutan as soon as she could.

So this was originally just a presentation trip, a chance for Tovya to display the baby to the monks, the governor, the Jakar festival organizers, and everyone else who had bestowed their blessings on her. Then she began to wonder whether she could bring other Americans to Chime Lhakhang and

Jakar. The governor and the festival organizers said she could, even though the idea of childless Americans flooding the holy sites of Bhutan was not perfectly in keeping with Gross National Happiness goals. Tovya advertised the trip in travel magazines as "Fertility Blessing: Spiritual Bhutan," but the fine print noted that you were not required to be seeking fertility as a condition of travel ("Don't worry, you can just observe — not be blessed if having a child is not what you are seeking"), and most of the people in the group — a retired schoolteacher, a couple in their sixties from Washington, an unattached lawyer, and Tovya's mother and husband — were just observing, not trying to conceive. The wishful thinkers were two couples from California, professionals in their forties. The women had tried and failed to become pregnant by other, more conventional and technological means. One of them — I'll call her Ellen — was a lawyer turned artist, and her husband was a lawyer turned actor. The other woman, whom I'll call Dina, ran a business in Los Angeles; her husband managed a restaurant. Both couples were fed up with science, having had no luck with anything, from hormone treatments to gamete transfers. Ellen hadn't even been planning to go to Bhutan; she had contacted Tovya with some questions about China, but once she mentioned her efforts to get pregnant and Tovya mentioned Rachelle, she felt that the trip was fated. Dina, who had miscarried several times, was skeptical but hopeful. "Anything that keeps me hopeful has got to help," she explained. "You need to feel hopeful somehow."

We drove to Chime Lhakhang on the twisting Indian-built roads, along the edges of the high hills and the rims of the riverbanks, in the shade of bamboo stands and under the shadow of Gangkar Punsum, the tallest unconquered mountain in the world. White farmhouses bunched together in the valleys like sheep. Once in a while, we noticed a house high up on a mountainside that had no visible means of support or access — or, for that matter, method of construction. It was as if it had been launched up to its perch by a rocket. Most of the oncoming traffic was baggy-kneed cattle. Golden langur monkeys — lucky creatures, in Bhutanese custom — loafed by the side of the road. An old woman appeared around a foggy bend, herding a dozen piebald goats and walking a good-luck pig on a leash. Almost every mountain pass and every bridge and every curve in the road bristled with prayer flags that whipped and snapped in the wind. In a schoolyard near the National Mushroom Centre, kids on recess lurched around on stilts. Next to the school was the Family Planning Centre and the turnoff to Chime Lhakhang. An hour later, we were there.

The temple is a mile and a half off the road, so we parked as close as we could, beside a handful of houses, and set out. A group of Nepalese watched us coolly as we walked by. Bhutan and Nepal are uneasy neighbors. Nepal is Hindu and has laid itself open to tourism, becoming a motley way station in the Himalayas. Almost no Bhutanese leave the country; Nepali emigration, by contrast, is constant, and so many Nepalese have settled in Bhutan that they make up almost a quarter of the country's population. In the eighties, Bhutan became aggressively nationalistic in an effort to preserve its cultural identity: Nepali ceased to be a language of instruction, and Dzongkha was mandated in addition to English; the prohibition against television was strengthened; and, in public, citizens were obliged to wear traditional Bhutanese dress (handwoven knee-length robes, or *go*s, for men and ankle-length jumpers called *kira*s for women). During this time, many illegal Nepalese immigrants departed, and tens of thousands more who had lived in Bhutan for decades were encouraged to leave — or forced to leave, according to human rights groups.

We passed farmhouses decorated with penis paintings, where old men sat playing checkers and a few spotted dogs were chewing their nails, and then we crossed onto the terraced fields. It was a bright, cold day, and the puddles in the fields were milky with frost. A woman in a striped *kira* stood amid hairy haystacks, separating wheat from chaff. The temple was visible from a mile away. Its walls were white and bare, as if they had been scoured; against the green fields and the green hills, it looked like a cue ball on a pool table. At the gate of the temple, a young monk, perhaps ten years old, met us and led us the rest of the way — up the side of a hill and around a column containing religious offerings, which was called a "chorten." To ensure good fortune, we circled around the chorten clockwise. Then we filed through the courtyard of the temple, where a few dozen monks in burgundy robes stood watching us. The wall behind them was covered with an enormous painting of the Divine Madman, who was portrayed as a sort of unstoppable galloping force, in rich reds and cobalt and gilt. In an alcove stood a prayer wheel as big as a cement mixer — hundreds of prayers had been handwritten on cloth and then stuffed inside a wooden cylinder; spinning the wheel sends all its wrapped prayers to heaven on your behalf.

At last we got to the guts of the place, the dim, sweet-smelling altar room, where there was a towering statue of Drukpa Kunley draped with flower necklaces and jewelry and surrounded by urns and candles and tiny golden jars. The young monk stepped aside for the senior monk, who would perform the ceremony. He was a big, quiet man with an egg-shaped head and an egg-shaped body and a grave, steady gaze. First he blessed Tovya's baby, then he motioned the group to draw together. Ellen placed butter, Krackjack Biscuits, Pizza Flavor Chicken Brand Chips, and candy at the foot of the statue of Drukpa Kunley; in the low light, I could make out other packages of biscuits and chips, which had been left earlier in the day. The rest of the ceremony was sort of a dream — a tap on the head with Drukpa Kunley's fifteenth-century archery set, a drink of holy water, a tap with the ivory penis, and another with the wooden one. The monk spoke in a low, flowing voice and in a sinking sigh, something that sounded achingly sad and kind and went on for a long time. Dice were thrown to get lucky numbers for the women; then names for the predestined babies were drawn from a tiny, ancient deck of name cards; and, as soon as it was over, everyone started to cry.

"I don't know why I'm crying," Ellen said. She and Dina embraced. "I'm going to have a girl," Ellen went on.

"I know it." Dina nodded and dried her eyes on her sleeve.

"A little Bhutanese girl," Ellen said. "A little divine madwoman." We walked back through the farm fields by moonlight. Some children from the village, singing a warped, Bhutanese version of "Happy Birthday," serenaded us all the way.

There was an advertisement for a vasectomy clinic ("No Incision, No Stitch, Walk Home in Ten Minutes!") behind the front desk of our hotel in Punakha and a desolate family-planning booth in Jakar — the government is trying to reduce Bhutan's overly vigorous birth rate to two percent within the next five years — but otherwise we kept seeing fertility symbols everywhere we went. Plus we couldn't stop talking about babies: the marvel of Tovya's conception; complaints from those who had received hormone injections; the delivery sagas of the three women on the trip who had had children decades ago. Perhaps because we were so far from home, in a place as unusual as Bhutan, we didn't notice how odd it was to discuss episiotomies and sperm motility with a group of relative strangers.

The festival in Jakar, our stop after Chime Lhakhang, is notoriously phallocentric, and Tovya wanted to have the group blessed there, because she believed that it had made the difference between her first, disappointing trip to Bhutan and her second, fruitful one. Jakar is a dot of a town in the Bumthang district of central Bhutan, a gold green valley of rice terraces bordered by the Black Mountains and the wall of the Himalayan foothills. The festival was held on a flat, dusty lawn beside an old stone temple. A small stage had been erected for dignitaries at one end and a shade tent set up on the other. When we arrived, the current governor of Bumthang, Jigme Zangpo, and several of his assistants were already seated on the stage, snacking on cracked corn and cookies, watching the huge crowd that had formed on the perimeters of the lawn. Everyone was dressed in Bhutanese clothing made of bright woven material of claret red and deep blue and piney green and yellow, in a scramble of patterns — glen plaids, rep stripes, geometric rickrack — and in the full, sharp mountain light they looked lucent, jeweled. Now and again, you might see a pair of Nikes or a Yankees baseball cap, or a Tommy Hilfiger T-shirt peeking out of a robe, but otherwise it was a vision without reference to time or place or to any world outside this one.

The governor's assistant noticed Tovya and the baby across the lawn and motioned for us to join the group onstage. He reached for the baby and said, "I knew it. The spiritual leader of our festival is very auspicious. We are very happy to see our successful outcome."

The governor leaned over to tickle the baby. He was a portly, handsome man with a walrus mustache and a Caesar haircut. I asked him whether he was prepared for Bumthang to become a mecca for reproduction if word of Tovya's success circulated. He tilted his head and thought for a few moments. On the lawn, the festival dancing had begun. The jester, the *atsara*, was sashaying around, swinging a wooden phallus. He wore a red wooden clown mask and a long robe that looked as old as time. Behind him, four dwarfs in puffy skirts and two dancers dressed as cows feinted and boxed. A pregnant dog with swollen ankles wandered onto the lawn, made a few tight circles, and then lay down and took a nap.

"It would be nice if many Americans came for the festival," the governor said. "I'm proud to say we can host two hundred and fifty-six tourists at a time in Bumthang. We don't have any limits, but we would want only as many as we are capable of accommodating. The festival has always been a neat family event. If there are too many outsiders, the family feeling isn't there."

Does the ritual work?

"You have to have inner respect for it, but it will work if you have any type of devotion," he said. On the lawn, two clowns had captured the *atsara;* a monk dressed as a tree stole the wooden penis from him and then raced around waving it at the crowd. The children in the audience clapped and screamed.

The governor turned to Tovya and asked, "Did you have an easy delivery? It's often risky to have a baby at your age."

She dandled the baby on her knee. "Very easy," she said. "And I felt great throughout the pregnancy."

"Maybe it was your faith," the governor said. "Some things are simply beyond science." He leaned over and cooed to the baby, *"Taa-shi! Taa-shi!"* The baby squeezed his nose and then began chewing on one of Tovya's credit cards. "Does she take up most of your time? Or do you have a nanny?" the governor asked. He adjusted his prayer shawl on his shoulder and shifted his ceremonial sword around his waist. An old man spinning a squeaky prayer wheel rambled across the stage, dipping respectfully toward the dignitaries. The clowns had released the *atsara,* and the fertility-blessing ceremony was about to begin. We were each handed a penis of stone or wood and lined up so the *atsara* could drip water from his phallus onto our heads. As we left, the governor shook hands with us and whispered, "I know you'll be back with your tiny tots someday."

One of the most sacred days in the Bhutanese calendar is Lhabab Duechhen, the day Buddha is believed to have descended from heaven; this year, it happened to fall on the day we were heading back to Thimphu — and would be driving past Chime Lhakhang again. To visit Chime Lhakhang on Lhabab Duechhen is to be overdetermined, luckwise — sort of a providential belt and suspenders. So of course we stopped again, leaving the car in the same spot in the tumbledown village, tramping again across the broad, wet meadow and up the round hill to the Divine Madman's temple. The young monk again met us at the gate of the temple, and we climbed to the top of the hill along with a score of other people, all Bhutanese, who were there on account of its being an especially lucky day. Many of them were kids praying for good grades on their upcoming exams, but the rest were young women — dark haired, slim, somber in their brilliant *kira*s — who had come to ask Drukpa Kunley for help in having children. It was, just then, a particularly propitious moment in the history of the kingdom of Bhutan. The king was about to celebrate his forty-third birthday, and he and his four wives — four sisters from a prominent Bhutanese family — were traveling around the country in their royal blue Land Cruisers, dropping in at local birthday events. Also, the only remaining district in Bhutan that was without telephones had at last been connected; the phones were being turned on that day. The weather was especially fine, too — cold enough to suggest that winter would be coming, but so sunny that it was impossible to believe it would be anything other than a favorable day. We hadn't had a chance to do any grocery shopping, so we didn't have cookies and candy and butter and wine, and we wondered whether we would be welcomed in the temple on such a holy day. The monk who blessed us the last time came to the door and saw that we were empty-handed, but he made it clear that he remembered us and waved us in anyway.

I went back to Bhutan a few months later, to take another look around. Right away, I recognized people I had met on my first trip, and they recognized me. "You were here with the American baby," a lot of them said to me, then asked, "What happened to the women who came to Chime Lhakhang and the festival at Jakar?" I told them what I knew. Dina had become pregnant a few weeks after getting home but then had miscarried. Ellen was working with a healer and a nutritionist but so far hadn't had any luck. Tovya had decided to spend more time with Rachelle Tashi and less time on the road, although she had organized another group to come for the fertility blessings in the fall.

At the time, though, it was still spring: The rhododendrons were blooming, and the mist in the Paro Valley was as thick as goose down. The airport was blanked out, invisible. For days, no planes could come in or out of the country. It was as if Bhutan had once more withdrawn from the rest of the world. Anyone planning to travel to the country was turned back. Those who were already on their way when the airport disappeared were billeted in crummy airport hotels in Kathmandu and Calcutta until the mist cleared and planes could find Bhutan again.

Do We Transcend
Before or After We Purchase
the Commemorative Eel Cakes?

The smallest Mount Fuji I saw while I was in Japan was next to a Tokyo fire station and across the street from a grocery store where you can buy sake in a box and eighteen-dollar cantaloupes. The shrine is called Ono-Terusaki, and the little Mount Fuji in its backyard is called Fujizuko, and they are located in Shitaya, an unfancy low-rise neighborhood you would never visit unless you were looking for miniature mountains. I went to see Fujizuko on a blazing hot July Sunday, when the sky was the color of cement and the air was so thick that it felt woolly. The real Mount Fuji is only sixty miles from Tokyo, but the scrim of smog around the city cut off the view. No one was on the streets of Shitaya that morning; all the houses were perfectly still except for a few damp kimonos flapping on balcony clotheslines. I wandered around the neighborhood for half an hour before I finally found the shrine, a homely ninth-century building dedicated to a scholar of Chinese classics who died in A.D. 852 and was said to have enjoyed landscapes. I walked around to the back of the shrine, and there I came upon the mountain. It was made of blackish lava chunks and was shaped like a piece of pie propped up on its wide end, exactly like the real Mount Fuji, only this Fuji was about 16 feet high, whereas the real one is 12,388. Someone who really liked Mount Fuji built the mountain in 1828. The mountain was flanked by a pair of stone monkey-faced dog-lions, and there was a sign that said, FUJIZUKO IS A MINIATURE MOUNTAIN THAT AN IMITATION MAN MADE IN THE IMAGE OF MOUNT FUJI. THIS PRECIOUS MOUND IS PRESERVED ON GOOD CONDITIONS.

I looked at the mountain for a while and rang a doorbell, and after a moment a student priest came out and gave me a look. He was dressed in a snowy white robe and slippers and had kissy lips and a grave, handsome face. He didn't speak English and I don't speak Japanese, so we just smiled at each other until a middle-aged gentleman who was also visiting the shrine said he would attempt to translate for the priest. The gentleman said that the priest said that there was a time when Japan was not in order and people felt a pain about the abuse of the land, and there were problems, lots of problems, with the gods, or maybe it was problems with the crops, but anyway then a man went climbing Mount Fuji and by climbing he tried to make the world in order and he prayed many crops or gods would come in good condition and then the world of Japan became in order and through his feelings he built the mountain. As the gentleman was translating, I felt a profound sense of mystery and confusion in my very own mind, but I also understood what he was trying to say. I then asked the gentleman to ask the priest if he had ever climbed the full-scale Mount Fuji. The priest giggled and shook his head, so I asked whether the priest planned to climb it anytime in the future. The two men chatted for a minute. At last the gentleman turned to me and shrugged and said, "I believe he says, 'No way.'"

The reasons people don't climb Mount Fuji are various. Sometimes they just forget to do it. There is approximately one Japanese cabdriver in New York City, where I live, and he is one of the people who happen to have forgotten. He also happened to be the cabdriver who took me to the airport for my flight to Japan. He was driving a new, nice-smelling Honda minivan cab and had a silver Mount Fuji key chain swinging from the ignition. He became excited when I told him I was going to Japan to climb Mount Fuji. He said that he had always planned to do it himself but kept forgetting, and the next thing he knew he had moved permanently to the United States.

Sometimes the reasons people have for not climbing are more existential than forgetful. When I first got to Tokyo I went to visit Kunio Kaneko, an artist who makes wood-block prints of Mount Fuji. At his studio, every wall was hung with pictures of the mountain — in indigo blue, in orangy red, covered with gold leaf, outlined with silver ink. There were drawers filled with Fuji prints and racks of note cards of Fujis and one wall with pictures of kimonos and *happi* platform sandals that make you walk as if you're drunk. Kaneko is in his late forties and has longish hair and broad shoulders, and he was wearing beat-up khakis and green Converse sneakers. He spread out his pictures for me to see and told me that he divided his life into two: the years before 1964, when the air was still see-through and Fuji was always visible from his backyard in Tokyo, and the post-1964 years, when pollution got so bad that he almost never saw Fuji except on rare stainless winter days. Kaneko said that he thought about the mountain all the time. Since he seemed slightly outdoorsy and had devoted so much of his work to the mountain, I assumed that he had climbed it, maybe even several times. When I asked him about it, he looked bashful and replied, "No, I have never climbed it." He shuffled together some of his prints and slid them into a drawer. "I always stay at a distance at the bottom so I have a perfect view," he said. "I don't climb it because if I were on the mountain, I couldn't see it."

There are lots of reasons the Japanese do climb Mount Fuji. They climb it because it's tall and pretty and has a grand view, because some of them think God lives inside it, because their grandparents climbed it, or because climbing Mount Fuji has been the customary Japanese thing to do for as long as anyone can remember. In a way, the enduring attraction of a Mount Fuji pilgrimage is a remarkable thing. The Japanese have always revered their landscape and scenery, but they seem perfectly at peace with fake nature, too — only in Japan can you surf at an indoor beach and ski on an indoor slope and stroll through exhaustively manipulated and modulated gardens of groomed pebbles and dwarfed trees and precisely arranged leaves. Sometimes it seems that the man-made Japan has eclipsed the country's original physical being. Still, the symbolism and reality of Mount Fuji remain. The mountain may have pay phones on the summit and its own brand of beer, but otherwise it persists as a wild and messy and uncontrollable place — big, old-fashioned, and extreme. That is, nothing like what I expected Japan to be. I wanted to go to Mount Fuji because I imagined it would be a trip to the un-Japan, a country I wasn't even sure existed anymore except in nostalgic dreams.

It was a terrible year to climb Fuji, really. The official climbing season opens July 1 with a ceremony at the base of the mountain in the Sengen Jinja shrine, and usually thousands of climbers would attend the ceremony and ascend the mountain that day. Some would be dressed in traditional pilgrim costumes: white kimonos and pants, straw *waraji* sandals, a mushroom-shaped hat, a walking stick. Most of the rest would be in Gore-Tex and T-shirts saying MOUNT FUJI: THE MOST HIGHEST MOUNTAIN IN JAPAN and WELCOME TO MELLOW VILLAGE and JOYFUL MY SCENE MORNING BUNNY MOUNT FUJI. In Tokyo that same day, less ambitious climbers hold another ceremony at the Ono-Terusaki shrine and scramble up all sixteen feet of the miniature Fuji: Similar observances would take place at each of the forty or so other miniature Mount Fujis in greater Tokyo. But this was the summer of ghastly weather in Japan. In the weeks before opening day, two typhoons passed through; the first one hit Tokyo and raked across Fuji, covering the climbing routes with snow and filling access roads with mud and rocks, while the tail end of the second typhoon added to the mess on the mountain. The opening ceremony was held but was sparsely attended, and access to Fuji itself was postponed until July 10, then postponed again for another twenty-four hours. The day I arrived in Japan, the tanker *Diamond Grace* had run aground and was bleeding crude oil into Tokyo Bay. In the south yet another storm struck, and on the island of Kyushu mud slides killed almost two dozen people. In Tokyo a heat wave jacked the temperature above one hundred degrees, and everyone walked around looking broiled and stoic, dabbing their foreheads with washcloths and flapping lacquer fans. I was so hot that I had to hide from the sun every afternoon in my hotel room. I would fall in a heap on my futon and crack open a Kirin beer and turn on a Japanese program called *Jungle TV*, which was hosted by two guys who did things like race each other on rowing machines while wearing business suits and teach themselves to cook bouillabaisse while being harassed by a pet monkey. I started wondering why exactly I wanted to climb Mount Fuji, but I did, and even after an earthquake bounced me around my hotel room, I was still good to go.

Mount Fuji is the highest mountain in Japan. Its peak is nearly two and a half miles above sea level, and its base has a circumference of seventy-eight miles and spans both Yamanashi Prefecture and Shizuoka Prefecture. The mountain is a ten-thousand-year-old volcanic cone that last erupted in 1707. Scientists believe it is dormant rather than extinct. A nearby mountain named Yatsugatake used to be higher than Fuji, but then the jealous and bellicose Fuji goddess Konohanasakuya-hime decided to knock over the Yatsugatake so Fuji could be supreme. The first documented ascent of the mountain was made by a Shintoist pilgrim named En no Ozunu in the eighth century; the first Westerner to climb was Sir Rutherford Alcock, the British consul, who ascended in 1860 with his Scottie dog Toby. The world's oldest mountain-climbing picture, painted in the fifteenth century, depicts monks climbing Mount Fuji. Only religious pilgrims were allowed to climb until the nineteenth century; women were not allowed at all until 1871.

Fuji's six climbing routes are divided into stations; the route I planned to take has ten. The Fuji Subaru highway to the Fifth Station was opened in 1965, and with it came millions of visitors by tour bus and subsequently tons of trash and erosion problems that continue to threaten the mountain. Mount Fuji is so pretty and so weirdly symmetrical that people have always believed it was supernatural and sanctified. The most fervent Fuji worshippers are the Shintoist sect Fuji-ko, whose founder, the sixteenth-century monk Fujiwara no Kakugyo, supposedly climbed Fuji one hundred and twenty-eight times and lived to be one hundred and six years old. Fuji-ko pilgrims stay in special shrine lodges at the base of the mountain, wash themselves in the purifying water of the five lakes nearby, get blessed by a priest, and then time their ascent so that they arrive at the summit at sunrise. During the seventeenth and eighteenth centuries, as many as ten thousand Fuji-ko would climb each year, but these days they are far outnumbered by ordinary Japanese and tourists.

Before I left for Japan, I obtained an introduction to a man in Tokyo named Fumiaki Watanabe, who was going to have me over for dinner as part of an official international friendliness program. All I knew about him was that he recently retired from his position as an internal auditor at an Exxon subsidiary. The minute he heard from our intermediary that I was planning to climb Fuji, he proposed skipping the dinner and instead going with me on the climb. This to me was a huge surprise. I kept being told that every year half a million people drive to the Fifth Station of Fuji and two hundred thousand climb to the summit, but so far I hadn't managed to find a single person who had done either. I was starting to wonder how much of the Japanese devotion to climbing Mount Fuji is abstract and conceptual and how much of it involves the material experience of putting on shoes and walking. It turned out that Mr. Watanabe was a materially experienced climber. He had climbed Fuji more than ten times, had skied into its crater and down its side, and was seventy percent of the way to his goal of climbing the hundred highest peaks in Japan.

It was decided that Mr. Watanabe and I could climb together but that our dinner would go ahead as planned, and one evening I rode the subway to the southern edge of Tokyo, where he and his wife and son live. He met me at the station and almost without a word gestured toward the exit. He walked quickly, pushing his bicycle, which like every Japanese bicycle I saw was low-built and sturdy, like a fifties Schwinn, and had a plastic bag wrapped around its seat. Mr. Watanabe was low-built and sturdy himself, with a baldish head and bright eyes and a small, solid body. In the very best possible way, he looked a little like Jiminy Cricket. That night we spoke about the beautiful dinner Mrs. Watanabe had made for us, about the differences between Americans and Japanese, about how tradition in both countries is melting away. Mrs. Watanabe was wearing Western-style casual clothes, but she decided to show me the formal kimono that she said she hardly ever wears anymore. Once she brought it out, she decided to dress me in it. The kimono was cool and silky and as heavy as water. It required special underwear with multiple belts and bows and had a wide sash tied over a pillow that sits in the small of your back. It took about fifteen minutes to get the whole thing on. Then, as I sat there trussed up like a fancy turkey, Mr. Watanabe began laying out his plans for our climb.

We left two days later on a bus that threaded through the steep hills and rice fields between Tokyo and Fujiyoshida, the town at the base of the mountain where we were going to spend our first night. The bus was full of vacationers carrying take-out *bento*-box lunches with overnight bags. Mr. Watanabe brought a big rucksack and was dressed in a long-sleeved shirt, a gray pin-striped vest, wool knickers, and hiking boots with bright red laces. The boots looked well-worn. He said that he managed to go climbing about ten times a year. I wondered whether he was going more often now that he had retired. "Yes, I have had the opportunity," he said. He shifted in his seat. Everything he said sounded measured and elegant. "My plan now is to climb the highest peak on each continent. I would begin with Kilimanjaro, then Aconcagua, and then, of course, Mc-Kinley."

"Will you start soon?"

He lifted an eyebrow and said, "Perhaps I'll have the opportunity."

"Alone?"

"Yes, I believe alone," he said. "To tell the truth, Mrs. Watanabe has a problem because she becomes very . . . *tired*. She also walks a bit slower than a . . . *normal* person." He paused again and then added, "I believe I should learn to be more patient."

Entering Fujiyoshida, you pass a Mc-Donald's and a *pachinko* gambling parlor and then a Mount Fuji made of flowers — a mound of red salvia and impatiens in pink and white. Just beyond it was the famous Sengen Jinja shrine. The long pathway to the shrine was dim and unearthly and lined with stone lanterns and tall red trees. Mr. Watanabe said the trees were called *fujitarosugi*, which translates as "boy cedar tree of Fuji." There are thousands of cedars encircling the mountain, forming what people call the Sea of Trees or the Forest of No Return. This forest is one of the most popular places in Japan to commit suicide — every year several dozen bodies are recovered in it — and it is one of the most popular places to headquarter a religion. There are almost two thousand officially registered religious organizations located around the base of the mountain, including a number of Nichiren Buddhist sects, the faith-healing Ho no Hana Sanpogyo group, and the ancestor-revering Fumyokai Kyodan religion. Until it was evicted recently, the subway-gassing Aum Shinri Kyo cult had its headquarters here, too.

We stopped at the Sengen Jinja shrine and walked under the boy cedar trees to the main structure, an ornate building made of reddish wood that had been slicked to a dull shine by the drizzle. The place was deserted except for a little boy who was studying his reflection in a puddle and a priest who was padding around in his white *tabi* socks, closing up for the day. The priest was in a hurry to leave, but he agreed to give us a condensed version of the traditional Shinto preclimb blessing. He motioned for us to stand in front of the shrine. As he chanted and banged on a small brass drum, the rain began to patter and a gust flicked the water in the trees onto the ground.

We finally arrived at our hotel, a

Western-style high-rise building that had its own amusement park, called Fujikyu Highland, whose attraction included a Ferris wheel and the highest roller coaster in Japan. On the hotel grounds there is a perfect 1:200 scale model of Mount Fuji and the five lakes to the north; guests can climb the small mountain and also visit the Mount Fuji museum located inside the artificial peak. The enormous picture windows in the hotel lobby would have offered a staggering view of the real Fuji if the weather had been clear, but it wasn't, so that night after dinner we sat in the lobby and gazed in the direction of the rain-shrouded Fuji, over the top of the scale-model Fuji, to an outline of Fuji made of neon glowing in the spokes of the Ferris wheel.

You can walk up Mount Fuji, or you can run up (the Mount Fuji Climbing Race has been held every year since 1948), or you can roll up in a wheelchair (first done in 1978), or you can wait until you're really old (as old as Ichijiro "Super Grandpa" Araya, who climbed it when he was one hundred, or Hulda "Grandma Whitney" Crooks, who did it at ninety-one). Or you can ride a horse to the Seventh Station, the rental horse drop-off point, and then walk the rest of the way. The next morning, as Mr. Watanabe and I were sitting in a cold mist at the Fifth Station getting ready for the climb, a horse rental guy walked over and introduced me to his pony, Nice Child. The guy was wearing a Budweiser hat and rubber boots that had articulated toes. Nice Child looked like a four-legged easy chair, and I was really tempted to take the man up on his suggestion that I ride rather than walk. It was a lousy day to climb a mountain. Many of the pilgrims at the trailhead were wearing garbage bags, and the only scenery we could see was the Fifth Station gift shop and a cigarette vending machine that had the phrase TODAY I SMOKE printed on it at least a hundred times. "I believe only crazies will be climbing today," Mr. Watanabe said, looking at a group of climbers who were eating rice balls and hot dogs and shouting at one another.

After Mr. Watanabe talked me out of renting Nice Child, I put on my pack and tightened my laces and went into the gift shop and bought a traditional pilgrim's walking stick — plain and squared off, with jingle bells hanging from the top to ward off evil spirits and plenty of room for *yakiin,* the brands you can get burned onto your stick at each station along the way to the top. I also wanted to buy the Fuji-shaped cookies or cheesecakes or bean-paste patties or jellies, or the Milk Pie biscuits in a box that said, FUJISAN: NATURE IS A GREAT EXISTENCE. IF YOU BECOME ANGRY OR NERVOUS HOLD COMMUNION WITH NATURE. The trouble was I'd already picked up some eel jerky and some octopus jerky at a 7-Eleven near the hotel.

We planned to climb to the Eighth Station by sunset, spend the evening in a mountain hut, and wake up at two a.m. to finish the climb so we would reach the summit by sunrise. We had reserved a space at a hut called Fujisan Hotel. From the sound of the name I thought maybe it was a luxury hut, but Mr. Watanabe rolled his eyes and assured me that all the accommodations on the mountain were more hut than hotel. "Do you know how silkworms live?" he asked. "They live on wooden shelves. That is what the huts are like — silkworm shelves."

I was taken aback. "You mean the huts are infested?"

"No," Mr. Watanabe replied, "the huts have shelves, and we are the worms."

I walked a few feet behind him, stepping on and around nubbly black lava rocks and loose pebbles of red pumice. The terrain was sheer and treeless. On a sunny day it would have been beastly. Rock larks flittered around, and green weeds grew under some of the overhangs, but otherwise the mountainside was blank. After about an hour I started wondering where one would relieve oneself in such a lunar landscape. "We will be at the Sixth Station in just a few more minutes," Mr. Watanabe said. He hesitated for a moment, pressed his finger to his lips, and then said, "There you will find a cozy adjacent hut."

In a few minutes we did in fact reach the station, a big wooden lean-to hut with a cozy adjacent unisex hut beside it, both clinging to the mountainside like barnacles. Inside the big hut you could get your walking stick branded and buy crackers and souvenirs and any one of a dozen brands of beer, as well as a twelve-dollar canister of Mount Fuji Congratulations Do It Now Oxygen. About forty climbers were milling around, dripping and sweating and gobbling snacks. One delicate-looking older woman dressed in what looked like pajamas was taking gulps from a canister of oxygen, and the man with her alternated gulps of oxygen with swigs of beer. Four U.S. Navy enlisted men came into the hut. They seemed quite excited. "Hey!" one of them hollered. "Anyone got any sake?"

I went outside on the deck, where a bunch of Chinese students were eating dried fish and cookies and taking snapshots of one another. Two of them were speaking to each other on their cellular phones and were shrieking ecstatically. One of the Chinese girls came over to me and gasped, "We are wanting to speak *Japanese!* We are wanting to speak *English!* But our heads are filled with *Japanese!*"

Mr. Watanabe wanted to push ahead, so we soon left and plodded up the jagged trail for another hour. By then the clouds had broken up, and below them we could see a big green patch that Mr. Watanabe said was a Japanese Self-Defense Forces training ground and some of the one hundred and seventeen golf courses that lie at the base of the mountain. I wanted to look at the view for a while, but the trail was getting clogged with other climbers, so we turned and continued. We beat the Chinese students to the Seventh Station and went in to get my walking stick branded. The stationmaster was a young man with bristly black hair and bright red cheeks. He motioned me over to a fire that was burning in the center of the hut and then pulled out a branding iron that had been heating in it. After I paid two dollars, he branded my stick with his symbol — some Japanese characters and a drawing of Fuji. Then he told me that he was the sixth generation of his family to run it. In the winter he works at a gas station. During the two-month-long climbing season, he leaves his wife and children in the flatlands and comes to the Seventh Station with his mother, and they don't go back down until after the Yoshida Fire Festival, which marks the season's close. On a busy day he brands the sticks of six hundred climbers. On a slow day, he said, he gets lonely.

Mr. Watanabe and I reached the Eighth Station two hours later. That is, we got to the first of the seven Eighth Stations. The seven Eighth Stations are strung out along about an hour's worth of trail. All of the stations on Fuji are family businesses that have had the same owners for a hundred years or more, and they enjoy the spirited competition of the free market system. The first Eighth Station calls itself the Authentic Eighth Station; the second one calls itself Originator of the Eighth Station; the third is the Real Eighth Station. As it happened, our Eighth Station, the nonluxurious Fujisan Hotel, was the seventh of the Eighth Stations. By the time we wended our way past the preceding six stations it was dusky, and I was eager for dinner and the use of a cozy adjacent hut. The Fujisan stationmaster was a jolly guy with a mustache and tobacco-stained fingers. When we arrived he and a few friends were sitting inside the hut, watching the Yankees game in which Japanese pitcher Hideki Irabu made his debut. The television and a fire were the hut's sole amenities. Otherwise it was outfitted with a couple of wooden benches in the main room and, in another, two levels of wooden platforms that formed a communal bunk bed — the silkworm shelves. Mr. Watanabe grinned when he saw me surveying the quarters. "On the mountain for women is very . . . *harsh*," he said. "I believe the goddess of Fuji was said to be very jealous and did not favor women climbers."

Because of the lousy weather, the mountain was unusually quiet that night. Typically there would have been about a hundred people at the hotel, but instead there were only two young Sony employees from Nagasaki and three of the stationmaster's friends. The Sony men went to sleep almost immediately. The rest of us ate a dinner of rice and then tried to warm up by the fire next to the television set. I stepped outside to see what I could see from eleven thousand feet up. It was a cold, black night, and the cloud cover was still cracked open; below I could see the little lights of Fujiyoshida and the carnival neon of the Fujikyu Highland Ferris wheel.

After I went back inside, Mr. Watanabe offered everyone refreshments: banana chips and cocktails of Johnnie Walker Black and Takara Multi-Vitamin water. "Very healthy," he said to me, holding up a can of Takara water and a plastic cup. "It has many important minerals. Please, allow me to give you some." The stationmaster's friends introduced themselves as Boss-o Guide-o, Guide-o Carpenter-o, and Mr. Shinto Priest. Boss-o explained that he was in charge of all the guides working on Mount Fuji. After his second Scotch and Multi-Vitamin Water, he offered to make me an assistant guide next summer. Guide-o Carpenter-o was an assistant mountain guide in the summer and a carpenter in Fujiyoshida during the winter. He was the brother of Mr. Shinto Priest, who was a Shinto priest and also a part-time carpenter. Mr. Priest was a wild-eyed semi-bald-headed man who chain-smoked Virginia Slims Menthols and was wearing a padded coat, a terry-cloth towel around his neck, a wool beanie, and high-knee rubber boots, which had the combined effect of making him look like a cross-dressing Tibetan heavyweight boxer. He kept lighting his cigarettes with one of the station branding irons and then whipping off his beanie and rubbing his remaining hair while growling something crusty sounding in Japanese.

"That's a joke!" Guide-o Carpenter-o yelled to me, pointing at Mr. Priest. "That's a Japanese joke!"

Even Mr. Watanabe, who may be the most gracious and proper human on earth, was roaring at the priest. "To tell you the truth, I believe he's quite crazy," he whispered to me. By then we had all had lots and lots of multivitamins. Mr. Priest was getting sort of sentimental, and when he was done with his hair routine, he wanted me to sit on his lap or next to him and look at snapshots. I had my doubts, but they turned out to be pictures he'd taken of the shadow thrown by Mount Fuji at sunrise — a perfect sheer gray triangle cast across an ocean of clouds, as amazing a sight as I've ever seen.

By then there was no real point in going to sleep, since we were going to wake up in an hour to finish the climb. I lay down on my shelf and listened to the Sony men snoring and the rain as it started to dribble, then pour, then slam down on the tin roof of the Fujisan Hotel. At about two in the morning, I heard the rustling of ponchos. Some two dozen climbers had arrived at the hotel, rain running off them in rivers, and outside on the trail I could see a dotted line of lights zigzagging up the mountainside. Most of the climbers wore their lights on their heads, so for a moment the scene looked like a subterranean mining expedition rather than the final stretch of a mountain climb. We dressed in a rush, and then Mr. Watanabe warned me about the end of the climb. "What we have left is the heart-attacking final eight hundred meters," he said, looking at me solemnly. "You must inform me before you become completely exhausted." Climbers were materializing all around us in the dark mist, each with a Cyclops headlamp shining in the middle of his forehead. We took our places on the trail and began trudging up the final steep stretch.

The line of the climbers' lights now reached up to the summit and down to the seventh Eighth Station, where it vanished into the fog. The rain was falling in gobs, coming down harder and harder, and the fog was building up into a solid white wall; I would never have known we'd reached the summit except that Mr. Watanabe said we'd reached the summit and should stop at a shelter and have something to eat. The crater was there but I couldn't see it, and the whole of Japan was spread out underneath us but you'd never know it, and there were scores of people all around us but I couldn't make them out even though they were probably just a few feet away. I didn't really care. I was completely thrilled just to be on the summit. I was the highest thing in Japan! I wanted to run around the crater, but the wind had picked up to about sixty miles an hour, which would have meant running sideways, if at all.

It is traditional for climbers to mail a letter at the Mount Fuji post office on the summit and to hike around the crater to each of the two shrines on the rim before descending. Mr. Watanabe suggested we should skip the post office and the shrines and simply head down right away. I wanted to stay. We held a vote and it was a tie, but then the wind punched me so hard that I changed my mind. I got the official summit brand burned into my walking stick and then started down into the fog, sliding heel first into the loose pumice, the sheets of rain in my face.

For a while, everyone who saw Mount Fuji wanted to write a poem about it or tell a story or make pictures of it. It was described by a writer in the eighth century as "a lovely form capped with the purest white snow . . . reminding one of a well-dressed woman in a luxuriously dyed garment with her pure white undergarments showing around the edge of her collar" — in other words, like a lady with her bra straps showing. Unquestionably, the consummate Fuji artist was the nineteenth-century printmaker Katsushika Hokusai, who made pictures of the peak for seventy years. Hokusai often called himself a crazed art addict and sometimes used the name Hokusai the Madman. *Thirty-Six Views of Mount Fuji*, a collection of his prints, was published around 1823 and was a huge hit in Japan. Hokusai depicted Fuji covered with snow, half-covered with snow, bare, hidden by mist, capped with an umbrella cloud, in nice weather, with pilgrims climbing, with storks bathing in front of it, as seen from the bow of a boat, and viewed from a bridge in Tokyo. In some of the pictures the mountain fills up most of the space, whereas in others it is just a pucker on the horizon while the foreground is dominated by geisha girls loafing around or a guy building a barrel or someone trying to talk his horse into walking over a bridge. A few years later, when Hokusai was seventy-four and worried about his career, he recharged it by publishing a new collection, *One Hundred Views of Mount Fuji*. It was another huge hit. Hokusai was an inconstant man who moved ninety-three times in his life and changed his name twenty times, but for the seventy years he made pictures of Fuji, his image of the mountain never changed; it was always steep sided, narrow peaked, wide bottomed, solitary, and simply the loveliest mountain you could ever hope to see.

When we got to the bottom of the mountain, Mr. Watanabe apologized for the weather and said he very much wanted me to come back so I could see Mount Fuji on a good day — that is, so I could see Mount Fuji at all. I told him that I wasn't the least bit disappointed and that anyway this seemed like the Japanese way of seeing the mountain, less with my eyes than with my mind's eye. I was a material climber, but I had been won over to the conceptual side.

If we wanted a view, I told him, we could always go back to the Ferris wheel at Fujikyu Highland. "I suppose," Mr. Watanabe said. "However, I do not believe we will have the time or opportunity to ride such a vehicle." He was right, so we just blotted our soaked clothes and kicked the pebbles out of our boots and caught the next bus back to Tokyo, and before I left Japan I bought myself a copy of Hokusai's *Thirty-Six Views of Mount Fuji*.

Game Plan

Millie, a spiny anteater with Betty Boop eyes, is the homeliest of the Olympic mascots and also the least athletic. I went to see a real Millie the other day at Sydney's Taronga Zoo and waited an hour for it to exert itself — to run or walk or do rhythmic gymnastics or even to lap up an army of ants with its tongue, which is what spiny anteaters do best, even though ant lapping is not yet a recognized Olympic sport — but this Millie wasn't moving. The Summer Olympics were only a few weeks away, but it was still sharply cold in Sydney, and most of the animals at the zoo had their noses tucked under their tails and their backs to the snappy wind. Even in the finest weather, though, spiny anteaters (or echidnas, as they are properly known) are clumsy-looking mammals the size of bowling balls, who toddle around like little drunks and roll up, spines bristling, when they get upset. They are not what you would call "sporty." The other two official Olympic mascots, Syd the platypus and Olly the kookaburra, are much more athletic than Millie but just as peculiar. Kookaburras are small, husky king-fishers that laugh hysterically at absolutely anything. Platypuses, with their big beaks, furry bodies, flat tails, and webbed feet, look like what mothers always warn you will happen if you buy separates rather than a nice outfit. However un-Olympian Millie, Syd, and Olly may be, they are plastered all over Sydney in what has been described as the biggest Olympics marketing effort in history; you cannot walk down a Sydney street without encountering an Olly stationery set, a Syd bumbag, a Millie sunvisor, or a sheet of stickers showing Olly playing basketball, Syd swinging a bat, and Millie — sluggish, nearly immobile Millie — gaily tapping a Ping-Pong ball. "I'm a typical Australian," Millie says in a children's book explaining her Olympic career move. "I'm tough, clever and occasionally a bit spiky. I'm an expert at my chosen occupation, namely digging, and I really like my food."

Everyone I met in Australia seemed awfully cranky about the Olympics. Maybe sour moods are typical in cities about to host events that are expensive and complicated and guaranteed to tangle traffic for weeks, but Australians seem to have brought cynicism to record-breaking new heights. One of the few things anyone raved about to me was the fact that Air New Zealand was offering a special, all-time-low round-trip airfare out of Australia during the two weeks of the Games. Another was an acidly satirical television series called *The Games*, about the machinations of the local Olympic committee. Otherwise, attitudes seemed to span the range from indifference to despair. This summer, a new website, www.silly2000.com, was launched to further skewer Sydney 2000; its motto is "Keeping You Sane Through the Games," and the site includes a countdown to the end of the Olympics and mock stories on equestrian hooliganism and where to buy guns and fast food in Sydney.

I had arrived in Australia expecting — dreading, actually — Olympic delirium, since Australians are usually portrayed as unironic enthusiasts. Once I got over my surprise at their cynicism, though, it struck me as perfectly appropriate; this is, after all, a post-Salt-Lake-City-scandals Olympics. What was going around was a distaste for the local Olympic Committee, antipathy toward the corporate nature of the Games, annoyance at the logistics of the thing, and a bit of anticipatory defensiveness about whether Sydney can actually pull it off.

"We're probably going to be reading a lot of nasty stories about Sydney now," a talk show host said to me, sighing heavily. Nasty stories about Sydney, one of the most beautiful, pleasant cities on the planet?

"Ha-ha," I answered, assuming he was kidding.

He sighed again and said, "Well, I guess we have it coming." (There have, it seems, been goof-ups. The Sydney medals, for example, appear to depict the Colosseum in Rome rather than the Parthenon in Greece, the birthplace of the Games. "The Australians," sniffed *Avriani*, a Greek daily, "have confused a sports arena with a public execution arena.")

Even children in Australia are being inoculated against Olympic fever. I figured that Kokey Koala, the main character in *Kokey Koala and the Bush Olympics*, would embody heroics and prowess, until I turned the book over and read, "Watch Kokey's disasters as he participates in the Bush Olympics."

The general grumpiness about the event meant that it was still possible, four weeks before the opening ceremonies, to get tickets to just about anything you wanted — that is, unless Australian postal workers went on strike, as they were threatening to do, and refused to deliver any Olympic tickets unless they got a special bonus.(Sydney hotel workers, keeping pace with the post office, staged a walkout for an Olympic bonus as well.) "We were glad when we got it, so let's get into it!" one radio campaign scolded.

My first night in Sydney, I flipped on the television and saw a commercial that showed an elderly man sitting in a stark white room, talking mournfully into the camera. At first, I thought it was one of those public service ads urging you to wear seat belts or quit smoking, because the man looked so depressed. "No, I didn't go to the Olympics in '56," he was saying, referring to the last time Australia hosted the Games, in Melbourne. And, he went on, his life had been a welter of regret ever since. "Rarely do you get a second chance in a lifetime," he said. "Why would you pass up that opportunity?" Which of course meant, "You will never, ever outlive the remorse and sorrow that I guarantee you if you don't at least go to a water-polo match or something." Maybe the ads will work eventually, but for the moment, the *Sydney Morning Herald*'s "Holiday Accommodation" classified section still listed apartments far from Sydney, under the headline ESCAPE THE OLYMPICS!

When it comes to Olympians rather than Olympics, everyone cheers up. There were billboards all over town featuring Cathy Freeman, the Aborigine runner who won a silver medal in Atlanta, and daily reports on Ian Thorpe, the seventeen-year-old swimmer, nicknamed Thorpedo, whose stupendous foot size is a matter of national pride. As cool as they are about the Olympics, Australians are mad about sports. They surf and swim and golf and ride and sail, and they play tennis and cricket and soccer, and they totally worship "footy" — Australian Rules football, a rugbylike concoction derived from an Aborigine game called *marngrook*. "Sport is a prime metaphor for Australian life," the art critic and historian Robert Hughes writes in the Sydney Games official souvenir program — which is called, inventively enough, "Official Souvenir Program" — "and because of it, many of our heroes (we don't have a lot) are sportsmen and women." In fact, six of the ferries to the Olympic venue in Homebush are named in honor of Australian Olympic athletes. Another hero might have been Richard Kevan Gosper, a working-class Sydneysider who won first place in the 440-yard sprint in the 1954 Commonwealth Games; a silver medal in track at the 1956 Melbourne Olympics; and a place on the Australian team in the 1960 Olympics, in Rome. Might have been, that is, if Gosper — now the most senior Australian Olympic official — hadn't queered his reputation by taking an eighteen-thousand-dollar ski vacation in Salt Lake City in 1993, a potential violation of International Olympic Committee rules. (He was finally cleared of any wrongdoing after five months of investigation.) Then, to forever ensure his lack of popularity in Australia, he allowed his daughter Sophie to accept an invitation to be the first Australian in the torch relay, bumping a young girl who had originally been chosen for the spot. Sydney's *Daily Telegraph* suggested that Gosper's name was actually an acronym for Greedy Obstinate Selfish Pompous Egotistical Reptile.

Except for the Sophie Gosper incident, the torch relay has been one of the happiest parts of the proceedings. As the torch has been circling the country, newspapers have been publishing maps showing its route, along with lists of the names of the various runners, most of whom are ordinary blokes, minor athletic heroes, community standouts, and kids. But even the relay has had snarls. Some joker tried to douse the torch with a fire extinguisher, and smart alecks have been lighting cigarettes from it. One town, Tingha, was so offended by being bypassed that its citizens conspired to pinch some of the flame with a homemade torch. Another town, Nimbin, in northern New South Wales, felt that it was deliberately left off the route because of its notoriety as a marijuana center and the fear that there would be too much enthusiasm for lighting joints from the Olympic torch. The manager of a local backpackers' hotel was quoted as saying, "The hemp Olympics come here, not the flame ones."

On my last day in Sydney, I went to Olympic Park in Homebush Bay, about fifteen miles west of the center of the city. From downtown, the easiest way to Homebush is by RiverCat, a long ferryboat that slips noiselessly from Circular Quay, beside the white half-shell of the Sydney Opera House, down the Parramatta River to Gladesville and Chiswick and Darling Harbour and Kissing Point and, eventually, to Homebush. The banks of the river are ragged, with long grooves and deep coves and jigsawed inlets and bays. Homebush is on a chunk of low, flat land shaped like the head of a golden retriever. The area has had an inglorious past. Besides being the site of a former racetrack, Homebush consisted of a drab collection of suburban bungalows, brick factories, and railroad tracks. For forty years, Homebush Bay and the surrounding wetlands were used as a dump for domestic garbage, construction debris, and commercial waste, including petroleum, tar sludge, asbestos, heavy metals, and dioxins. So much waste was deposited that the landscape was permanently redrawn. The area was considered, in the most generous terms, "highly degraded." After six years and a hundred and thirty-seven million dollars, it is now a green, or at least greenish, mostly man-made landscape called Millennium Parklands, replanted with native grasses and casuarina trees, and pocked with twenty-two man-made ponds. Even the most ornery of Australians would have to agree that this aspect of hosting the Olympics has been a success.

Most of the thirty-two Sydney Olympic venues are clustered at Millennium Parklands, including the two-hundred-million-dollar Super Dome, the Aquatic Centre, the Olympic Stadium, the Tennis Centre, the Baseball Stadium, Archery Park, and McDonald's Central. The Olympic site is such a spectacle that it has been swarmed by visitors who wanted to see the largest Olympic stadium in history (StadiumAustralia, which seats a hundred and ten thousand). By the time I got to Sydney, some of the athletes had arrived, and the site was in pre-Games security lock down. Though it was no longer possible to tour the facilities, my Olympic Explorer bus, which met the ferry, was nearly full; the passengers were mostly Italian and Japanese.

The bus driver was a middle-aged Australian with a craggy face and a bush hat covered with pins and insignia. Even he had succumbed to the prevailing cynicism. "We'll get the propaganda over with first," he announced, and proceeded to give the precooked description of the place. The passengers pushed toward the windows to take pictures of Olympic Boulevard, and Pavilions Two, Three, and Four, and Boral Olympic Dream Parkway, and Kronos Hill — a garbage mountain now capped and re-planted and hemmed in with retaining walls. Everything was bright and clean and beautiful and had the unnaturally gentle undulations of a landfill. As we passed the Homebush Bay Novotel, the bus driver said it was a fine hotel offering every comfort. "The only thing you won't see at the Novotel are Olympic officials," he said. "That's because it's only a four-star hotel. Olympic officials are only willing to stay at five-star hotels." The passengers tittered and put down their cameras. The bus driver chuckled and added, "They couldn't handle a four-star hotel, poor dears."

Some of the Olympic venues are outside Millennium Parklands. The equestrian events, for instance, will take place west of downtown at something called, remarkably enough, Horsley Park. Beach volleyball will be held at Bondi Beach, a choice that many Australians have found remarkable for other reasons. Bondi is not the prettiest beach in Australia, but it's probably the best loved — as familiar and iconic to Sydney residents as, say, Central Park is to New Yorkers. One of the closest beaches to downtown, it is a horseshoe of tan sand southeast of the harbor, in a hilly neighborhood of kabob shops and stores selling spotty-dog ice cream and Roxy bikinis and deep-fried coconut-battered Mars bars. Bondi has one of the oldest lifesaving clubs in Australia and one of the oldest surf cultures. Board shorts and rash-guard shirts with BONDI BEACH insignia sell like crazy, and most tourists to Sydney ride three stops on the Illawarra Line subway to look at the legendary waves.

There is no ballplaying allowed at Bondi Beach. When it was announced, two years ago, that the Olympic beach-volleyball competition would take place at Bondi, and that a stadium would be built to accommodate it, reaction in the neighborhood was immediate. A Stop the Stadium movement was launched, led by a group called Bondi Olympic Watch, which collected thousands of signatures on petitions opposing the stadium. Nevertheless, the stadium went up. The anti–beach volleyball groups kept complaining. BONDI OLYMPIC STADIUM TURNS INTO A DOLLAR DUMPER, one flyer raged. "The Olympic beach volleyball stadium has turned the centre of our world famous beach into what looks like a giant scaffold site and is gobbling up millions of tax payers' dollars. Originally costed at $13 million, this piece of ugliness has become the unspoken nightmare of the Olympic Coordination Authority."

The stadium is a gigantic tangle of risers and bleachers and fencing moored on some three hundred pylons sunk into the sand. Supposedly, it will be pulled down as soon as the Olympics are over and Bondi Beach will be back to normal, but many people I spoke to suspect that they'll be stuck with it forever, and others referred to a study alleging that if the pylons are removed, they will raise polluted soil to the beach surface. I spent my afternoon at Bondi walking around the stadium, reading the "Fuck the Olympics" graffiti, and peeking through the fence to get a look. Anyone who really wants to see the inside will have no trouble once the Games begin, because at last count tens of thousands of beach-volleyball tickets remained unsold. In Martin Smith's Bookshop, just off Campbell Parade, I picked up a sticker that said, KEEP TAKING YOUR MEDICATION. OUR OLYMPIC VISITORS MUST SUSPECT NOTHING, and considered buying a T-shirt with a mock IOC logo that said, IDIOTS ORGANIZING CHAOS rather than INTERNATIONAL OLYMPIC COMMITTEE and had five lemons arranged like the five Olympic rings.

"There's a lot of bad odor about the Olympics," Martin Smith told me. "I'm just disillusioned. I'd like to not be here at all. Instead, I'm leaving for Spain halfway through."

A customer, overhearing him, came over and said angrily, "Not all of us feel that way. I live here, too, and I'm very proud to share the beach with the world for a few weeks."

I was surprised that the store owners in the area weren't more enthusiastic, since the event will probably bring thousands of visitors who might shop around. "People who come for an event like that don't go shopping," Lee Ross, the owner of Parade Music, explained. "They come for the event and they leave. It's a myth that it will be good for the stores. It won't help my business to have a bunch of idiots in G-strings lobbing around."

I thought that the most outrageous thing about the Sydney Olympics would be its colossal merchandising campaign — a projected billion dollars' worth, the biggest in Olympic history, protected by a revolutionary anticounterfeiting device patterned on DNA taken from the hair of an unnamed Olympic athlete. But that was trumped by the announcement, made a few days before I left Australia, that a float featuring a dozen or so drag queens would appear in the closing ceremonies. According to published reports, Mitzi Macintosh, Portia Turbo, Chelsea Bun,

Trudi Valentine, and Vanessa Wagner — a few of Sydney's most glamorous transvestites — will "frock up in *Priscilla, Queen of the Desert* outfits" as part of a celebration of Australian culture. One newspaper reported that "bitchy comments about who will have the most expensive costume and how some allegedly unreliable drag queens have missed out are also flying about. . . . But there are hopes that a group of 'muscle marys' — or well-toned men — may perform alongside them."

Suddenly, the public debate left the question of whether Cathy Freeman should be allowed to carry an Aboriginal flag and whether members of Parliament were right to accept expensive tickets from corporate sponsors and picked up the drag-queen controversy. The "Letters" columns of Sydney's newspapers were swamped: "The billions watching the ceremony on worldwide TV will no doubt be left with the enduring memory, not of our champion athletes, but of abnormal men prancing round in atrocious feathers and frocks." "Sydney, the City of Sleaze. Well, it does have a certain alliterative quality." "After observing the tasteless self-serving arrogance of the ruling AOC/IOC aristocracy, I conclude that even a bunch of drag queens would, by comparison, provide a classier act." "That boofy bronzed [Australian] macho sort of thing is fearfully passé. Although, to tell the absolute truth, there are some people I know who wouldn't mind a boofy bronzed [Australian], if only they could lay their hands on one. What bliss!"

The drag queens had signed confidentiality agreements, so they weren't talking, but as I left Australia the people of Sydney definitely were, and I suspect the debate over the opening ceremonies, the closing ceremonies, the mascots, the venues, the disfiguring of Bondi Beach, the ticket prices, the ticket delivery, the traffic, the price hikes, and, of course, the judging of the events will continue until the torch is passed. Certainly, that debate is already a little more trenchant and a little more cantankerous than I had anticipated. My favorite souvenir — besides my Millie the Spiny Anteater stickers — was a letter addressing the drag-queen issue with what I had come to understand was classic Australian reasoning. "Transvestites and poofters at the Olympic Games to illustrate the Australian sporting culture?" the writer asked. "Why not add a few prostitutes to give their sport some quality?"

The Place to Disappear

All languages are welcome on Bangkok's Khao San Road, including Drunkard. "Hold my hand," a man fluent in Singapore slings commanded a Scottish hairdresser one night at Lucky Beer and Guest House — only in his dialect it came out soggy and rounded, more like "Hole mah han."

"Not right now," the Scottish hairdresser said. She was a slender girl with the pinkish pallor of a milkmaid, blond hair, gray eyes, and a nose ring. She was on a six-week trip through Asia with two cute friends from Glasgow. They'd just arrived on a superdiscount flight from Scotland and had checked into a seven-dollar-a-night room at one of the several hundred or so cheap guesthouses around Khao San Road — Happy Home Guest House or Nirvana Café and Guest House or Sweety's or Lek Mam's or something; they actually couldn't re- member what it was called, but they knew how to find their way back. They also knew how to get from their guesthouse to the new branch of Boots, the English drugstore, which opened recently amid the T-shirt shops and travel agencies that line Khao San. Within their first few hours in Bangkok, the girls went to Boots and blew their travel budget on English soap and shampoo — same soap and shampoo they could get at home but somehow more exotic seeming when bought in Thailand — and on snack packages of Oreos, which they worship and which are not easy to find in the United Kingdom. They thought Khao San was horrible because it was so crowded and loud and the room in the guesthouse was so dingy, but it was brilliant, too, because it was so inexpensive, and there were free movies playing at all the bars, and because they'd already run into two friends from home. On top of that, finding a branch of Boots right here was almost too good to be true. What's more, Boots was super-air-conditioned, and that distinguished it from many of the other Khao San Road shops, which were open to the hot and heavy Bangkok air.

Now it was close to midnight, and the girls were sitting at a rattletrap table outside Lucky Beer, eating noodles and drinking Foster's Lager and trying to figure out how to get to Laos. "Hole mah han," the drunk repeated, and thrust his arm across the table.

The three girls studied his arm, then shifted away from him. "Wow," one of the hairdresser's friends said. "He looks kind of . . . old."

"Shut up," the man snapped. He yanked his arm back, wobbled to his feet, and then fell across the table, sending a salt shaker and a napkin dispenser to heaven. All the while, the girls kept talking about their schedule. It was as if the strangeness of where they were and what they were doing was absolutely ordinary: as if there were no large, smelly drunk sprawled in front of them, as if it were quite unexceptional to be three Scottish girls drinking Australian beer in Thailand on their way to Laos, and as if the world were the size of a peanut — something as compact as that, something that easy to pick up, shell, consume, as long as you were young and sturdy and brave. If you spend any time on Khao San Road, you will come to believe that this is true.

Finally, the hairdresser glanced at the man, who had not moved. "Hello, sir?" she said, leaning toward his ear. "Hello? Can you hear me? Can I ask you something important? Do you remember where you're from?"

I went back to Lucky Beer the next night, but the Scottish girls were gone — off to Laos, most likely. At their table was a South

African woman who taught English in Taiwan and was on her way back from massage school in Chiang Mai, in northern Thailand. The next night, she was gone, too, replaced by an American couple in their twenties who'd just finished a Peace Corps assignment in Lithuania and were taking the long way home; the night after that, it was five Israelis who had just finished their military service and were stalling in Southeast Asia before starting college in Tel Aviv. Khao San Road, one long packed block in Bangkok's Banglamphu neighborhood, was the jumping-off point for all of them, a sort of non-place they went to in order to leave from, so they could get to the place they really wanted to go. People appear on Khao San just long enough to disappear. It is, to quote the Khao San Road Business Association's motto, "Gateway to Southeast Asia," provided you are traveling on the cheap and have a backpack fused to your shoulders. From here you can embark on Welcome Travel's escorted tour of Chiang Mai, which guarantees contact with four different hill tribes, or the Cheap and Smile Tour to Koh Samui, or a minibus trip to Phuket or Penang or Kota Baharu, or an overland journey by open-bed pickup truck to Phnom Penh or Saigon, or a trip via some rough conveyance to India or Indonesia or Nepal or Tibet or Myanmar or anywhere you can think of — or couldn't think of, probably, until you saw it named on a travel agency kiosk on Khao San Road and decided that was the place you needed to see. Everything you need to stay afloat for months of traveling — tickets, visas, laundry, guidebooks, American movies, Internet access, phone service, luggage storage — is available on Khao San Road.

Thailand, the most pliant of places, has always accommodated even the rudest of visitors. For hundreds of years, it was the junction between Chinese, Burmese, Indian, Khmer, and Vietnamese traders. Many Americans first came to know Bangkok as the comfort lounge for troops in Vietnam and, later, as the capital of sex tourism. Starting in the early eighties, when foreigners began trekking to such places as Myanmar and Tibet and Vietnam, Thailand took on another hostessing job, because Bangkok was the safest, easiest, most Westernized place from which to launch a trip through Asia. Until then, Khao San was an unremarkable working-class neighborhood. It had a large temple called Wat Chanasongkhran, a small Muslim enclave, bakeries, motorcycle shops, grocery stores, and a surprising number of residents who were employed as traditional Thai dancers. There were some hotels in the neighborhood, frequented by Thai businesspeople.

In 1985, Bonny and Anek Rakisaraseree noticed how many budget travelers — mostly young French and Australian men — were drifting around Bangkok, so they opened Bonny Guest House, the first on Khao San catering to foreign wanderers. Locals were not even permitted to rent rooms. Dozens of other guesthouses opened soon afterward, most with forbidding signs in the lobby saying "Not allow any Thais to go upstairs." Drugs were fantastically cheap and available and quietly tolerated, despite wishful signs saying "We do not welcome use or possession of heroin in guesthouse." More than a third of Thailand's seven million annual visitors are young, and undoubtedly many of them pass some time on Khao San. Some are Americans, but even more of them are from other countries: Australians having what they call their "o-s experience," their overseas experience, which begins in Sydney and ends six or eight months later with requisite *Rough Guide–* and *Lonely Planet*–advised stops in Goa for Christmas and in Nepal for a winter trek and in Angkor Wat for sunrise; hordes of

Israelis, fresh out of the army — so many, in fact, that the best kosher food and the only Hebrew bookstore in Thailand are on Khao San Road. There are such large crowds of Japanese kids that a few guesthouses are de facto Japanese only, and you can buy a logo T-shirt of any Japanese baseball team from the vendors on the road. There are French and German and British and Canadians.

Altogether, they have turned Khao San into a new sort of place — not really Thai anymore, barely Asian, overwhelmingly young, palpably transient, and anchored in the world by the Internet, where there is no actual time and no actual location. Khao San has the best foreign bookstores in Thailand, thanks to the books that backpackers sell before heading home, and it probably has the fewest prostitutes in Bangkok, partly because the guesthouses frown on overnight Thai guests and partly because, one backpacker explained to me, most of the travelers would rather have sex with one another than with someone for hire. Khao San is now the travel hub for half the world, a place that prospers on the desire to be someplace else. The cheapest tickets on the most hair-raising of airlines can be bought in the scores of bucket shops that have collected in the neighborhood. Airlines you've never heard of, flying routes you never imagined, for prices you only dream of, are the staple of Khao San travel agencies. The first time I ever heard of Khao San Road was from an American backpacker whom I met on a Bhutanese airline flight from Calcutta to Bangkok. He'd bought his ticket on Khao San Road. "I told the travel agent I didn't care how or when I got there," he said. "As long as it was cheap, I was ready to go."

I have a persistent fantasy that involves Khao San. In it, a middle-aged middle-brow middle manager from Phoenix is deposited at the western end of the road, near the Chanasongkhran police booth. He is a shocking sight, dressed in a blue business suit and a red tie and a white Oxford shirt, carrying a Hartmann briefcase, and wearing a Timex. He wanders through the snarl of peddlers' carts and trinket booths. First, he discards his suit for batik drawstring trousers and a hemp vest and a Che Guevara T-shirt or knockoff Timberland cargo shorts and a Japanimation tank top, and he sells his Timex to a guy with a sign that says, WE BUY SOMETHING/CAMERA/TENT/SLEEPING BAG/WALKMAN/BACKPACK/SWISS KNIFE. He then gets a leather thong bracelet for one wrist and a silver cuff for the other, stops at Golden Lotus Tattoo for a few Chinese characters on his shoulder, gets his eyebrow pierced at Herbal House Healthy Center, has blond extensions braided into his hair, trades his briefcase for a Stussy backpack and a Hmong fabric waistpack, watches twenty minutes of *The Phantom Menace* or *The Blair Witch Project* at Buddy Beer, goes into Hello Internet Café and registers as "zenmasterbob" on hotmail.com, falls in love with a Norwegian aromatherapist he meets in the communal shower at Joe Guest House, takes off with her on a trek through East Timor, and is never seen again.

The sidewalk vendors changed a little every day I was on Khao San. The road has a jumble of small businesses — travel agencies, Internet cafés, souvenir stores, bars — and the sidewalk and the edge of the roadbed are lined with stalls offering bootleg tapes, bogus Teva sandals, Hindu-print camisoles, and flyweight silver jewelry, along with the hair braiders and the banana pancake makers. A few spots had more transient occupants, and except for the daily twitches in the exchange rate at Khao San's foreign currency shops, they were one of the only things that distinguished one day from the next. The morning I arrived on Khao San, a nerdy Thai teenager had got a foothold halfway down one block, between Shaman Bookstore and Nadav Bead Shop, and was peddling electronic pagers. The next day, he was gone, and a chatty young woman was there selling handmade burlap handbags. I began to think of the days that way — as "burlap bag day" or "pager day" — to help tell them apart. One morning — it was miniature mirrored disco ball day — I stopped to check my e-mail at Khao-San Cyber Home, a computer center set a few paces back from the sidewalk beside a stand of banana trees and a fishpond full of carp. On the street, the open-air Siam Oriental Inn was blasting a Swedish-dubbed version of *The Phantom Menace* on wide-screen TV, while across the way Buddy Beer, also open-air and also maximum volume, was showing *Wild Wild West*, and at the big bootleg-cassette booth next door an early Santana album screeched out of tinny speakers. The sounds collided like a car wreck, and even early in the day the wet, warm air smelled like Michelob and pad thai.

Inside the Khao-San Cyber Home, though, it was mercifully cool and quiet. In the front room were eight computer terminals with Pentium III microprocessors, a large and solemn photograph of King Bhumibol Adulyadej on one wall, and a Buddhist altar in the corner across from the front door. I left my shoes by the landing and padded across the floor to an open computer. On my left, a thin kid with a blond braid was instant messaging someone in Australia. On my right, two girls were squeezed together at one terminal, tapping out a message in romanized Japanese. The more slowly and more uncomfortably and more dangerously you travel around Asia, the more rank you pull in backpacker culture — in other words, it's much cooler to go somewhere by cargo boat or pickup truck or milk train than to fly — but when it comes to computers, Khao San is all speed. The first Macintosh computers in all of Thailand appeared here, and one Internet service owner complained sourly to me that backpackers refused to use anything with Pentium I microprocessors anymore, so he had to upgrade all his machines to Pentium IIIs. There are so many Internet outlets on Khao San Road now that the price to use a computer is probably the best in the world, and certainly the best in Asia — around three cents a minute, compared with, say, five dollars a minute, which is what I paid to check my e-mail in Cambodia. In the past, a six-month odyssey through the Far East might have meant a few letters home and the rare long-distance phone call; now it's possible for a few cents to e-mail friends and family every day, order clothes from the Gap, and even read your local newspaper online. Some computer centers on Khao San stay open twenty-four hours a day.

Hello Internet Café was the first in the neighborhood. Khao-San Cyber Home is one of the most recent. Until eight months ago, it wasn't a cyberhome at all: It was an actual home of an actual Thai family, the Boonpojanasoontorns, who had been living on Khao San for many years. Until Chanin Boonpojanasoontorn learned about the Internet when he was at college and pushed the family to capitalize on their location, Khao-San Cyber Home computer center had been the family's living room. Urasa Boonpojanasoontorn, the second youngest daughter, was behind the desk that day, and from time to time her father toddled by on some household task and then disappeared behind a door again. Urasa is twenty-five and has a round face and a square body and a quick, crumpled-up smile. She was wearing a white polo shirt and pleated khakis — nearly a nun's outfit on Khao San Road, where the skimpiest camisoles and the filmiest skirts are the usual backpacker gear. Urasa and her brother and sisters grew up playing soccer in the middle of the street with the other neighborhood kids, buying candy at the stores that back then stocked everyday groceries and household goods.

"When I was in seventh grade," Urasa said to me, "I went outside and everything was different. The foreigners had arrived. It happened so fast! It was such a quiet place before. There were no foreigners. It changed, like, overnight, and I never went outside again." Her parents were afraid of the backpackers. Once the neighborhood changed, they insisted that the kids come home directly from school and stay away from the street. I asked her what they were afraid of.

"They thought the backpackers had a different lifestyle than us," she said carefully. "Their language and their behavior were different. There were boys and girls traveling together, and the problem of drugs. And when I first saw the way the backpackers dressed . . ." She hesitated. The door behind her desk opened, and I could see her father in an easy chair, watching TV. "The way the backpackers dressed was shocking. My father and mom thought it wasn't good. I can't say what happens in other countries, but if I saw a Thai girl dressed like that, I would think it wasn't good." She brightened and added, "Sometimes it was fun to hear the music from the bars. It wasn't sad when it changed. There was no more playing in the street, but then I grew up and I had other things to do. I studied hard. It's different from your culture. I had a tutor for two hours every day after school and on Saturday, too."

The front door opened and three Israeli girls in pastel tank tops came in to use Khao-San Cyber Home's international long-distance service. They took off their shoes and left them by the door, a Thai tradition that most shops on Khao San forgo. Urasa decided to uphold it because she wanted her customers to see a little bit of her culture, her lifestyle, even though it meant that some backpackers in twenty-four-eyelet hiking boots chose to check their e-mail somewhere more lenient. A similar impulse accounts for the Buddhist altar and the king's portrait, though not for the enormous framed Michael Jordan poster beside her desk. "He's mine," Urasa said, tapping the glass above Jordan's eye. "I never heard about him until my sister went to college in Illinois, and she said to me, 'Urasa, you have to see this man. He is a god.' "

Something about Khao San Road makes you feel as though it could eat you alive. The junkies and the glue sniffers lurking in the alleys are part of it, and so are the clean-cut kids with stiff, Ecstasy-fueled grins dancing at the cafés; the aimlessness that pervades the place is both pleasantly spacey and a little scary when you glimpse an especially blank face. Travelers do vanish in all sorts of ways. The first cybercafé I stopped in had a ten-thousand-dollar-reward sign on the wall that said, "Have you seen my son? He was back-packing around India and was last heard from in May 1997 from Northern India." Urasa said she sees lots of lost souls. One day, an American girl came into Khao-San Cyber Home to call her mother and could hardly talk because she was crying so hard. "She had lost her boyfriend," Urasa told me. "He disappeared from her in Nepal." Sometimes visitors planning another kind of trip are busted and subsequently relocated to Bangkok's Ban Kwan Prison. Guesthouses often post lists of foreigners who are locked up on drug charges and encourage you to visit Lyle Doniger of Australia, or Alan Jon Davies of Britain, or any number of Americans and Danes and Italians at Ban Kwan if you find yourself with nothing to do one afternoon.

The day begins at night on Khao San Road. Usually a soccer game is being broadcast from one bar, and five or six movies are being broadcast from the others, and the cassette dealers are demonstrating the quality of their bootleg tapes by playing Global Trance Mission or Techno Trance Mania or Earth, Wind and Fire at top volume. Kids clutching copies of *Bangkok Groovy Map & Guide* and *Teach Yourself Indonesian* and *Teach Yourself Card Games for 1* and *The Swahili Phrasebook* amble up and down the street. They emerge from the guesthouses — and their bottom-dollar rooms with wafer-thin walls and battered mattresses — to collect in the cafés for ten-cent plates of curry chicken and "Stogarnov steak" and beer and to shop. The first Thai head of state to travel outside the region was King Rama V, who visited Europe in 1897. He brought back Waterford crystal from Ireland, Sèvres porcelain and Baccarat goblets from France, Murano glass from Italy, Royal Crown Derby plates from England. When you visit Khao San Road, you can bring back Indian undershirts decorated with Hindu imagery, Australian Billabong sweats, Nike jackets made in Indonesia, rubber-platform faux-fur thongs from another planet, Game Boys from Japan, and a used copy of *Memoirs of a Geisha* that was published in England and sold to a secondhand bookstore in Bangkok by a New Zealander on his way to Vietnam.

Around midnight, I ran into the South African English teacher from Taiwan who had been on her way back from massage school in northern Thailand the other time I'd met her. Seeing her again was both a shock and not a shock, because Khao San is so transitory a place that you imagine each encounter there to be singular, but then you realize that the world is small and this particular world of young adventurers is smaller yet, and that there is nothing extraordinary about seeing the same people, because their great adventures tend to take them to the same few places over and over again. Her name was Elizabeth, and she and I stopped at a street vendor and bought corn on the cob and sat on a curb near My House Guest House to eat. This time she'd just come back from a full-moon party on the southern Thai island of Koh Phangan, a party of two thousand travelers, most of them high on Ecstasy or pot or psychedelics, painting a herd of oxen with Day-Glo colors and dancing for hours on the edge of the sea. She now had a terrible headache, but she didn't think it was from the drugs or the late hours. She blamed a Sikh psychic she'd met that morning on Khao San who had tricked her into paying him a hundred dollars so he wouldn't curse her karma.

I felt sorry for her, so I treated her to a bowl of noodle soup from a stand at the western end of the street. We were, at that moment, on the very edge of the rest of the city. Thirty paces away, on Chakrabongse Road, were a dozen bridal shops where Thai girls shopped for their big white gowns; a few paces beyond that was the temple, Wat Chanasongkhran, where monks in yellow were chanting their daily sutras. All of it seemed surreal and sort of irrelevant and much farther away from Khao San Road than almost anywhere else in the universe, including outer space. Elizabeth had a travel tip for me. *The Phantom Menace* was starting at one a.m. at Buddy Beer, and if she finished her soup, and we hurried, we could make it back for the opening scene.

EVERYWHERE
Part Three

Homewrecker

Recently, my friend Gene asked if I'd let a friend of his use my apartment while I was away. I declined, and then, later, he mentioned that the person needing a place to stay happened to be Tina Turner. I was sorry I'd said no, because even though I don't know Tina personally, I had just seen the movie about her — *What's Love Got to Do with It* — and I think that it would have been cool to have her stay in my apartment. It's a two-bedroom on the Upper West Side, which I have decorated as if it were owned by a midranking official of the Chinese Communist Party. I like how it's turned out.

However, I don't know if it would be to Tina's liking. In the movie, Ike and Tina's apartment (or mansion, or whatever) has a different look from mine, but maybe Ike did their decorating.

I'm a size 2, and I bet that Tina is also a 2, or maybe a 4 on her fat days. I'm sure she'd end up rummaging around in my closet — something I ordinarily wouldn't like, but I'd love to be the person who turned Tina on to

J. Crew plain-front relaxed-fit khakis. On the other hand, if she visited on a fat day and tried on something of mine and split a seam, would she fix it? Or would she hide it and hope I'd never notice? Or — worst of all — would she throw away the ruined outfit and then let me spend the next year of my life trying to figure out where I lost my pants? I'd hate having to worry that some celebrity who hadn't worked out her shame-and-denial issues was going to be destroying my stuff and then pretending it had never happened.

Also: Does Tina Turner cook? I'll bet that she doesn't cook a lot but that she has mastered one fancy party dish — something that's not actually hard to make but looks complicated, like smoked-bluefish pâté or nachos. It's become her signature dish: Whenever she goes to pot lucks, people see her coming up the driveway and instead of saying, "Hey, here comes Tina," they say, "Hey, here comes that smoked-bluefish pâté," or, "Here come the nachos." Anyway, my kitchen is typical for New York City, so there wouldn't be much for her to see, except that I have one cupboard absolutely loaded with cans of water-packed tuna. This could have a downside. It might tempt her to just "borrow" a few cans, with every intention of replacing them at some future

400

date, and we all know how often guests spend their vacation running to the grocery store to replace what they've filched. The answer is: not very often. I also have these great boar-bristle hairbrushes that I think a show business person with a lot of hair and an elevated hair consciousness — for example, Tina Turner — would adore. Unfortunately, I'm not crazy about sharing combs and brushes — this is something I was taught as a child — but if Tina had just shampooed and had forgotten her own stuff, she would probably use them, even if I had specifically asked her not to. No comment. I've done it myself.

I think my neighbors would like Tina, but I'm not sure they'd like her clattering around the apartment in those spike-heeled pumps of hers. I would have to ask her to limit her clattering — she could borrow my socks if she wanted to, but I would appreciate their being washed afterward. Moreover, if she had friends over — I'm assuming her friends also wear noisy shoes — she'd have to insist that they also take theirs off, but they'd have to bring their own socks. If she's too uncomfortable to ask them to do something like that, then maybe she ought to get new friends, or maybe she should look for somewhere else to stay. Isn't that what hotels are for?

The World

The first time we saw the World was in a friend's bathroom in the East Village, and we knew in an instant that we had to have it. It had been some time since we'd thought of ourself as a colonial power, or even a post-isolationist neocolonial power, but once we saw the World, the Gulf of Bothnia and the Strait of Malacca started to look irresistible instead. We wanted the own the World. We wanted hegemony. We hankered to expand our sphere of influence globally. The greatest thing about owning the World, which is a transparent vinyl shower curtain imprinted with a pastel geopolitical world map, is that if you hang it with plastic rings on a good strong rod, you can exercise expansionism at will. Moreover, by applying proper antifungal treatment, you can also control worldwide growth, especially where the curtain hangs against the side of the tub.

Ray Faragher, who makes the World, told us over the phone the other day, from his office in Cincinnati, that he hadn't expected to sell many copies of the World at all, and certainly hadn't expected it to become his bestselling shower curtain in New York City. But that is what has happened. The World has supplanted curtains featuring frogs, fish, and parrots as the shower curtain of choice. According to Mr. Faragher, it sells particularly well at the United Nations gift shop.

Mr. Faragher, who is something of an international bath accessories kingpin, grew up in a house in Kentucky that had no indoor plumbing. "I named my shower curtain company Saturday Knight, because Saturday was bath night when I was growing up," he said. "Plus I'm an Anglophile. Which reminds me: The World is being very well received around the world. It's quite a conversation piece. After all, how many people have a world map hanging in their bathroom? I'd heard about a survey that showed that most people don't know where Iran is, and I thought that with the World they'd be able to find it in their shower." Mr. Faragher went on to say that he's not always sure what makes one shower curtain work and not another one. This year, for instance, he thought that pigs would be big, but pigs flopped — instead, hippos were a hit. As for the World, he thinks some people like it because it transforms their bathroom into something like the Situation Room of the National Security Council. "I knew it would appeal to people with imagination," Mr. Faragher said, "and to people with young minds."

Margo Warnecke Merek, who has an apartment in the East Sixties, originally bought the World just because the colors — creamy pink, yellow, gray, and light green — looked good in her bathroom. Then the real benefit of the World ownership dawned on her. "I had just started doing crossword puzzles," she told us, "and I realized that the curtain would be a good way to check countries."

The apartment in the East Village where we first saw the World belongs to Paula Klausner, who first saw the World when she attended a party on Central Park West three years ago. "The minute I saw it, I knew I had to have it," she told us. "I was enjoying the party, but I spent a lot of time in the bathroom that night just admiring the curtain. I'd never known where Swaziland was. I'd also just heard of Gambia that year, and I liked it that the World had Gambia on it. I even liked the mistakes — the way they spelled 'Manila' just like 'vanilla' on those early curtains."

Beth Shulman, who lives in Morningside Heights, bought the World last winter to cure her wanderlust. "My husband and I used to travel a lot, and then we had our son, and we cut back on our traveling, but we missed it," she said. "We have friends who are on a six-month trip through Asia and Australia, so I've been monitoring their trip on my shower curtain."

Mrs. Shulman, like everyone else we know who owns the World, spends a certain amount of her shower time planning imaginary trips and a certain amount trying to figure out whether there's a pattern to the way the countries are colored. For example, the Soviet Union, Ethiopia, and Bolivia are pink; the United States and China are gray; Canada and South Africa are yellow; and Greenland and Kenya are green.

We asked Mr. Faragher to explain the World.

"There's no pattern at all," he said, and laughed. "Pastels are very popular in the market these days, and the design just worked out that way." He then seemed to reconsider and added, "Of course, I thought we should at least do the Soviet Union pink."

Skymalling

One characteristic of the Skymall customer seems to be an excess of body hair. In fact, as you leaf through the hundred or so pages of the Skymall catalog, you begin to suspect that its customers have luxuriant growth everywhere, sprouting out of their noses, ears, cheeks, legs, underarms, and what is always delicately referred to as "the bikini area." In the world of Skymall, though, hirsutism is not an obstacle: It is a challenging and market-exploitable opportunity, with exciting products attached to it. Just look at last summer's issue of the catalog. On page 23, you are offered the Turbo-Groomer 5.0, with superior Swiss surgical stainless-steel blades, for those hard-to-reach nose and ear hairs; on page 42, the immersible long-use travel shaver, for hair removal underwater; on page 74, the Igia Forever Gone Plus, "the permanent solution to hair removal"; on page 81, the Discrette Plus by Epilady, which announces itself as "Always one step ahead in hair removal." There are also line extension hair-removal-associated products, such as the Chrome-Plated Fog-Free Shower Mirror and the AM/FM Shower Radio with Lighted Mirror, which allows you to listen to traffic reports while you shower and shave, satisfying another Skymall trait, the desire to do more than one thing at a time, especially if one of the things you're doing is removing hair. I never used to think about hairiness when I flew, but then I began to read Skymall regularly, and as a result, much of my air time is now devoted to wondering if I have too much hair and, if I do, what system I should use to get rid of it. I also wonder, persistently, whether or not I should at last surrender and order myself a solar-powered cascade fountain or a jewelry organizer with sixty-six pockets or a Pop-Up Hot Dog Cooker — three Skymall items I have thought about buying time after high-flying time. I have dog-eared enough copies of Skymall to fill a kennel. I fly all the time, and even on those overscheduled days when I fly somewhere in the morning and somewhere else in the afternoon, I always pull Skymall out of the seat pocket and browse through it, savoring each and every brass guest towel holder and hand-painted Russian balalaika and foldaway closet ladder and pocket pepper mill. For me, Skymall is the land of products I never think I want, serving needs I never thought I had, and which I can't quite bring myself to buy but can't help considering once they have been brought to my attention.

Skymall is a weird entity. It is a go-between that packages other mail-order companies and offers them in a virtual shopping mall in the virtual megalopolis of the sky. In the trade it is known as a "multichannel specialty retailer." It actually has no products of its own: It doesn't produce anything or manufacture anything or even customize anything it offers for sale. Its closest precedent is probably the Yankee peddler. Skymall is offered in some hotel rooms and airport lounges and on some Amtrak trains, but its singular and fundamental microenvironment is the airline seat pocket — that grimy pouch sagging from the seat back, where it is tucked between the evacuation-slide instruction card and the airsickness bag and whatever previous travelers' rubbish the ground crew failed to clean out. Skymall debuted in 1990. It is now distributed on nineteen airlines, including American, Delta, Southwest, United, Continental, and Alaska. More than five hundred million air travelers see the catalog every year; its sales in 2000 were a whopping sixty-two and a half million dollars — that's sixty-two and a half million dollars' worth of garden toad ornaments and FM radio/ballpoint pens and Old Fashioned Nachos & Cheese Makers, ordered, in a few instances, from the Skymall website but in most cases purchased while at the comfortable cruising altitude of thirty-five thousand feet. According to a company spokesperson, the founder of Skymall, Robert Worsley, came up with the concept of the catalog when he was on a flight and noticed how bored passengers were. In the words of the corporate legend, Worsley "decided to start a business that would alleviate the boredom factor and give passengers something useful to do with their time." Skymall gobbled up another in-flight catalog along the way and then was in turn gobbled up by Gemstar–TV Guide International in 2001. The Skymall vision, though, has remained the same from the day the company began. "Passengers tell us they think we have something for everyone," the spokesperson e-mailed me recently. "Their reaction to products in the catalog range from 'Wow! That's something cool that I must have!' to 'Who on earth would buy that?'"

I began reading Skymall during a period in my life when I had developed a ferocious fear of flying. Because of the itinerant nature of my work, I have to travel all the time, regardless of the state of my nerves. Like all sissy fliers, I gorged compulsively on airplane disaster news, became fluent in traffic controller lingo, and developed a self-taught genius in diagnosing aircraft thumps and rattles. During takeoffs and landings, in particular, I was very busy assisting the pilot. At the same time, of course, I was scared witless and needed to distract myself or I would have jumped out the emergency exit. There were also a few unfortunate episodes of me clawing the arm of the stranger in the next seat when I thought the plane was moments from hurtling out of control. I always carried dozens of magazines and books with me, but honestly, who can concentrate on reading when at any moment she might be called upon to pull a 767-200 jumbo jet out of a nosedive? No, the reading I wanted to do during my flying phobia days was not actual reading: I just wanted to flip through something, the pages sticking slightly to my clammy hands, while running my eyeballs over text. This is how I discovered, and grew to deeply love, Skymall.

My discomfort in the air reached its peak — or was it its nadir? — on a flight between Cleveland and New York some time ago. In addition to pawing through Skymall, I often tried to calm myself by jabbering to my seatmates, and on this particular flight I was next to an older gentleman who told me that he was a magazine publisher. Pay dirt! I was just starting my writing career, so I considered the chance to schmooze a real live publisher a major opportunity — major enough for me to put aside my Skymall completely and focus on cultivating my bit of good fortune. Things were, in fact, going very nicely. The gentleman told me that his magazine was distributed all over the United States and was published in scores of languages as well. He even suggested that I come by the office and meet the staff. I was so excited and so afraid of looking too eager that I didn't dare ask him the name of the magazine. Then, somewhere over Altoona, we hit what felt like an air trampoline. I say this not as the sissy I was then but as the flying strongman I am now: It was really wild turbulence, with service carts clattering down the aisle, overhead compartments flapping open, flight attendants tumbling like tenpins. In the midst of the commotion, my seatmate/future editor/publisher swiveled to face me. "Susan, are you ready to meet your Maker?" he gasped. "Have you accepted Jesus Christ as your personal savior?" Well, I wasn't, and I hadn't, and I twisted away from him, fumbling in the seat pocket to find my lucky Skymall and silently repeating nonsense verse to drown out the sound of his prayers. At last, the plane stopped bucking, and we wafted uneventfully down toward New York and onto the runway. At this point my neck was practically dislocated from craning it away from my seatmate, but he still managed to push his business card into my very sweaty hand before we got off the plane. "I do hope you'll come visit," he said sweetly. "I think you'll find that the *Watchtower* is a wonderful magazine."

Right after that ride, I signed up with a hypnotist and got myself bedazzled into thinking airplane rides were fun — or, at the very least, nonlethal. It worked, and I soon abandoned most of my flying anxiety behavior, but my attachment to Skymall endured. What had started as a palliative had become a passion. Mostly I found myself a little obsessed with the idea of the Skymall customer — the person the catalog evoked. Even when catalogs don't include pictures of people with the products, they do bring to mind a particular individual; they really need to, since there is no salesperson at your elbow giving you the narrative that all retail experiences imply — the story of who you are and who you will be by acquiring a particular item. I can decode a lot of other catalog personas, such as, say, the horny trust funders of Abercrombie & Fitch; the nerd-ball pipe-smoking Levenger guy; the swingers who live and die by Design Within Reach. But Skymall? Who was this person that Skymall described?

Well, there's the hairiness, as I mentioned previously. In fact, despite those bikini-area shavers, I would say that there is, overall, a distinctly masculine aura in the catalog. Skymall man is a businessperson — maybe a middle-level database adminis-trator or regional field sales trainer. He lives in a house and has a backyard. He is an intrepid traveler but is afraid of fire (for which Skymall provides smoke hoods and fire escape ladders), insects (no problem: he can use the Bug Cap to protect his face and neck or, better still, the Keep Your Distance Insect Vacuum), and germs (be-sides the Daisy-Lift toilet-seat lifter, Skymall offers vibrating tongue cleaners, ultraminiature personal air purifiers, and bacteria-resistant utensils — "Your old wooden cooking spoon may be teeming with bacteria — replace it with the new-tech ExoGlass Spoon!"). The Skymall man also worries about his privacy (for which Skymall offers wide-screen Caller ID displays, driveway alert systems, and a listening device detector — "Find Out Who's Eavesdropping on You!") and mean dogs, who, thank goodness, can be stopped in their tracks up to fifty feet away using Dog Off, "a great gift for joggers, walkers, repairmen, and postal delivery people." (Just one question: Are we supposed to be giving gifts to repairmen these days? Maybe Skymall men are raising the generosity bar.)

Mean dogs aside, the Skymall man is a pet lover, forking over a fortune for automatic pet dishes, deluxe dog beds, ramps to help older dogs into cars, wheelie bags for pet transportation, and, most touchingly, pet headstones made of Vermont slate. (Skymall also features a garden stone of composite granite, cement, and resin with a prewritten "sentiment" of either "My Beloved Pet" or a four-line farewell that is generic enough to use for either a pet or a human buried in the backyard.) The Skymall man likes a drink. He appreciates the value of having a martini atomizer and a Barmaster Electronic Mixing

Assistant ("It's the PDA of the Cocktail Circuit") close at hand, as well as, appropriately enough, two different digital Breathalyzers. He likes to barbecue (see the array of tools and grills and even the personal steak branding iron with up to three initials, "to show your guests the pride you take in a great barbecue!"). But, as much as he likes to be the boss of the backyard grill, he likes to relax while doing it, which he can do once he orders the Remote Cooking Thermometer, which allows him to sit inside and, say, practice his golf game on the amazing DivotMat until the remote alarm beeps to let him know that his personally branded steaks are ready.

Commitment to utter laziness is another signature Skymall attribute. The Skymall man may make gestures of activity by purchasing the appurtenances of the sporting life (digital golf scopes, electronic fish finders, and a luxuriously padded, synthetic leather, motorcycle-seat bar stool, which is particularly desirable, since it is both a sport-related item and a drinking accessory), but the quintessential Skymall sport product may be the ExerCHIzer. "If regular aerobic exercise is too strenuous, try the ExerCHIzer for health, fitness and stress reduction!" the catalog suggests, explaining that the device "helps you perform vital aerobic exercises with minimal effort."

Skymall does celebrate items that perform more than one task at a time — for example, the binoculars that are also a camera, or the Fire & Ice Grill, which is both a barbecue and a cooler, or the world's first digital camera/recorder/PDA stylus pen — but it really exalts in the single-function product, the thing that does one thing and one thing only and is wholly useless otherwise. It's a bold move to tout products like battery-operated automatic eyeglass cleaners and five-foot-tall popcorn poppers when doctrines like voluntary simplicity, arguing that we could live very well with one blanket, one frying pan, and a knife, are in vogue. What kind of house could accommodate not only a five-foot-tall popcorn popper, but also a carnival-style snow cone maker and a soft-serve ice-cream maker, and the Old Fashioned Carnival Cotton Candy Maker, and the Nachos & Cheese Maker, and the plastic salad-bar set ("The Mother of All Salad Bars!")? Is it the biggest house in the known universe? Does it have a storage room just for makers of specific foods? Does Skymall represent the ultimate in human ingenuity — the ability to devise a machine that makes cotton candy — or is it addressing our lack of ingenuity in not being able to figure out a way to make cotton candy ourselves?

I am not totally immune to Skymall's beckonings. I once bought a little handheld scanner after seeing it in the catalog, and fell for not one but two sets of vacuum-sealed storage bags that were going to banish forever — or at least compress — the clutter in my closets. And this Christmas, at last, my husband got me a Pop-Up Hot-Dog Cooker. I used the scanner approximately once; the vacuum bags just added to my closet clutter. The hot-dog cooker will probably get a brief workout and then be retired, first to my even more cluttered closet and then to my neighborhood Goodwill collection center. This is perhaps proof that the ultimate, best product of Skymall is Skymall itself — this document of the misbegotten inventiveness of humankind; the magical thinking that leads us to believe that some material item, however nutty it is, will improve our existence; and the heart-warming, affirming fact that we humans are the only life force that would — or could — conceive of, market, and purchase goods such as French Maid toilet paper holders, talking Christmas ornaments, dryer vent brushes, Tan Thru bathing suits, CD shredders, World's Largest Write-on Map Murals, and personal neck-mounted cooling systems. In the words of another Skymall product — those framed instructional thought inducers, known in Skymallese as Inspirational Artwork That Shares Your Values — this takes CHARACTER (aluminum or wood framed), EXCELLENCE (double matted), and the ESSENCE OF LEADERSHIP. Or you can just — wood framed and double matted — DREAM.

We Just Up and Left

A guy known as the Catman lived in Portland Meadows Mobile Home Park for a while; he had a hundred cats and a mouse-colored trailer, which he parked in Space 19, near a knobby maple tree. This happened to be prior to the animal weight restriction — that is, the rule that residents in the park could not own a pet that weighed more than twenty pounds. None of the Catman's cats weighed more than around ten, but if you added them together, they would probably have weighed close to a thousand, and if the twenty-pound rule had been in effect, they might have required some sort of waiver. This is all academic, because before the rule was enacted the Catman had hitched his trailer to his pickup and packed up his animals, and in a matter of minutes all hundred and one of them were gone. In Portland Meadows, as in all trailer parks, people come and go. Everyone everywhere comes and goes, but people who live in trailers live in a constant state of possible mobility.

Some people come to Portland

Meadows, on the outskirts of Portland, Oregon, and then leave after no time; some people stay too long. A man who hated everyone and used a battery-operated bullhorn for normal conversation stayed in the park only a few years, but everyone could hardly wait for him to go; when he finally did, he pulled his trailer out and then sowed broken glass and planted pieces of barbed wire and crisscrossed fishing line all over his parking space. Some people stay for ages and are nearly unseen. They could disappear and no one would look for them, because no one would notice they were gone. Last April, the park newsletter noted one of the hazards of being invisible: "We must request that persons please not be getting inside the Dumpsters. . . . A person could be knocked out trying to get into or out of a Dumpster by a slip of the hand or foot and not be discovered before the Dumpster is emptied." Some people who live in the park, though, make a big impression. A phony blind priest with a Great Dane Seeing Eye dog lived in the park for just a couple of months, but no one will forget him: He had lots of high-spirited friends who used to visit and who didn't seem to mind at all that he wasn't really a priest, that the dog was blind, and that the priest, in fact, was the one with excellent vision.

Victor Nicolaevich Gorbachev, who told me he is Mikhail Gorbachev's cousin, lives in Portland Meadows, in a crumbly camper with busted pipes. He works as a driver for Space Age Fuel. He has lived in the camper since shortly after he arrived in America, except, he said, for five months he spent in prison. He has moved the camper three times — from Fairbanks to Phoenix to San Francisco to Portland. He says that life in Alaska, Arizona, and California was not particularly pleasant, but he loves Oregon, and for the moment he is planning to stay. Drifting in a house with a license plate is something that Victor Gorbachev considers distinctive about the United States. "In America, the houses are light as wood and you move them around," he says. "In Russia, our houses were made of bricks."

Portland Meadows is in a saucer of land rimmed by the Columbia River, the Willamette River, and the stagnant, coffee-colored Columbia Slough. Downtown Portland is a few miles south. To the north and the east lie the snowy tops of Mount Adams, Mount St. Helens, and Mount Hood. To the west are a race-car track and a horse track and the bundled black strands of the railroad tracks. It is an empty-feeling landscape of big, homely things — big trucks, big truck stops, a big toy warehouse. In 1915, when the park opened, it was called Portland Auto Camp, and on advertising placards its address was given as "Union Avenue and North Edge City Limits." The park lies low. The land it sits on is two feet below sea level. It may be the lowest point in Portland. It is part of the Columbia River floodplain; several times in this century, it has been underwater. Jim Benson, who manages the park with his wife, Jan, says, "We're way down. We're really down in a hole." Now the address is 9000 Northeast Martin Luther King Jr. Boulevard, but from the road there is no sign of the park, no front gate or portal: There is only a steep-pitched driveway, unmarked and unremarkable, that looks like one of the narrow off-ramps that truck drivers use when their rigs are running away. At the bottom of the driveway are a speed bump and a pothole, and then the asphalt levels off and the park spills out in every direction, like a puddle. Except that it is older and bigger, Portland Meadows is a lot like any other trailer park. It has some two hundred trailer spaces, a beauty parlor, and a dusty box of a building called the Country Store. It has an office and a Laundromat. It has a dozen narrow lanes that even have names — Main Street, A Street, Twelfth Street. At any given moment, several hundred people live here. Some are single, many are divorced, some are old; there are babies and children; there are people living on welfare and people with more money who just like low-maintenance living that they can take on the road. There are Elkhart Travelers and Airstreams and cab-over-campers, bulky Detroiters and Travelezes and double-wide longs. None of this is visible from the road. I lived in Portland for five years and drove up and down this block of Northeast Martin Luther King Jr. Boulevard a million times and never saw anything to suggest that scores of lives were unfolding a few feet below me. People find their way here anyway. One recent afternoon, a boyish-faced man with wheat-colored hair stopped by the trailer park office. "You got any trailers for rent?" he asked.

"No rentals," Jan Benson told him. "You rent the space, but not the trailer. I'm sorry, honey, you have to own your own."

"I've been moteling it for two months," the man said, jiggling his keys. His eyes had pink edges. He leaned on the counter, mussing a pile of Post Office change-of-address forms and flyers advertising pizza delivery and one noting the next meeting of the Portland Meadows Mobile Home Park Bible study group. "I come here from Missoula. I been bouncing from place to place. It's me and my two kids."

Jan clucked at him soothingly. She is as big as a fullback, with thin, streaky hair and flushed cheeks and the tiniest, twangiest voice you've ever heard. "Why don't you buy yourself a trailer, hon?" she said. She pulled out a map of the park. "Let's see. Number eighty-six is for sale, she can't pay her rent, she's deceased is why. Sixty-five is for sale — they're wanting more acreage, and our spaces aren't that humongous. Sixty-three is a repo, seventy-three is a repo."

"What kind of money are they wanting?" he asked.

She went over prices — four thousand for an old single-wide of about eight hundred square feet, ten thousand for something bigger. She told him the rent for a space was two hundred and sixty dollars a month. It is probably the cheapest possible way to live in Portland, and buying a trailer is certainly the cheapest possible way to live that would allow you to own something. He said he liked the idea of owning. Then she mentioned that all applicants in the park have to obtain and submit a police report detailing any criminal record they might have.

"Let me be totally honest," he said. "I been to prison. Eight years ago, though, and now I'm all done with my supervised parole."

"It'll probably be okay," Jan said. "But we have to visually see the report before we can rent to you." They talked a moment more about his parole, about his bouncing around from motel to motel, about how he'd come to Portland to settle some legal matters and that he didn't know if he would stay very long, but that if he bought one of the trailers, he could take it along with him no matter where he wandered next. Then Jan mentioned the twenty-pound rule — the restriction on the size of pets in the park. He listened, and a broody look crossed his face.

"I'm just thinking," he said after a moment. "How would that apply to a Rottweiler puppy?"

Dreamers come up with dreamy names for trailer parks. In Oregon, there is Shady Rest, Cedar Shade, Cherry Grove,

Rockwood, Fir Haven, Tall Firs, Stark Fir, Pine Cove. There are trailer parks with restful, poetic names in every state in the country. Often, nothing about them is actually bucolic. Chaos and sadness always visit poor people's lives, but some trailer parks like Portland Meadows seem to attract extra tragedy — tornadoes seek them out, fires race through them, shoot-outs take place in them. People I met in parks in Oregon seemed matter-of-fact about disaster. One morning, I drove from Portland Meadows to Carver Mobile Ranch, which is about twenty miles south. It is a more serene place, full of retirees. The endpoint of the Oregon Trail is a few miles down the road. A portion of the old trail lies just behind two of the trailers. I had been invited to drop in on a weekly crafts group that meets in one of them. When I arrived, the women in the group were stitching needlepoint Christmas trinkets. I sat next to a woman named Edith, who was working on a Santa Claus paper towel holder. She had springy brown curls and a narrow chest; her elbows were pointed and bony, and she poked them out as she stitched. She and her late husband used to work in a trailer factory in Loveland, Colorado, and they lived in a trailer then, too.

"When the wages dropped in the sixties, we just up and left," she said. "Up and left." She eventually got to Oregon and went to work at a packinghouse, and then a pottery factory, and then a cherry-packing plant, and then a printing press. Before she and her husband got out of Colorado, a storm hit their trailer. She said, "We were blowed over, and we couldn't get out. We were tipped over onto our side, and I opened the door and I was looking upwards. But that wasn't so bad. We were used to it. The wind would get to blowing all the time, and then the hitch would flap and the dresser drawers would come wide open."

The women then began reminiscing about which of their neighbors had been washed out in the 1964 flood or blown away with the Columbus Day windstorm in 1962. "That time, there were three trailers smashed together," one woman was saying.

Edith looked up from her stitching and said, "Not yours, though, I remember. Yours got wrapped around the light pole."

Trailers are cheap housing, and cheap housing often looks rough and plain and worn out, but trailer parks, on top of that, look lonesome. In the West, trailer parks are often set outside the city on bare sheets of land; the sweep of the sky, the walls of mountains, the vacancy around them, make them look tossed down at random and as insubstantial and easy to crush as a pile of cardboard boxes. John Bunnell, the sheriff of Multnomah County, whose jurisdiction includes Portland Meadows, told me that trailer parks are populated with elderly folks and migrant workers and people with no money who need shelter, but that he mostly thought of trailer parks as places to go if you want to get lost, so they are the first places he heads when he's looking for a suspect. He said that because trailer parks are isolated and secluded, they harbor a lot of crime, like drug dealing and prostitution; law enforcement people have nicknamed the worst parks "Felony Flats." Portland Meadows, he said, had been cleaned up recently, but for years it was famous for its vice. He said that trailer parks are exactly where he would have gone looking for someone like Timothy McVeigh, someone who wanted to live in the margins, to be self-contained, to conduct business unnoticed. Then he added that he never passes a trailer park without getting the creeps, because the first crime scene he ever investigated was in a park near Portland: In the middle of the night, a drunk, half-asleep in his trailer, had heard a noise, grabbed his gun, and fired. The bullet pierced the wall of the trailer as if it were cutting through a cracker; it struck a three-year-old boy, who was peeing outside, and killed him.

It takes only twenty minutes to unhitch a little trailer and get it on the road. It takes only a couple of hours to unhitch and mobilize a big one. A strong wind can blow a trailer loose in a second or so. Trailers are hardly attached to anything. In a park, small ones sit on their wheels; large ones sit on blocks. Sometimes they are secured by chains to a chunk of concrete sunk six feet belowground, which trailer people refer to as a "dead man."

Jim Benson was doing some maintenance work around the park when I arrived, so I rode in his pickup as he made his afternoon rounds. We bumped along, past a tan Buddy, a cream-and-brown Lamplighter, a turquoise Vagabond with an Astroturf-carpeted porch, a Traveleze with two American flags and bumper stickers saying SUPPORT AMERICA and NO CASH ON PREMISES. A school bus had just dropped off the trailer park kids, and three little girls with pale shaggy haircuts were chasing behind us on bikes. Jim pointed to different trailers as we passed them: "That one's horse people, they left it behind to sell it. This one's a truck driver. That next is a shipyard fellow, retired. This is a trucker, been here a month only. This one's a truck driver and his wife, her dad owned the trailer before and now they got it, so they're second generation. This one's — I don't know them, they're people that keep to theirselves. This one's a young woman and her son. That one's a fellow who owns five other trailers in the park and rents them. In that double-wide shorty, that's a couple that has a boat, a trailer, a van, a dog, and a lot of kids, and they home-teach their kids. This one's a lady who's been here thirty years, and this one's Art Powers, and he's been here probably thirty-five. Art's wife just died. She fell, and when they went to the hospital she said, 'Dad, I won't be coming home,' and she didn't."

A wide woman who was crouched in front of her trailer stood up and waved as we drove by. She was wearing green shorts and a mechanic's jacket. Her hair was piled and twisted like a French cruller. Jim banged on the brakes when he saw her and then rolled down his window. The woman rested her elbow on his side mirror. "Just look at two forty's yard," she said to Jim. "It sure looks pretty."

"They're getting there," Jim said. "Two forty-one's not bad, either." The two of them looked up and down the row of trailers. After a moment, Jim said, "What are you up to?"

"To tell you the truth," she said, "I'm out here murdering."

"Sugar ants," Jim said, nodding. "Murder some for me, will you?"

A long-haul trucker was working in his garden, tearing out a dead rhododendron bush and putting in a new one. The plot of land was about the size of a tablecloth. The trucker told me that he lived in the trailer with his bartender bride. His family had lived in Oregon for five generations. "We owned all the land from here to the mountains," he said. "We were into building. My family built half the houses in southeast Portland. I lived in a house in southeast for a while, but it got too built up for me. Everyone pays attention to your business, and I don't like that. You can't even cut a shrub without getting a permit." His trowel crunched the dirt. He said that several roads and one neighborhood in the city had been named for his family and that his grandfather eventually sold all his land to the Port of Portland for three cents an acre. "I own my trailer, and I can go when I want to," he said. "But, as far as land, I don't even have a sliver."

A bulky man in a plaid shirt was sitting in his trailer with the door open, and from my seat in the pickup truck I could see his living room and kitchen and even what he was watching on TV. I got out and went over to his open door. He said he didn't want to talk to anybody, and then he started telling me that his trailer was the exact same brand as Lucille Ball's trailer in a movie called *The Long, Long Trailer*, which he saw once when he was messing around watching TV. I asked him where he'd been living before he got his trailer, and he said, "In a motel, I guess." He was watching a daytime talk show about women discovering that their boyfriends are transvestites, and every few minutes he would stop talking to watch the show for a moment, and then he would exclaim, "Now, would you get a load of that!"

He told me he'd moved into the motel after he got divorced and moved into a camper after that. "Then I bought a little bitty travel-trailer, and moved here, and then I traded up for this one. I had a little poodle at the time, and she went crazy when she saw this much space." The poodle had been run over by someone backing a trailer out, and he hadn't got another dog, because the whole thing made him too sad. Hanging above the television set were two framed photographs of racehorses, and I asked about them. "Well, I never had any interest in horses," he said. "The park's right by the track, but that made no matter to me. But in 1987 I was talking to my neighbor and he was a racetracker, and I told him that I was looking for an investment, and he said, 'Buy a horse,' and well, you know what? I did. I was sober at the time, too."

On my way back to the office, I saw a man I had noticed around the park buying candy in the Country Store or just loafing around outside his trailer. He told me his name was Paul May. He had a blocky upper body and long graying hair and a frozen, startled look in his eyes. Most days when I had seen him, he was wearing a black cowboy hat decorated with plastic animal teeth, a souvenir sweatshirt from New York City, and jeans. I told him I'd seen him around, and he said, "I saw you, too. I spent two and a half years in Vietnam. I got an extra set of eyes." He told me that his stepdaughter from his first marriage hadn't talked to him in years, and he wondered whether it had something to do with the fact that he'd fought in Vietnam. He had been in the park for only a month. He was staying in a ratty old trailer that someone who had been evicted had left behind. His own trailer hadn't yet arrived. It had been his grandmother's trailer, and she had recently died, so he was having it hauled here and was going to share it with his brother. Paul said he was a floor-care maintenance man working a graveyard shift and that his brother was a forklift operator. His grandmother's trailer had three bedrooms and two baths, and he said it was beautiful.

He used to be an eighteen-wheel long-haul truck driver, and after he got divorced, he decided to just live in his truck or on the road. Then, for a while, he tried living in an apartment in Oregon City, and he hated it — hated having somebody over his head, underneath him, and on both sides. Trucking, he said, ran in his family. His mother, who is seventy-two, is a long-haul interstate driver. "She just got a new truck, she and her husband," he said. "They'll be driving it coast to coast." Paul asked me where I lived, and I said New

York. He whistled and said, "That's pretty spendy living. I like to save my money." Right now, he was saving his money to buy gifts for his girlfriend. He said, "I like buying her things that make her feel special. She works really hard. She's an exotic dancer, and she has a little boy, and she's scraping to make things happen." For Mother's Day, he had paid to send her and her mother to Glamour Shots, a service where for a fee you get a fancy makeup session and then a photo session. Now he said he was planning to surprise her with a diamond ring and tickets for an all-expenses-paid trip to Mexico by herself — both of which he thought would help her decide to make a commitment to him. He said he was ready for the relationship. I asked where his girlfriend lived. "I'm not precisely sure," he said slowly. "I know it's some kind of neighborhood."

I walked up the path to a trailer that belonged to a young woman named Celina, who worked as Jan's assistant manager until she got pregnant. Jan told me that Celina had recently broken her leg trying to do the hokey-pokey on roller skates and also that she had her hands full with her baby, so I thought she'd be home, but the trailer was shut tight. The windows were high slits, and they were curtained; there was no way even to peek in. The trailer seemed more than closed — it seemed sealed and seamless and impenetrable. I knocked anyway. My knock rattled the door and made a flat, metallic sound, as if I were knocking on a can of tuna.

How Jan and Jim came to manage the trailer park is a roundabout story. Jan was explaining to me once how fast an old trailer can burn down, then told me a story about one night when she was the assistant manager here. She and Jim were asleep in their trailer when they got a call about a fire. Jan called the fire department, and as she went out the door to check out the burning trailer, she tripped and fell and hit her head hard, then got up and steadied herself and continued. She arrived at the burning trailer, saw that no one was inside, went looking for the tenant, found her at her parents' trailer, broke the news to her, and then, while heading back to the fire, noticed a couple of people sleeping in a doghouse beside another trailer. She then briefed the fire department, comforted the hysterical tenant, and reported the squatters in the doghouse to the police. Only about twenty minutes had passed, but by this time the trailer had burned to the ground. Nonetheless, Jan considered the evening a success: When the manager's position opened up, she decided that if she could handle so many things in the middle of a crisis, all the while dizzy headed from a fall, she ought to apply for the job. It keeps her busy. "We've worked like Trojans to make the place better," she says. "And not everyone's easy to deal with. But as a manager I'm not allowed to cuss people out or hit them. It's considered unprofessional behavior."

The week I spent at Portland Meadows fell at the beginning of the month, when rent was due. There was a lot of turnover, because some people weren't making their rent and because the horse-racing season had just ended and all the track people who'd been living at the park had left for the southern Oregon circuit. In the Laundromat, a sign was still up, saying NO WASHING OR DRYING OF HORSE BLANKETS, THANK YOU. THE MANAGEMENT. New people were moving in. A forklift operator had just bought a trailer from one of the horse people who'd had a losing season. One afternoon, he came into the office while I was talking to Jan, waving a syringe with a crusty-tipped hypodermic needle. He was holding it with a pair of pliers. He said he'd found it while he was cleaning the trailer. "Second one, Jan!" he exclaimed. Then, still waving the pliers, he started chatting about the racecar track just west of the trailer park. "Some of the big drivers come through here," he said. "I like being around them. I got some cars myself. I run Bumpin' Bombers, they're like jalopies. There's Street Stocks, Limited Sportsmen, Late Models, fantastic stuff."

The phone rang. It was someone from one of the trailers calling to tell Jan that there was a woman running around the park dressed only in her underwear. "We can't allow that," Jan said into the phone. "This is a family park."

She clamped the receiver with her shoulder, reached for another phone, and called the police, saying, "Yes, sir, this is Portland Meadows Mobile Home Park. We have an individual walking around here just in her panties." While she was talking, I flipped through the new park newsletter. There was a calendar showing a happy face on Sundays and a sad face on the day that seventy-two-hour-late rent notices would be sent out, and a puzzle with hidden words in a grid of letters; some of the hidden words were *neighbor, maintain, fix, weeds, trash, rats, rent, manager, pain, bugs, garbage*, *mailbox*, *hog*, and *notice*. At the counter, a man with lank black hair stood with his arm draped over the shoulder of a weary-looking woman with chopped blond hair and a soft, saggy chin. When Jan hung up the phones, he said, "Jan, this is my long-term sister. She's looking for a For Sale."

Jan said, "We have quite a few. Especially because this is the time of the racetrackers' leaving out." She started reading the list of trailers for sale. She was interrupted by a woman who came in to ask if she knew a way to remove a tattoo that wouldn't cost a fortune. Jan suggested blemish concealer or bleach water. The woman said, "Well, bless you," and left. The phone rang again; now the nearly naked woman was partially clothed but still roaming around the trailers. Jan called the police with an update and then went back to reading the list of trailers for sale.

Kathie Eyler, Jan's assistant manager, had been writing up eviction warnings, and she put down her pen and listened. She has been in the park eight months. Her husband works in construction and is an ordained minister — he runs the Bible study group in the park. She had lived for years in North Dakota on a sheep ranch thirty miles from anything. Her husband used to own his own company, but it went bankrupt, and then they moved in their trailer four times in four years. "Don't get a single-wide," she cautioned the couple. "Ours is a single-wide, and some parks won't take a single-wide. I don't know what we're going to do, because we want to take ours with us when we retire."

The Avon man came in with a delivery for Jan. The postman came in. "Space twenty-three?" he asked, holding up a wrinkled envelope. Jan said they were gone.

Another envelope. "Space ninety-eight?" Gone, moved back to southern Oregon to work on a potato farm. Another envelope. Gone, but just to another space in Portland Meadows. I had talked to the guy who'd moved to the other space; he had told me that he'd bought a trailer after living in Chicago, then moved around for work or to follow better weather or when the mood struck him. He worked now as the assistant manager of a quick-repair auto shop. He said at first he worried that everything about the trailer would be strange — even just getting used to living in something shaped like a shoebox. He worried that it would be noisy, but he said he was used to noise. He said, "After all, I spent years listening to clowns playing bumper tag at midnight in the city of Chicago." He said it was now twelve years since he'd had a real house, and he thought he'd miss something about his old neighborhood and his old life, but he didn't.

Art for Everybody

One recent sultry afternoon, inside the Bridgewater Commons mall in central New Jersey, across from The Limited, down the hall from a Starbucks, next door to the Colorado Pen Company, and just below Everything Yogurt, a woman named Glenda Parker was making a priceless family heirloom for a young couple and their kid. This was taking place in the Thomas Kinkade Signature Gallery, a plush and flatteringly illuminated, independently owned, branded distribution channel for the art-based products of America's most profitable artist, Thomas Kinkade. The young couple were from a moderately priced gated community not far from the mall, and they were bashful and pleased because they had never bought a family heirloom before. Also, they had never bought a painting before. Actually, they still hadn't bought a painting, since what they were buying was not a painting per se but a fifteen-hundred-dollar lithographic reproduction of a Thomas Kinkade painting, printed on textured brushstroke canvas with an auto-pen

Kinkade signature in the lower right-hand corner.

This was not an ordinary day at the gallery: It was a Master Highlighter Event, a two-day guest appearance by one of Kinkade's specially trained assistants, who would highlight any picture bought during the event for free. Highlighting a picture is not that different from highlighting your hair: It entails stippling tiny bright dots of paint on the picture to give it more texture and luminescence. The customer could sit with the highlighter and watch the process and even make requests — for a little more pink in the rosebushes, say, or a bit more green on the trees. Some highlighters — Glenda was one — would even let the customers dab some paint on the picture themselves, so it would be truly one of a kind.

"Is this your first Kinkade?" Glenda asked the young woman. They were sitting in front of a large easel, on which the couple's picture had been propped. Beside Glenda was a digital kitchen timer, which she had set for the highlighting time limit of fifteen minutes, and a Lucite palette heaped with small blobs of oil paint.

"Yes," the woman said. "It's our first."

"Well, congratulations," Glenda said. She smiled warmly.

"My grandmother just passed away," the young woman said. "The money she left for me — it wasn't quite enough to invest, but I didn't want it to just disappear. My sister also inherited money from my grandmother, and she bought a Kinkade, too."

"Well, that's wonderful," Glenda said. "You picked a great one."

"I just wish I'd heard of him sooner," the young woman said, twisting a piece of her hair. "There are so many that I love now that are already sold out."

"Oh, yes, that does happen," Glenda said. She dotted some white paint on the underside of a cloud.

"I can't believe I never knew anything about Thomas Kinkade before this," the woman went on. "I had passed the gallery before, but I didn't really know anything about it or about how . . . huge he is. I mean, he's just this really huge thing! It's almost like a whole world."

The painting that the young couple bought was called *Evening Majesty*. It is one of Kinkade's most popular images. It features mountains and quiet shadows and the purple cloak of sunset, but it could just as easily have featured a lavishly blooming garden at twilight, or maybe a babbling brook spanned by a quaint stone bridge, or a lighthouse after a storm; it's hard to distinguish one Kinkade from the next, because the effect is so unvarying — smooth and warm and romantic, not quite fantastical but not quite real, more of a wishful and inaccurate rendering of what the world looks like, as if painted by someone who hadn't been outside in a long time. In a Kinkade painting, if there is a bridge or a road or a gate (as there often is, since Kinkade likes visual devices that carry you into the picture frame), the bridge or the road or the gate is finely detailed, and the burr on the cobblestone or the grain in the brick is so precise, it could have been drawn with a whisker. But every edge and corner is also softened slightly, as if someone had stuck it in an oven or left it in the sun. The effect is wee and precious — the cottages look as if they had been built out of cookie dough and roofed with butter cream, more suited to elves or mice than to human beings. Even big things, like the Golden Gate Bridge and the Yosemite Valley, look tiny and darling, like toys.

Kinkade's paintings are filled with lampposts and windows and images of the sun, and the lampposts are always lit, the windows are always illuminated, the sun usually in a dramatic moment of rising or setting. Light is Kinkade's hallmark. His pictures have a weird glow even in dim settings. If you go to a Kinkade gallery, you will be taken into a special room where the picture you're interested in will be shown to you under bright light and then the light will be turned down slowly, and as it gets darker, the dark areas of the painting will get lighter, an effect Kinkade has said is produced by layering the paint on the canvas. Kinkade has trademarked the slogan "Painter of Light," and receptionists at Media Arts Group, in California, the company that produces all Kinkade art-based products, answer the phone, "Thank you for sharing the light!"

By and large, art critics consider Thomas Kinkade a commercial hack whose work is mawkish and suspiciously fluorescent and whose genius is not for art, but for marketing — for creating an "editions pyramid" of his prints, each level up a little more expensive, which whips up collectors' appetites the way retiring Beanie Babies did. This view annoys Kinkade no end, and he will talk your ear off — even talk past the company's strictly enforced one-hour interview limit — about the ugliness and nihilism of modern art and its irrelevance compared to the life-affirming populism of his work. He will point out that he has built the largest art-based company in the history of the world and that ten million people have purchased a Kinkade product, at one of three hundred and fifty Thomas Kinkade Signature Galleries that carry his limited-edition prints, or through his website, or at one of the five thousand retail outlets that sell Kinkade-licensed products, including cards, puzzles, mugs, blankets, books, La-Z-Boys, accessory pieces, calendars, and night-lights. Last year, Media Arts Group had a hundred and thirty-two million dollars in revenues. It has been traded — first on the Nasdaq, then on the New York Stock Exchange — since 1994, making Kinkade the only artist to be a small-cap equity issue. He owns thirty-seven percent of the company, which makes him, by his calculations, one of the wealthiest artists in the world.

Kinkade is forty-three years old. He has short, brushy brown hair, a short, brushy brown mustache, a chest as broad as a beer keg, and a leisurely and booming laugh. If you see his paintings before you meet him, you might expect him to be wispy and pixielike, but he is as brawny and good-natured as the neighborhood butcher. He has the buoyant self-assurance of someone who started poor and obscure but has always been sure he would end up rich and famous. He is so self-assured that he predicts it's just a matter of time before the art world comes around to appreciating him. In fact, he bet me a million dollars that a major museum will hold a Thomas Kinkade retrospective in his lifetime.

What Thomas Kinkade's fans will tell you about his paintings is that they are much more than just paintings — overlooking, of course, the irony that they are also much less than paintings, since they are really just reproductions. Anyway, they will tell you that Kinkade pictures are an emotional experience. People get attached to them in a profound way. While I was at the highlighter event, I asked the gallery consultant — the person who can help you match a Kinkade to your sofa upholstery — how she came to have her job, and she said that she had hung around the gallery so often that all concerned decided she just had to be given a job. Her name was Janice Schafer, and when she talked about Kinkade, she was as animated as a jumping bean. "We actually met him!" she exclaimed. "It was such an absolutely amazing thing! He's even better than the way he is on QVC! A lot of times, the icon doesn't live up to the image, but he did. He really connects to people. He was so friendly when we met him. You never felt you were in the presence of genius, which you were, and you never felt you were in the presence of someone a lot more affluent than you, which he is."

Suddenly, Glenda's timer buzzed. Janice peered over to examine *Evening Majesty.* "Oh, I love the way the smoke came out!" she said. "Oh, and look!" she said, pointing to the bottom corner of the picture. "She highlighted the puppy dog, too!" Everyone nodded.

Janice went to help a customer choose a picture for his wife's birthday, and Glenda freshened her paints. She is one of thirty master highlighters. Her training involved a seven-day workshop followed by an exam testing her knowledge of the paintings and how to highlight them and her knowledge of Kinkade himself: his birthday, the names of his children, where he met his wife, details of his childhood — in other words, the sorts of intimate tidbits that could be sprinkled into the conversation during the highlighting and that would make people feel they were getting not merely a reproduction of a painting, but a chance to connect with Thomas Kinkade. Glenda said she had been highlighting for almost a year. During the week, she works in a gift shop in California, and two or three weekends a month she travels to a gallery event. Her dream is to travel with Kinkade to Europe and do gallery events there.

Currently, there are signature galleries in Canada, England, and Scotland; the company plans to expand throughout Europe and then take on Japan. Glenda said that while she is highlighting, customers tell her about their lives and often about some sadness they feel is lifted when they look at Kinkade's work. "I get a lot of cancer survivors," she said. "I meet a lot of people who have just lost someone. I send the most special stories I hear back to Thom."

Another customer plunked down in the chair next to Glenda. She reset her timer for fifteen minutes. "I'm getting *Hometown* something," the customer said. "I already have *Hometown* something else. What is it? *Hometown Morning*? *Hometown Evening*? I don't know."

"You're building a great portfolio," Janice Schafer said. "They're nice investments. And this one's almost sold out. And they do have a history of appreciation. We have some secondary-market pieces here. This one, *Julianne's Cottage*, was released for a few hundred dollars in 1992, and now it's thirty-seven hundred and thirty dollars."

"Well, I like the one I'm getting," the customer said. "It's like a picture of some tightly knit neighborhood where everything is well and everyone is friendly to each other. It's nice."

"It would be nice with this one, too," Janice said, pointing to another piece hanging across the gallery. She admired it for a moment and then clasped her hands and said, "You know, he's like a national treasure."

Not only the highlighters, but the gallery staff, the Media Arts receptionists, even the people who build the frames and stretch the canvases know Kinkade's biography by heart: that he was raised in Placerville, California; that his father left home when Thomas was five; that his mother told him he would be the man of the family. That he was good at everything he tried — math, civics, and especially drawing — that when he was about fourteen he set up a little concession selling his drawings for two dollars each, and that every time he sold one he would marvel at how he could make money on something that had taken him only fifteen minutes to do. That he went to what he jokingly calls "a nice little conservative Christian school," Berkeley, and left after two years to attend the Art Center College of Design, in Pasadena. That when he was twenty he experienced a Christian awakening and that it changed his art — it stopped being about his fears and anxieties and became optimistic and inspirational, with themes like hometowns and perfect days and natural beauty, and millions of people responded. It's as good a story as you could hope for if you want to make a point about perseverance and pulling yourself up by your bootstraps and appreciating life's bounty; even the bad parts of the story are good, because it's easier not to begrudge Kinkade his fortune when you are reminded that he was a poor kid who had to struggle, who rejected the smarty-pants liberal establishment to follow his heart, and who is proud of having earned his way into the ultimate American aristocracy of successful entrepreneurs.

Kinkade's commercial awakening occurred in 1989, when he formed Lightpost Publishing with a business partner, Ken

Raasch. His paintings were selling well, but he decided that he wanted "to engulf as many hearts as possible with art," a goal that would be hindered by selling only original work. Instead, Kinkade opened a chain of galleries and began producing high-quality digital reproductions of his paintings on specially treated paper, which sold for a few hundred dollars each. A digital image could also be soaked in water, peeled off the paper, and affixed to a stretched canvas, so that it showed the texture of the canvas the way a real painting would. These canvas transfers could be sold as they were, or they could be accented with paint by a master highlighter or by a special apprentice to Kinkade ("Studio Proofs" and "Renaissance Editions") or by Kinkade himself ("Masters Editions"); the transfers now fetch anywhere from fifteen hundred dollars for the standard numbered editions to thirty-four thousand dollars for the prints that Kinkade highlighted himself. The originals were no longer for sale at any price, and the number of each edition was restricted, and the image was "suspended" once it was sold out.

In 1994, Kinkade was named Artist of the Year by the National Association of Limited Edition Dealers, and the demand for his pictures was growing so fast that he was able to take his company public. *Business Week* named it one of the "hot growth" companies of 1995. A Kinkade picture had become "collectible" — one of the countless items valued not just for their own merits, but for their supposed rarity and potential to appreciate because they have been intentionally produced in a restricted quantity. According to a 1999 survey, the collectibles market is worth an estimated ten billion dollars a year. The market includes limited-edition Boyds Bears, which are costumed teddies; Adam Binder's Fruit Faeries, which are marble-powder-and-resin creatures with names like Humble Umhalubhala the Apple Faerie; the Ebony Visions sculptures of Thomas Blackshear, who describes his work as Afro-Nouveau; a series called Just the Right Shoe, which are miniature right shoes in different styles, made by an artist who calls herself Raine; and all varieties of dolls and unicorn figures and paperweights and Olszewski Miniatures and Cameo Girls vases and Snowbabies and Precious Moments moppets and Steinbach limited-edition nutcrackers, and, of course, Hummel figurines.

There are scores of limited-edition

painters in addition to Kinkade, and they account for some seven hundred million dollars of the collectibles market each year. They include every sort of landscape and still-life painter, and wildlife and marine-life painter, and Christian-themed painter, and sports painter (and at least one multi-dimensional painter, Arnold Friberg, whose subject matter is described on one website as ranging from "the Bible to American football").

Kinkade is not the only multimillionaire among the limited-edition artists: Bev Doolittle, whose art is described by dealers as whimsical, mystical, and spiritual, has sold sixty million dollars' worth of prints in the last decade; Wyland ("the world's premier ocean artist") has sold more than fifty million dollars' worth of whale pictures; Terry Redlin, according to *Time* magazine, sells twenty million dollars' worth of Americana images each year. Like Kinkade, Redlin has stopped selling his originals. He now displays them in the Redlin Art Center in Watertown, South Dakota, which opened in 1997 and drew four hundred thousand visitors in its first six months. According to the museum's website, "Certainly no one would disagree that Terry's artwork, which holds such a special place in the homes and hearts of so many Americans, should be preserved in a public setting." Redlin limited editions — "Affordable Decorator Art by Terry Redlin," as one dealer advertises it — are available instead, although only just available. Because they are expensive and might "sell out," the prints seem more precious than ordinary reproductions that are issued in unlimited quantity.

People like to own things they think are valuable, and they are titillated by the prospect that the things they own might be even more valuable than they thought. The high price of limited editions is part of their appeal: It implies that they are choice and exclusive and that only a certain class of people will be able to afford them — a limited edition of people with taste and discernment.

"I created a system of marketing compatible with American art," Kinkade said to me recently. "I believe in 'aspire to' art. I want my work to be available but not common. I want it to be a dignified component of everyday life. It's good to dream about things. It's like dreaming of owning a Rolex — instead, you dream about owning a seventy-five-thousand-dollar print." In fact, a lot of limited-edition art is about dreaming; so many of the paintings portray wistful images of a noble and romantic past that never was, or the anti-intellectual innocence of fairies and animals, or mythical heroes who can never fail and never fade.

Last May, I visited the Media Arts Group headquarters, in a plain brown building in a commercial district near San José Airport. Inside, the office had the décor that characterizes all the Thomas Kinkade Signature Galleries: The furniture was plump and chintz covered, and the walls were a soothing forest green, and a gas flame in the fireplace lapped at a ceramic log, so that whether you were in a mall in central New Jersey or an industrial park in Northern California, you would feel you had entered Thomas Kinkade's world, where it is always a dusky autumn evening in a small but prosperous English town. The day I visited was actually hot, dry, and blindingly bright, the height of spring in the middle of Silicon Valley, and dust from airport construction gave the air a blurry glow. I had come at a lively moment for Media Arts: The company had recently launched a new chain of stores called the Masters of Light Galleries, featuring three artists whose work had been selected from the more than two thousand who applied. The Masters of Light Galleries are part of a plan to diversify Media Arts Group, because stock analysts have worried about the company's reliance on one charismatic figure and about the possibility that Kinkade's popularity has crested and will inevitably ebb, his paintings going the way of so many collectibles before them.

"Analysts are fascinated by the company," Craig Fleming, the Media Arts CEO, explained. (Fleming has since left Media Arts.) "But they were never excited about the company based on just Thom. Now, with the diversification, they're starting to do due diligence and pay attention to the stock."

Fleming is not an art guy. He was a sales guy who came to Media Arts after twenty-five years of working for nutritional product companies, home party businesses, and the Kirby vacuum-cleaning company. He said that when he first got to Media Arts, he would go around asking, "What's our number one product?" and would then supply the answer himself: "Our number one product is the Thomas Kinkade business opportunity!" In 1998, shortly after he took over, the stock price pitched downward, suffering from the industry's weakness, the company's overexpansion, and Wall Street's coolness toward small-cap companies. Fleming oversaw the sale of most company-owned galleries; all but two Thomas Kinkade galleries are now owned by franchisees. According to a recent quarterly report, the company also developed "a new retail promotional event involving appearances by Thomas Kinkade at selected Galleries which substantially reduced the decline in same store sales, increased product pull-through, lowered retail inventory, improved accounts receivable and strengthened our cash position." In other words, wherever Kinkade appears, customers buy pictures.

"Thom will go to a gallery, and twenty-five hundred people will show up," Fleming said. "He speaks for about thirty minutes, and afterward they come up to him and talk. It's very emotional, some of them are crying and saying, 'Here's how you have affected me.'" He paused and then gestured toward a large Kinkade hanging in his office. "We believe that the walls of the home are the new frontier for branding. Thom always says that there are forty walls in the average home. Our job is to fill them."

Last month, Taylor Woodrow Homes and Media Arts Group opened the Village, a Thomas Kinkade Community, a gated development in Vallejo, California. According to promotional material, it is a "magical community" featuring "meandering sidewalks, benches and water features, which are designed to enrich home owners' lives with endless visual surprises and delights." There are four house models available, and they are named after Kinkade's four daughters — Chandler, Merritt, Everett, and Winsor — and will be priced from four hundred thousand dollars up.

Thomas Kinkade lives in a large, handsome house in a magical suburban community the name of which I am not at liberty to disclose. It is easy to understand his wish for privacy: Ten million people own some product featuring his name, and most editions are signed with ink containing DNA from his hair or blood, to prevent fakes. He likes to say he has a retro — "but not Amish" — lifestyle. His children are homeschooled by his wife, Nanette, and they don't watch television, but he owns "a hell of a lot of stuff, a nice car and so forth." He works in an old stone cottage on the grounds of his house. The cottage is filled with his favorite paintings: an original by his idol, Norman Rockwell; a seascape by Glenn Wessels, who taught him art when he was a teenager; a pastel by his father, an amateur artist who, according to Kinkade, never made anything of his life. In the main room of the cottage are easels, shelves of reference books, and a high-tech color-balanced lighting system that provides the constant effect of overcast midday sun. At the time, Kinkade was working on a painting of two horses grazing in the yard of a trim stone cottage. The horses weren't finished yet, and next to the easel he had pinned a photograph of a horse that appeared to have been torn out of a cigarette ad. The room was clean and orderly and didn't smell of turpentine or brush cleaner.

"I have this certain ability to have in my mind an image that means something to real people," he said, sitting on a sofa across the room from the easels. "The number one quote critics give me is, 'Thom, your work is irrelevant.' Now, that's a fascinating, fascinating comment. Yes, irrelevant to the little subculture, this microculture, of modern art. But here's the point: My art is relevant because it's relevant to ten million people. That makes me the most relevant artist in this culture, not the least. Because I'm relevant to real people." He sat up and started to laugh. "I remember that quote, man! It was a great quote! It was, 'The Louvre is full of dead pictures by dead artists.' And you know, that's the dead art we don't want anything to do with!" He laughed again and slapped his thighs. "We're the art of life, man! We're bringing the life back to art!"

The door of his studio opened and a slight blond girl walked in. "Daddy, how do you spell 'schedule'?"

"That's an important question," Kinkade said. "S-c-h-e-d-u-l-e, honey." The girl drifted out of the room. "The fact is we have a grassroots movement emerging in my art and in the country, and there's ten million people out there that if I give the word will go out and picket any museum I want them to," he went on. "I won't give the word, but they're dying to have an art of dignity within our culture, an art of relevance to them. Look at someone like Robert Rauschenberg. What's his Q rating? How many people have his art? A hundred? Where is the million-seller art? What about the crafts-manship of expression?"

I asked him why he even cared how the

art establishment viewed him, since it hadn't had any effect on his work.

"It's irritating," he said. He cocked his head and grinned. "I'm thinking of starting this program of loaning a few of my paintings to some of these critics and letting them live with them for a year or two and see what they think then. Because art really grows as you live with it. See, I have faith in the heart of the average person. People find hope and comfort in my paintings. I think showing people the ugliness of the world doesn't help it. I think pointing the way to light is deeply contagious and satisfying. I would want to argue that I'm not an antagonist to modernists. I just believe in picture making for people. I'm a firebrand. I will sit down and debate the grand tradition with anyone. I am really the most controversial artist in the world."

I asked him what he would have done with his life if he hadn't become a painter. "What would I have done?" he repeated, gazing across the room. "I would have probably become a motivational speaker."

When I was in the gallery in Bridgewater, I wandered into the stockroom. I had toured the manufacturing area of Media Arts in California and had watched a crew of Hispanic workers peel images off wet paper and smooth them onto canvases and then slide them onto racks like pies set out to cool. Now, in the Bridgewater stockroom, I came across a stack of boxes fresh from the factory, with the names of the pictures scribbled on the side: one *Light in the Storm*, one *Clearing Storms*, two *Conquering the Storms*, and one *Sea of Tranquility*.

By then, it was midday. Several more paintings had been highlighted and taken away by their owners; Glenda was now sitting with a man and a woman, meek and awkward, their new painting, *Clocktower Cottage*, on the highlighting stand.

"Is this your first Kinkade?" Glenda asked. They nodded. "Well, congratulations. Let me tell you a little about what is here. This is about the changes of time. You see, everything changes. The sky changes, and the clouds change, and life changes." They leaned in so that they could follow Glenda's finger as she pointed to details in the picture. "Do you see this?" she asked, resting her finger on the clocktower. "Here the clock says five oh-two, which is Thom and Nanette's wedding date. And here are the initials NK —

that's for his wife, that's how he honors her. It's his love language for her."

They were transfixed now. Glenda took a brush and dipped it in the green paint, then with quick, short strokes dappled the underside of a tree. It was just a touch, but the tree suddenly stood out from the other trees, and it seemed newly bright and full. "Wow!" the man said. He glanced at his wife and then back at the picture. "I hadn't even noticed that before."

Intensive Care

These are the questions I've been asked since I worked on Show No. 6079 of *All My Children*, which will be broadcast on Tuesday, June 29:

Q: What's Susan Lucci like?

A: Perky, sharp, thin, underappreciated — but I'm just speculating, since she wasn't in my episode.

Q: What was your part?

A: I was a nurse. I appear in act three, in the hospital sun porch scene, and I say, in a mean voice, "Intensive care patients are only allowed two visitors per hour," and then, "We don't want to overtax him," and, finally, "Rules are rules." I say this to Hayley, to stop her from seeing Adam, who is in intensive care after he and Natalie are in a car wreck while speeding to someone's wedding — I forget whose — after Natalie has had a big fight with Trevor, who has recently discovered he was duped by Laurel Banning, who then mysteriously disappears, although she — Laurel — has just sent a note to Natalie's son Timmy, which he reads to An Li, Tom, Trevor, and Myrtle, who are sitting around keeping one another company and are beginning to suspect that Jack and Laurel might have eloped.

Q: Wait a minute — what were Adam and Natalie doing in a car together? They hate each other!

A: I have no idea. I'd never seen the show.

Q: What did you wear?

A: A white pinafore, a white blouse with big shoulder pads, homely white oxfords, white pantyhose, tasteful jewelry, no hat. I was hoping I'd be dressed in something skimpy, but the costume department informed me that only one nurse on the show is ever allowed to wear something really tight and short, and that's Nurse Gloria.

Q: Why?

A: I have no idea. I'd never seen the show.

Q: What's going to happen to Adam and Natalie?

A: The powerful and mercurial Adam, who is married to Nurse Gloria, and is the twin of shy, gentle Stuart, discovers he can't move his legs, although in real life he went jogging between the morning camera blocking and the afternoon dress rehearsal. I get the feeling he will recover. Natalie, on the other hand, is definitely going to die. I was told this by Natalie herself while I was having my hair done and she was getting her head bruise applied. "I'm flatlining either this Thursday or next — I can't remember which," she said. "Natalie's sweet, so she's got to die. If you're on a soap, you want to be a bitch or be miserable, because then you'll last forever."

Q: How were you?

A: Really good. In fact, Conal O'Brien, the director, told me that I was "very steady" and that the sixteen million people who watch the show will probably appreciate my work. And this is a guy who can be tough: For instance, during camera blocking, he told Christopher Lawford — Charlie — that he was giving the camera "too much tush."

Q: How did you prepare?

A: I studied my script, I practiced my lines, I got to the studio at seven a.m. for all the rehearsals and dry blocking, and during lunch I called my doctor for some authentic insight on nursing.

Q: What did she say?

A: She recommended that I consider my character's back story; avoid wearing my hair in a bun, because nurses don't do that anymore; work on understanding my motivation; and forget about a tight uniform, because only Nurse Gloria gets to wear one.

Royalty

My first apartment in Manhattan was on West End Avenue near Seventy-second Street or, as I soon came to think of it, about two blocks from Gray's Papaya, which is at Broadway and Seventy-second. My husband's office was around the corner from Papaya Kingdom, which was Broadway and Fiftieth. My gym was down the street from Papaya King, which was on Eighty-sixth between Second and Third. My best friend lived near Papaya Prince, in the West Village. I spent a lot of my afternoons at the mid-Manhattan branch of the public library, a few blocks from Papaya World. I can't remember exactly where Papaya Princess was, but I know I passed it now and then, in cabs. Before I moved to New York four years ago, I hadn't had much contact with papayas. I knew they existed, and I saw them in supermarkets — stickered with their country of origin, like luggage — but they never figured greatly in my life. Now papayas were everywhere I was.

My preoccupation with papayas didn't

hit me all at once. A few nagging questions only gradually turned into a full-scale fixation. It's not that I was especially interested in consuming papayas, which I think taste like a vague memory of something that tastes a lot stronger; it's that I grew increasingly determined to understand the phenomenology of papayas in New York. How did a tropical fruit come to be so prominent in a temperate-zone city? Why were there so *many* papaya stores? Why did all of them sell frankfurters, too? (I mean, were they health food stores or junk food stores?) Why did so many papaya stores include references to royalty in their names? Why were all of them decorated with signs using stilted, hyperbolic descriptions of papayas, like THE ARISTOCRATIC MELON OF THE TROPICS, THE FAMOUS MAGICAL PAPAYA MELON, and GOD'S GIFT TO MANKIND IS OUR PAPAYA DRINK? That nobody I knew could answer these questions, or had even considered them, came as no particular surprise; one characteristic of the New York personality I had noticed right away was an ability to overlook prevailing conditions, such as high taxes and sidewalk bridges. Papayas seemed to be just another prevailing condition.

I did what I could to get answers. I put

questions to countermen at various papaya outposts and got strangely specific but unsubstantiated reactions, among them "Eighty-five percent of all people in the world love papaya" (the bun man at Papaya Kingdom) and "The relationship between the hot dog and the papaya is very good" (the juice man at Gray's). I also talked to Peter Poulos, the owner of Papaya King, which, I learned, was the original papaya store in New York. He said that his father had traveled to Florida decades earlier and had come back fired up with the idea of introducing New Yorkers to the tropical delights of papaya juice. The outbreak of other papaya stores, he said, was an attempt to copy Papaya King's success. The romantic paeans to the papaya were his father's own words and cadence, and the other stores duplicated them. The other stores' reference to royalty were meant to fool customers into thinking that all the papaya stores were affiliated, like some tropical fruit juice House of Hapsburg.

A few days after talking to Mr. Poulos, I came across a United States District Court opinion in a 1989 case involving Papaya King and Papaya Kingdom. The former had charged the latter with trademark infringement, on the ground that the papaya-plus-royalty name implied that the two businesses were associated. Papaya King had won. The owners of Papaya Kingdom then tried to satisfy the judgment by merely covering up the "K" on its sign with a piece of tape. Peter Leisure, the judge in the case, observed wryly that the defendant was "contented apparently to be known as 'Papaya ingdom.'" Less wryly, he imposed contempt charges on Papaya Kingdom — or, rather, Papaya ingdom: twenty-five thousand dollars in damages, seventy-five hundred for contempt of court, and more than thirteen thousand in attorneys' fees. I went down to Papaya ingdom a few days after reading the opinion to see whether the store had a new name and a new sign. It was gone, and a pizzeria had risen in its place.

It was about this time that I began to get used to living here: I knew uptown from downtown, and I had finally figured out that the guys in my parking garage were denting my car because I hadn't tipped them, and I had come to realize that there were certain things about the city that I would never understand. I wouldn't say that I gave up; I simply started taking things in stride. This was when Gray's was elling its frankfurters for fifty cents (they're now sixty), and business was particularly brisk; I rarely passed by when a House O'Weenies truck wasn't double-parked by the door, offloading product. (I never saw anything like a House O'Tropical Fruits truck parked nearby, so I assumed that the papayas were delivered late at night — just the way you'd expect exotic cargo to arrive.) I still dropped in for a hot dog now and then, but I stopped pestering the countermen with questions about papayas. The crowd at Gray's was always the same peculiar mix of panhandlers, with barely enough money for a Gray's special (two frankfurters and a papaya drink for two dollars), working people in a hurry, and one or two anxious-looking guys in suits. No one ever talked to anyone, and the radio was always blasting country music. I no longer drove myself crazy trying to figure out this combination of the tropics, street life, hot dogs, and Loretta Lynn. It had become a part of my neighborhood, period. In some ways, I felt relieved.

One day at Gray's, I ordered a hot dog and a small papaya — I had finally come around to drinking papaya juice — and got in line for the mustard, which was in a stout gallon jug with a plastic squirt top.

The man behind me was skinny and be-draggled, and in my best "I'm a New Yorker now" style, I pretended he didn't exist. I certainly expected that, in keeping with the custom at Gray's, we wouldn't converse. As we waited for the mustard, though, he leaned over my shoulder and muttered to me, "It's going to blow up." I took a deep breath and looked away. "It's going to blow up," he repeated. I tried to look more explicitly uninterested. Garrulous strangers with the urge to share their apocalyptic visions appeared often enough in my day-to-day life that I had gotten good at this; in fact, I took pride in staying unruffled. I was now just one person away from the mustard, and I planned to dress my dog quickly and find a place at the window far away from the skinny man. He said it again, this time very distinctly: "Hey. It's. Going. To. Blow. *Up*."

It was my turn. I set my papaya juice on the counter, positioned my hot dog under the nozzle, and pressed down hard on the top. It blew up. Mustard splattered all over my hands and my shirt. Most of the hot dog remained naked; the bun had a small mustard-filled crater, made by the impact. A plug of dried mustard that had caused the explosion was somewhere east of my papaya juice. "I *told* you it was going to blow up," the man said, shaking his head.

I looked at him and said apologetically, "I just moved here."

Uplifting

If you're the kind of person who gets a kick out of saying "bosom" and "breast" and "bustline uplift," you ought to go visit the Maidenform Museum on East Thirty-seventh. That way, you can walk around the display with the curator, Catherine C. Brawer, and ask questions like "Did the bandeau that preceded the brassiere squish the breast or just *smoosh* it?" and "When did natural shaping supplant the torpedo?" and "Can you please elaborate on the nipple?" If you pretend to be a scholar, you can then pause for a really long time in front of the best pair of breasts in New York City — which are on a miniature mannequin, are perfectly shaped and absolutely firm, and have a one-inch forward thrust — and say, "The semiotic evolution of window displays sure is *interesting,* isn't it?" and hope that Ms. Brawer is suddenly called away. If she isn't — and don't get your hopes up — she will probably stand there with you and point out that the mannequin with the terrific breasts is wearing a petite copy of a 34-B Interlude bra, made of

Alençon lace and broadcloth, with trapunto stitching on the undercup, which Maidenform marketed in the 1930s for women who prefer "the rounded as well as uplifted bustline." Then you will drop the scholar shtick and just observe that the Interlude and the other little bras made for this particular display — a teensy version of the Dec-La-Tay, made of fine peach netting with a lace edge and satin straps, and a Ves-T-Lace, which was designed for the fuller figure but, in this instance, would just about fit your thumb — are totally cute.

Then you might ask a reasonable question, like "Where did Maidenform get all these old bras for the museum?" and Ms. Brawer will answer that some guy who used to work for the company cataloged almost every single style that Maidenform made — the Chansonette, the Star Flower, the Tric-O-Lastic, the Twice Over, the Blue Horizon, the Maidenette, the Semi-Accentuate, the Hold-Tite, the Gree-Shen, the Allo, the Allo-Ette, the Allegro, and so forth — and when she is finished, you will definitely not say anything about leg men versus boob men. Because that would be childish. Especially when Ms. Brawer goes on to tell you that the museum has regular visits from the sixth, seventh, and eighth graders from IS 246 in Brooklyn and CS 211 in the Bronx and, to the best of her recollection, none of the students ever giggle. "They come here prepared," she will say. "They are here to work."

So you will work, too. You will take a lot of notes about the Maidenform war effort, which involved designing cotton-gingham bras, because nylon was requisitioned for parachutes, and also manufacturing carrier pigeon vests, which are almost as cute as the tiny 34-B Dec-La-Tay, and you will study the display highlighting the twenty-year history of the "I Dreamed . . ." ad campaign ("I dreamed I barged down the Nile in my Maidenform Bra"), and you might even copy down the text from an "I Dreamed . . ." ad that ran in Denmark (*"Jeg drømte, jeg blev forfulgt i min Maidenform b.h."*), commenting to Ms. Brawer that Danish is quite a poetic-looking language, just so you can take another long cheap look at some ladies in their underwear.

Okay. You're done, you stared at lots of breasts, you managed to maintain some dignity, you believe Ms. Brawer may actually still view you as an adult. Then she says, "Oh, I've got to show you something hilarious," and she leads you into a conference room and pulls out an atlas and turns to a map of the Grand Tetons — a name you always got a giant charge out of — and she says, "My husband and I went on vacation in Wyoming this summer, and, honest to God, we were looking at the map and look at *this*," and she points to a spot between upper Moran and Leigh canyons, about three-quarters of a mile south of Peak 49, and there it is on the map: Maidenform Peak, elevation 11,137. "Can you believe it?" Ms. Brawer says, grinning. "And it's a *twin* peak."

My Life:
A Series of Performance Art Pieces

1. Birth

As the piece opens, another performance artist, "Mom" (an affiliate of my private funding source), waits onstage, consuming tuna noodle casseroles. Eventually, she leaves the initial performance site — a single-family Cape Cod decorated with amoeboid sofas, Herman Miller coconut chairs, boomerang-print linoleum, and semi-shag carpeting — for a second site, a hospital. There she is joined by a sterile-clad self-realized figure of authority ("Sidney Jaffe, MD") who commands her to "push" and then externalizes through language and gesture his desire to return to the back nine. This tableau makes allusion to the deadening, depersonalizing, postwar "good life." "Mom" continues "pushing," and at last I enter — nude. I do this in a manner that confronts yet at the same time steers clear of all obscenity statutes.

2. Coming Home Extremely Late Because I Was Making Snow Angels and Forgot to Stop

Again, an ensemble piece. But unlike "Birth," which explores the universal codes of pleasure and vulnerability, "Coming Home Extremely Late" is a manifesto about rage — not mine, but that of the protonuclear family. The cast includes "Mom," "David," "Debra," "Fluffy," and my private funding source. In "Coming Home," I become Object rather than Subject.

The piece is also a metaperformance; the more sophisticated members of the audience will realize that I am "coming home extremely late" because of another performance: "Snow Angels," an earlier, gestural work in which, clothed in a cherry red Michelin Man–style snowsuit, I lower myself into a snowbank and wave my arms up and down, leaving a winged-creature-like impression upon the frozen palimpsest. Owing to my methodology, I am better at it than anyone on the block. Note the megatextual references to heaven, Superior Being–as-girl-child, snow-as-inviolable-purity, and time-as-irrelevancy. "Coming Home Extremely Late" concludes with a choral declaration from the entire cast (except for my private funding source, who has returned to reading the sports section), titled "You Are Grounded for a Month, Young Lady."

3. I Go Through a Gangly Period

A sustained dramatic piece, lasting three to five years, depending on how extensively the performer pursues the orthodontia theme. Besides me, the cast includes the entire student population of Byron Junior High School, Shaker Heights, Ohio — especially the boys. In the course of "Gangly Period," I grow large in some ways, small in others, and, ironically, they are all the wrong ways. I receive weird haircuts. Through "crabby" behavior (mostly directed at my private funding source), my noncontextual stage image projects the unspeakable fear that I am not "popular." In a surreal trope midway through the performance, I vocalize to a small section of the cast ("Ellen Fisher," "Sally Webb," and "Heather Siegel") my lack of knowledge about simple sexual practices. Throughout the piece, much commentary about time: how long it is, why certain things seem to take forever, why I have to be the absolutely last girl in the entire seventh grade to get Courrèges boots.

4. Finding Myself

This piece is a burlesque — a comic four-year-long high art/low art exploration. As "Finding Myself" opens, I am on-site — a paradigmatic bourgeois college campus. After performing the symbiotic ritual of "meeting my roommates" and dialoguing about whether boyfriends can stay overnight in our room, I reject the outmoded, parasitic escape route of majoring in English and instead dare to enroll in a class called "Low Energy Living," in which I reject the outmoded, parasitic escape route of reading the class material and instead build a miniature solar-powered seawater-desalinization plant. I then confront Amerika's greedy soullessness by enrolling in a class called "Future Worlds," walking around in a space suit of my own design, doing a discursive/nonlinear monologue on Buckminster Fuller and futurism.

Toward the end of "Finding Myself," I skip all my "classes" — spatially as well as temporally — and move into an alternative environment to examine my "issues." At this point, my private funding source actually appears in the piece and, in a witty cameo, threatens to withdraw my grant. Much implosive controversy. To close the performance, I sit on an avocado green beanbag chair and simulate "applying to graduate school."

5. *I Get Married and Shortly Thereafter Take a Pounding in the Real Estate Market*

A bifurcated work. First, another performance artist, "Peter," dialogues with me about the explicit, symbolic, and functional presentations of human synchronism. We then plan and execute a suburban country club wedding (again, with assistance from my private funding source). Making a conceptual critique of materialism, I "register" for Royal Copenhagen china, Baccarat crystal, and Kirk Stieff sterling. Syllabic chants, fragments of unintelligible words like the screeches of caged wild birds gone mad — this megatonality erupts when I confront my private funding source about seating certain little-liked relatives. At the work's interactive climax, "Peter" and I explode the audience/performer dialectic and invite the audience to join as we "perform the ceremony."

The second part of the piece — a six-month-long open-ended manifesto on the specificity of place — culminates with "Peter" and me purchasing a four-and-a-half-room cooperative apartment with a good address in Manhattan. Conran's furniture, Krups appliances, task-specific gadgets (apple corers, pasta makers, shrimp deveiners), and other symbol-laden icons are arranged on-site. Curtain goes down on the performers facing each other on a sofa, holding a *Times* real estate section between them, doing a performative discourse lamenting that they have "purchased the apartment at the peak of the market."

The series will continue pending refinancing.

Shiftless Little Loafers

Question: Why don't more babies work?

Excuse me, did I say "more"? I meant, why don't *any* babies work? After all, there are millions of babies around, and most of them appear to be extremely underemployed. There are so many jobs — being commissioner of Major League Baseball, say, or running the snack concession at the Olympic synchronized swimming venue — and yet it seems that babies never fill them. So why aren't babies working? I'll tell you. Walk down any street, and within a minute or so you will undoubtedly come across a baby. The baby will be lounging in a stroller, maybe snoozing, maybe tippling a bottle, maybe futzing around with a stuffed teddy — whatever. After one good look, it doesn't take a genius to realize that babies are lazy. Or worse. Think of that same baby, same languid posture, same indolent attitude, but now wearing dark sunglasses. You see it all the time. Supposedly, it has to do with UV rays, but the result is that a baby with sunglasses looks not just lazy, but lazy and snobby. Sort of like an Italian film producer. You know: "Oh, I'm so sorry, Mr. Baby isn't available at the moment. No, Mr. Baby hasn't had a chance to look at your screenplay yet. Why don't you just send coverage, and Mr. Baby will get back to you when he can."

This is right about when you are going to bring up statistics about show business babies. Granted, there are some show-biz babies, but their numbers are tiny. For one thing, there isn't that much work, and anyway most of it is completely visual driven, not talent driven. And everyone knows that babies lose their looks practically overnight, which means that even if Baby So-and-So lands a role in a major studio feature, she'll do the work and go to the big premiere and maybe even make a few dollars on her back-end points, but by the next day she's lucky if she's an answer on *Jeopardy!* Modeling superbabies? Same. Remember those babies zooming around in the Michelin tire ads? Where are they now?

The one job that babies seem willing and eager to do is stroller pushing. Well, big deal, since 1) they're actually very bad at it, and 2) am I the only one who didn't get the memo saying that there was a lot of extra stroller pushing that desperately needed to be done? Besides, it's not a job, it's a responsibility. For a baby to claim that pushing his or her own stroller counts as gainful employment is about as convincing as for me to declare that my full-time job is to floss regularly.

Elevator-button pushing? Not a job: a prank. Unless you really need to stop on every floor. And have you ever watched babies trying to walk? Is it possible that they don't work but still go out for a three-martini lunch? Of course, babies do a lot of pro bono projects, like stand-up (and fall-down) comedy and preverbal psycholinguistic research, but we all know that pro bono is just Latin for Someone Else Buys My Pampers.

One recent summery morning, I walked across Central Park on my way to my own place of employment — where, by the way, I have to be every day whether I want to or not. The park was filled with babies, all loafing around and looking happy as clams. They love summer. And what's not to like? While the rest of us, weary cogs of industry, are worrying about an annual report and sweating stains into our suits, the babies in the park are relaxed and carefree and mostly nude — not for them the nightmare of tan marks, let alone the misery of summer work clothes. And what were they doing on this warm afternoon? Oh, a lot of really taxing stuff: napping, snacking on Cheerios, demanding a visit with various dogs, hanging out with their friends — everything you might do on a gorgeous July day if you were in a great mood, which you would be if you didn't have to work for a living. That morning, I was tempted to suggest a little career counseling to one of these blithe creatures, but as I approached, the baby turned his attention ferociously and uninterruptibly to one of his toes and then, suddenly, to the blade of grass in his fist. I know that look: I do it on buses when I don't want anyone to sit next to me. It always works for me, and it worked like a charm for this "I seem to remember telling you I'm in a meeting" baby. I was outfoxed and I knew it, so I headed for my office. As I crossed the playground, weaving among the new leisure class, I realized something. The reason babies don't work? They're too smart.

Where's Willy?

It was a hell of a time to be in Iceland, although by most accounts it is always a hell of a time to be in Iceland, where the wind never huffs or puffs but simply blows your house down. This was early in August, and it was stormy as usual, but the summer sun did shine a little, and the geysers burped blue steam and scalding water, and the glaciers groaned as they shoved tons of silt a few centimeters closer to the sea. On the water, the puffins frolicked, the hermit crabs frolicked, and young people bloated with salmon jerky and warm beer barfed politely into motion-sickness buckets on the ferry sailing across Klettsvík Bay. The young people were on their way to an annual songfest and drinkathon on the Westman Islands, a string of volcanic outbreaks off Iceland's southern coast. During the trip, they spoke in Icelandic about Icelandic things, such as whether they had remembered bottle openers and bandannas, and then they turned greenish and stopped talking as the boat lurched up and down the huge cold waves. After two hours or so, the waves settled and the boat slowed and glided into Heimaey Harbor, which is ringed by cliffs of old lava as holey as Swiss cheese. Dozens of trawlers and knockabouts bobbed at their moorings, nudging the docks and making that clanging sound that is supposed to make you feel lonely.

A few of the young people, gummy mouthed and bleary-eyed, roused themselves and gazed out the portholes. We sailed past a row of white buoys strung across the mouth of a small bay.

"Hey! Keiko!" one girl exclaimed, pointing at the buoys.

"Huh?" another mumbled, looking where the first one was pointing. "Keiko?"

"Willy! Free Willy!"

"Oh, *Keiko*!" the others said, pushing up to the window, yanking one another's sleeves, and gawking at nothing but the empty inlet, the glassy water, the blank, looming cliffs. "Keiko! Oh, yeah! Oh, wow!"

The whale was gone, of course; he left in early July, after taking a watery journey with his human overseers to look at other whales — his kin, if not his kith — who had stopped near the Westman Islands for a midsummer feast. Keiko had seen wild whales before, having originally been one himself, and he had been reintroduced to them two years ago, after twenty years of captivity. He watched the visiting whales from a shy distance at first and a bolder one later, but he always returned to the boat that had led him out to open water. Back at his private pen in the harbor, an international staff of humans would massage his fin, scratch his tongue, and compose press releases detailing his experiences at sea. This July, however, Keiko ventured closer to the whales than ever, then followed them when they headed off past Lousy Bank, past the Faeroe Islands, onward to — well, honestly, who knows? Whales keep their own counsel. The truth about them is that they come and go, and you can't really know where they've gone — unless you've already fished them out of the water, drilled holes in their dorsal fins, and hung radio tags on them. Only a madman would suggest that drilling a hole in a whale's dorsal fin is easy. This is why no one is sure where the creatures that visit Iceland every summer spend the winter — and where, presumably, they were heading late in July.

But Keiko — which means "lucky one"

in Japanese — is the most watched whale in the world. He has a satellite tag and a VHF transmitter and three nonprofit organizations vested in him, along with millions of spectators waiting to see if this famous, accomplished, celebrated whale, who has lived most of his life as a pet, will take to the wild. Every day that Keiko is on his own, his location is tracked by satellite, relayed over the Internet, and then plotted on a marine chart in the Free Willy/Keiko Foundation offices in the Westman Islands, a row of neatly penciled X's tracing his arcing route through the sea.

What is known about Keiko is this: He is an *Orcinus orca,* commonly called the orca or killer whale; weighing as much as ten thousand pounds, the orca is the largest member of the dolphin family — big mouth, big teeth, big appetite. Like humans, orcas can kill and eat almost anything they choose. What they usually choose is herring, salmon, or cod, but some orcas prefer to eat sea lions, walruses, and other whales. They have been known to neatly skin a full-grown minke whale, bite off its dorsal fin, and eat only its tongue, a behavior that has been construed as either a tendency toward ostentatious epicurean wastefulness or a cross-species reenactment of an Aztec virgin sacrifice. Orcas seem to have no taste for humans. Only two people have ever been killed by captive killer whales, and both deaths involved the same whale, Sea World's Tillikum, who held his victims underwater to drown them but did not eat them afterward. Orcas are found in every ocean on the planet and have enjoyed relative invulnerability from hunting; they are twenty times less blubbery than sperm whales and have therefore been less valued for oil, and their meat is far less tender and flavorful than that of minke whales. They are, on the other hand, fiercely smart and remarkably educable. They are also handsomely outfitted in black and white with a grayish saddle patch — more appealing by far than, say, the transcendent horribleness, the blank ghastliness, the strange and awful portentousness, of a gigantic white whale. Therein lies the killer whale's real weakness: its suitability for being displayed and taught to perform silly tricks, made all the more marvelous by its reputation as a ruthless assassin.

In 1964, the Vancouver Aquarium commissioned a sculptor to kill an orca to use as a model for an artificial one. An orca was harpooned, but it managed to survive, so the aquarium decided to make the best of the sculptor's ineptitude and display the live whale rather than build the plastic one. The whale was named Moby Doll. She was the first orca in captivity. She died after eighty-seven days but had been observed enough to demonstrate the species's considerable intelligence. More than a hundred and thirty orcas have been captured for display since Moby Doll's misadventures. Many of them came from Iceland, until all whaling in the country was halted in 1989. Currently, there are about fifty orcas in aquariums and amusement parks around the world, and their scarcity has made them each worth a million dollars or more.

Keiko's beginnings, however, were humble. He was born near Iceland, in 1977 or 1978, and was captured in 1979. For a few years, he lived in a down-in-the-mouth aquarium outside Reykjavík, which raised most of its money by catching and selling killer whales to other aquariums. In 1982, Keiko was sold to Marineland, a park in Niagara Falls, Ontario. There he was bullied by older whales, and in 1985, Marineland sold him to Reino Aventura, an amusement park in Mexico City.

The whale facility at Reino Aventura was too small, too shallow, and too warm for an orca. There were also no other whales to keep Keiko company. He developed an unsightly pimply condition around his armpits and had the muscle tone of a wet noodle. He could hold his breath for only three minutes and wore down his teeth by gnawing the concrete around his tank. He spent much of his time swimming in nihilistic little circles and had a lethargy that some saw as foretokening an early death. In spite of this, and in spite of his droopy dorsal fin (which is symptomatic of nothing but made him look sad), he was much adored. He, in turn, was fond of children and cameras.

After Dino De Laurentiis's 1977 disaster epic *Orca*, Hollywood had shown little interest in cetacean films. Into this void, a writer named Keith Walker submitted to the producer Richard Donner a script about a mute orphan boy who lives with nuns and befriends a whale at an amusement park. In Walker's original script, the boy is silent until the end of the movie, when he releases the whale into the ocean and cries out, "Free Willy!" Donner, an environmentalist and an animal lover, liked the script's intentions and passed it to his wife, the producer Lauren Shuler Donner, and her partner, Jennie Lew Tugend, for development. Tugend and Shuler Donner thought that the story was too sugary. They rewrote the boy as a juvenile delinquent, the whale as a petulant malcontent, and the amusement park operator as a penny-pinching crook, but they kept the climactic release.

Once Warner Bros. agreed to underwrite the project, Tugend and Shuler Donner went out to audition the killer whales of the world to play Willy. Twenty-one of the twenty-three orcas in the United States belong to Sea World. The company's executives reviewed the script, shuddered at the message of whale emancipation, and declared all of its orcas unavailable for movie work. Shuler Donner and Tugend looked further. In Mexico, at Reino Aventura, they found not only Keiko but also a dilapidated facility that would be perfect for the film's fictional dilapidated facility, as well as park owners who were disposed to let their whale appear in a pro-wild-whale, anticaptivity movie.

Free Willy, which was shot on a lean budget of twenty million dollars, had a cast of mostly unknowns and starred a child actor named Jason James Richter, who was the same age as Keiko: twelve. No one imagined what a success it would become, although Shuler Donner had an inkling when, after an early research screening, a man approached her, held out ten dollars, and said, "Here, use this money to save the whales."

Free Willy pulled in huge audiences right from the start — mostly kids, of course, who insisted on seeing the movie over and over and over, thus answering the movie's tagline question, "How far would you go for a friend?" with a worldwide gross of a hundred and fifty-four million dollars. What's more, the producers had attached a message at the end of the movie directing anyone interested in saving the whales to call 1-800-4-WHALES, a number that belonged to Earth Island Institute, an environmental group. The resulting torrent of calls blew the minds of everyone involved — the executives at Warner Bros., the producers, the people at Earth Island Institute. And not just the number of calls, but the fact that many of the callers were asking something that hadn't been anticipated: Sure, save the wild whales, but more to the point, what about Willy?

"We had no clue that this would involve Keiko as an individual," says David Phillips of Earth Island Institute. "At that point, he was just a prop in the movie. Of course, everyone had fallen in love with him. The cast was in love with him. Everyone who gets near him gets Keiko virus."

Keiko, who had become infected with his own virus — a papillomavirus that had caused the pimply irritation on his skin — was still languishing in Mexico, but now he was in demand. The owners of Reino Aventura didn't want to part with him, but they recognized that he was in poor health and possibly even dying. They had already tried to find Keiko another home, having previously offered to sell him to Sea World, but Sea World hadn't wanted a warty whale. Now, suddenly, everybody wanted him. Michael Jackson sent representatives to Mexico, hoping to acquire Keiko for his ranch. Conservation groups wanted him for this or that aquarium. Scientists asked to keep him in a tank on Cape Cod for research.

David Phillips, with the support of the movie's producers, had formed the Free Willy/Keiko Foundation, whose mission was to rehabilitate and release Keiko. Reino Aventura's owners finally chose the foundation over other suitors and agreed to give Keiko away — but the expense of moving and housing him still had to be met. More than a million people had already contributed to the cause, but in amounts that were usually modest, raised at Free Willy bake sales and by kids breaking open their piggy banks. UPS agreed to fly Keiko free of charge, but the container and other incidentals would cost at least two hundred thousand dollars. Shuler Donner brought several bulging bags of letters to the studio executives — letters demanding to know whether Willy had really been set free and, if he hadn't, what they were going to do about it. The Free Willy/Keiko Foundation got a million dollars from both Warner Bros. and the film's other production company, New Regency. The Humane Society of the United States gave another million. Next, the telecommunications tycoon Craig McCaw put in a million, through the Craig and Susan McCaw Foundation.

"Craig's not really an animal person," McCaw's spokesman, Bob Ratliffe, said not long ago. "He's an environmentalist and is interested in the health of the oceans, and — well, long story short, Craig gives the million bucks. And then he gave another one and a half million to build a tank for Keiko in Oregon. His intention was never to be as involved as he became, but he really kind of bonded with Keiko. He went swimming with him. He was actually on the whale's back, and — well, long story short, he got very involved."

Mexican children cried bitterly when Keiko was loaded onto a UPS truck and taken away in January 1996, and who could blame them? The park used to allow kids to have pool parties with him in his tank, and now he was leaving for good, traveling thousands of miles north to the Oregon Coast Aquarium. In a documentary film about Keiko, his Reino Aventura trainers, two beautiful young women, were nearly hysterical about his departure, saying he was not just a whale or a job, but their closest friend. The truck carrying him to the C-130 Hercules cargo plane moved at a solemn pace with a police escort, as if it were the Popemobile, and more than a hundred thousand people lined the streets at dawn to say goodbye. In Newport, Oregon, the depressed, gray seaside town where the aquarium is situated, there were more crowds and more tears — Willy was almost free! — and there was the gorgeous new $7.3 million tank that the Free Willy/Keiko Foundation had built for him and the staff of six to care for him, cure him, and get him ready for the big, wide world. Throughout Oregon, there was Keikomania, with around-the-clock news reports and Keiko-cams and special sections in the newspaper about the whale, with instructions on how to fold a broadsheet into a whale-shaped cap.

"It was like New Year's Eve when he arrived," Ken Lytwyn, the senior mammalogist at the aquarium, said recently, sounding wistful. "I've worked with dolphins and sea lions and even other killer whales, but Keiko was . . . different. There was really something there."

By every measure, Keiko thrived in Newport. His skin cleared up; he gained two thousand pounds; he tasted live fish for the first time since infancy; he had toys to play with and a television set on which he could watch cartoons. His caretakers found him more Labrador retriever than orca: cheerful, affectionate, eager to please — the sort of killer whale who, if you were in the tank and he swam over to see what you were doing, would be careful not to accidentally crush you to death. Attendance at the struggling aquarium rose to an all-time high, and all those visitors, with their demands for snacks and souvenirs and motel rooms and gasoline, buoyed every enterprise around.

Wouldn't it have been great if Keiko could have stayed there forever? He was then twenty-one years old, a middle-aged piebald virgin living as good a life as captivity could offer. But the plan had always been to free Willy, even though a killer whale had never been set free before. However, Keiko was hardly an exemplary candidate for release. He had been confined for so long, had become so thoroughly accustomed to human contact, and was so much more a diplomat than an executioner that it was hard to imagine him chewing holes in walruses and beating schools of salmon to a pulp with his terrible, awesome tail.

When would Keiko be ready to take the next step toward freedom? Criteria had been set up, benchmarks had been established: Was he eating live fish? Could he swim great distances? Could he hold his breath underwater for a long time? But still, right-minded people could disagree. In fact, right-minded people could even litigate, as the Oregon Coast Aquarium did in 1997, to prevent the Free Willy/Keiko Foundation from moving the whale to Iceland, where he would be decanted into the actual ocean, into an open-water pen in Heimaey Harbor. The aquarium's position was that Keiko was not ready to leave; the foundation's position was that 1) Keiko was indeed ready to leave, and 2) he belonged to the foundation, not the aquarium. Relations grew ugly, then hideous. In early October 1997, the board members of the aquarium requested an independent evaluation of Keiko's health. A few days later, the Oregon Veterinary Medical Examining Board announced that it would investigate Keiko's care and the legality of his custody arrangements. There was talk in the Free Willy camp of moving Keiko to a pen in Oregon's Depoe Bay. Finally, a blue-ribbon panel of experts was formed to analyze Keiko's well-being and determine his fitness for release. To the dismay of the Oregon Coast Aquarium, the run of million-visitor years would soon be over: The panel announced that Keiko was ready and able to go.

Even then, there were skeptics who believed that the effort to free Keiko was doomed. Some of those skeptics also happened to be employed by Sea World, which had been picketed to free their own orcas in the wake of *Free Willy*: They warned that the poor whale would get frostbite if he was exiled to dark, cold, miserable Iceland — this in spite of the fact that Keiko was born in Iceland and that killer whales teemed in the waters offshore. But even among whale people — free-whale people, that is — there was doubt. Keiko, they argued, was already ruined. It was too late to teach him what a wild whale needs to know, and he repeatedly demonstrated an alarming preference for frozen fish over fresh, suggesting that his tastes had become completely corrupted by two decades in a fishbowl. What's more, there was a conspiracy theory circulating in the most radical anticaptivity ranks that Sea World might actually be behind the free-Keiko efforts, knowing that they would fail, thus inoculating amusement parks around the world from an upwelling of liberationist sentiment.

Skepticism was not the only impediment to moving Keiko to his ancestral home. Consider this: Icelandic fishermen view whales as annoying and gluttonous — blubbery fish grinders that consume commercial product by the ton. The government has asked the International Whaling

Commission to allow regulated whaling again, and Iceland recently accepted the first shipment of Norwegian whale meat in fourteen years. Now imagine that you are David Phillips of Earth Island Institute, and you represent a telecommunications billionaire, the Humane Society, and Ocean Futures, an environmental group founded by Jean-Michel Cousteau, and you are approaching various Icelandic ministries for permits to construct a million-dollar pen in the harbor; organize a fleet of boats, helicopters, and airplanes; and muster a crew of scientists, veterinarians, and animal trainers for the nurture and eventual discharge of one Keiko, aka Willy, a whale. Furthermore, the affront of having a whale so coddled in Icelandic waters would not even be offset by the comfort of cold cash, since Keiko would not be on display. There would be no Icelandair travel packages to visit Keiko — he would be living in a pen in the harbor, accessible only by boat, and he would be slowly weaned from human contact to ready him for life among his brethren. "The opposition from the Ministry of Fisheries was fierce," Phillips said. "This was antithetical to everything they do. There is very little by way of whale conservation awareness in

Iceland and a lot of hostility toward anything coming from the United States. So we started looking at other locations, in Ireland and in England, too. But Iceland was Keiko's home waters and really the best place for him, and after a long series of complexities, we finally got it approved."

So now there was another flight to pay for (three hundred and seventy thousand dollars), another pen to build (a million dollars), a staff to recruit and equip and pay. The annual costs of the project in Iceland were estimated at three million dollars; if Keiko never learned to live on his own, the foundation could conceivably be looking after him for thirty more years, at a cost of ninety million dollars. "Along the way, this had become a different kind of project," Bob Ratliffe, of the Craig and Susan McCaw Foundation, explained. "It was involving planes and helicopters and big boats and major expenses." But, Ratliffe said, a commitment had been made to the creature, and there was a desire to do something people said couldn't be done. The flight on an Air Force C-17 was booked, the gallons of diaper rash ointment to moisturize Keiko during the long flight procured, Familian Industrial Plastics contracted to build the new pen, the staff of fifteen lined up.

By September 1998, it was all ready. The goodbyes were again tearful. Keikomania had rolled on, unabated, since the day the whale arrived in Newport, and two more Willy movies had come out, further inciting whale devotion — *Free Willy 2: The Adventure Home*, and *Free Willy 3: The Rescue* — although these used computer-enhanced footage of wild whales and animatronic models rather than a real Willy.

"I went to his tank and told him goodbye and good luck," Ken Lytwyn, the Oregon Coast Aquarium mammalogist, recalled recently. "I would love to see the release work, but, because of who Keiko is, the kind of individual he is, I don't think it will. I was really sad when they said he was going, but it wasn't my call."

Ah, the Westman Islands! So raw, so rugged, ripped so recently from the earth's dermis — in fact, the youngest landmass on the planet may be the little rock pile called Surtsey, the southernmost Westman in the chain, tossed up above sea level only thirteen years before Keiko's mother conceived him. And as recently as 1973, a volcano erupted right in the middle of Heimaey, increasing the island's landmass by twenty percent. To make a living, people in the Westmans fish and they fish and they fish, and a few of them service the small but steady tourist economy. Slogans range from the somewhat inexplicable "Westman Islands, Capri of the North" to the more explicable "Ten Million Puffins Can't Be Wrong." Everywhere you look, you see dozens of these stout, clownish black-and-white birds: nesting in lava outcroppings, teetering on cliffs, plopping like stones into the sea. Every August, the baby puffins sail out of their nests to make their first trip on the ocean and instead crash-land in town, seduced by the lights of human civilization. This magical visitation and potential avian catastrophe is known as *pysjunaetur* — the Night of the Pufflings — and children and visitors await it every summer, armed with cardboard boxes for the rescue effort, and, in the morning, they release the babies at the water's edge. When full grown, puffins are enjoyed in the Westmans roasted, smoked, or sliced thin, like carpaccio.

The whale was not unwelcome here when he arrived, in September 1998, even though you couldn't see him unless you drove up to the ledge across the harbor and looked through a telescope that the foundation had installed; and even though not many local people got jobs; and even though the Keiko merchandise — the shot glasses and aprons and tea cozies decorated with his distinctive black-and-white face — wasn't flying off the shelves in the souvenir shops. He was met with what was becoming the standard greeting in Keiko's life — several hundred accredited representatives of the media and scores of ebullient schoolchildren, many of whom had first seen *Free Willy* when an Icelandic hot dog company gave the video away for free with a six-pack of franks. Everyone, certainly, liked Keiko, admired him for his gentle giantness, for being the good egg who tolerated being crated and shipped hither and thither, for suffering with a sort of martyred calm the strange, fickle circumstances of his life. If anyone thought that the money being spent on his rehabilitation was an insane extravagance, they didn't blame it on the whale: It wasn't his fault that he was captured to begin with and stuck in a lousy tub in Mexico. It wasn't his fault that he became a ten-thousand-pound symbol of promises kept (or not) and dreams achieved (or not) and integrity maintained (or not) and nature respected (or not). It also wasn't his fault that he didn't know how to blow a bubble-net and trap herring, and it wasn't his fault that he'd been torn from the bosom of his family at such a young age that now he was a little afraid of wild whales and that they viewed him as a bit of a freak.

Moving the Keiko project to Iceland wasn't easy. The storms were endless — wild, white, end-of-the-world storms, with screaming winds and waves so high and stiff that they looked set with pomade. A walloping squall hit Heimaey just two weeks after Keiko arrived. The pen net, held in place with what the staff called "the big-ass chain" — each link weighed five hundred pounds — broke apart and had to be rebuilt and reanchored. Keiko's living quarters were splendid, but everything had to be done by boat, since the land that formed the bay around him was a sheer ridge of petrified lava. A crust of grass grew on the lava, and every summer local farmers ferried their sheep out to spend the season grazing on the ridge. The staff agreed to restrain Keiko when the sheep were floated back and forth, since no one could guarantee that a killer whale wouldn't have a taste for mutton. And throughout the next three years the caretaking staff turned over again and again, because it was lonely and cold in

Iceland, even if you were crazy in love with your whale.

Then the stock market deflated. This would not ordinarily be a matter of much concern to a whale, but Craig McCaw now wanted to pay more attention to his other undertakings — some land-based conservation efforts, some world peace initiatives with Nelson Mandela — and it just so happened that his company, Nextel, had seen its stock price fall from a high of more than eighty dollars a share to somewhere around ten. He wasn't crying poorhouse, but the word went out at the end of 2001 that the three-million-dollar annual whale underwriting from the Craig and Susan McCaw Foundation was finished.

It was such an irony, in a way — just as everything in Keiko's life has been an irony — that the funding dried up just as the project was starting to accomplish what it had set out to do. In the summer of 2000, Keiko began taking supervised "walks" out of his pen into the ocean. At first, when he saw wild whales he did a spy hop to look at them and then swam back to the staff boat and followed it home. The next year, he dallied a little, and more than once he stayed with the wild whales when the staff boat sailed away. Meanwhile, the budget for the project was cut from more than three million dollars a year to six hundred thousand dollars, and the helicopter and pilot that McCaw had provided were furloughed, and the Free Willy/Keiko Foundation offices in Heimaey were consolidated into one drab waterfront space, a former grocery store (with, conveniently enough, a huge freezer for Keiko's herring).

Despite Keiko's progress, though, there was no irrefutable evidence that he would ever leave his bay pen permanently. During the winter, when the wild whales were gone, he was back in his pen full-time, and he was the same tractable fellow as always, ready in a minute to put his big wet rubbery head in your lap. If he was getting an idea of what wildness was, he was still a bit of a baby, and certainly daintier than you might think a killer whale should be. Once, when the trainers instructed him to bring something up from the bottom of the bay, he presented them with a puffin feather when they were expecting something more like a boulder, and then he accidentally dropped it, dived back down, and brought up the same tiny feather. Another time, he came up with a little hermit crab that was blithely scurrying up and down the long row of his teeth, oblivious of the fact that it was inside the mouth of a killer whale. When seagulls stole his food, he got angry, but he usually just grabbed them, shook them a bit, and spat them out.

Really, though, just how big a baby was he? There were plenty of people who wondered whether Keiko was being held back. "I worry about the trainers," David Phillips said recently. "Just who is more dependent on whom?" It was a question not simply of Keiko providing jobs for people, but of the emotional attachment. One of his trainers carried pictures of Keiko rather than of her children in her wallet. And if Keiko didn't leave — that is, if he didn't join a whale pod, learn how to hunt, eschew the easy life of a kept man, a Hollywood retiree — he would have to be funded with new money from somewhere. Whoever contributed to the Keiko project now would have to do it knowing that he or she would probably be underwriting not a magnificent mammal's colossal leap to freedom, but an ongoing day care program for an aging whale.

Then, on July 7, he was gone like a shot. The trainers had led him out to the waters near Surtsey, where several pods of killer whales were rounding up a ration of herring, and Keiko headed over to them and didn't turn back. Days went by, and he was still loitering with them. The project staff checked on him, noted that he was getting on nicely, and then slipped away without his noticing. More days went by. The summer was in full bloom. The sun hung in the sky until close to midnight; the ice creaked and melted; the sheep, now so heavy with wool that they looked like four-legged snowballs, clipped the grass down to the rock on the cliffs surrounding the empty bay pen. In late July, a huge storm muscled in on Heimaey, and for days it was too rough to send anyone out on the water. The satellite was still transmitting coordinates from Keiko's radio tag, but there was no way to tell whether he was with other whales and eating or floundering around, lost.

By the time I got to Heimaey, Keiko had been on his own for almost a month. I went down to the office the morning I arrived, during the three-hour window of the satellite feed. It is a large room across from the harbor, outfitted with a motley array of cast-off desks, boating magazines, foul-weather gear, and photographs of a loaf of bread that one of the staff members had baked in the still-warm crater of Heimaey's volcano. A handful of people wandered in and out: Fernando Ugarte, a Mexican scientist with a master's degree in the killer whales of Norway; John Valentine, an American whale-training consultant, in town from his home in Thailand; Colin Baird, a Canadian now running the Heimaey office; Michael Parks, a marine operations coordinator who is from Oklahoma but lives in Alaska; a Danish whale scientist; a sailor from Ireland; and three Icelandic staff members, one of whom was an awesomely musclebound former Mr. Iceland. Charles Vinick, the executive vice president of Ocean Futures, had flown in the day before from the group's Paris office to organize the effort to figure out where Keiko had gone. Naomi Rose, a marine-mammal scientist with the Humane Society, had also just arrived on what had been planned as a trip to check Keiko's physical fitness.

"It looks like he's spent all this time with wild whales," Vinick said. "To me that's, like, wow."

Michael Parks was plotting the satellite information on a marine chart. "He's south today," he said. "Jesus Christ, he's here." He was pointing to a spot southeast of Surtsey, several inches off the chart.

"He's making the decisions now. He's in charge," Vinick said. "He could be gone for good." People drifted over to examine the chart. It looked as though Keiko were traveling sixty or seventy miles a day and was now too far away to reach by the project's fast but open-deck workboat. It was decided that three people would take a sailboat in Keiko's general direction. This would put them out of regular radio range, making it impossible to receive the updated satellite coordinates. But one of the staff people knew a company in Reykjavík that rented satellite telephones that would work at such distances and arranged to have one flown from Reykjavík to Heimaey — or conveyed by ferry, if fog, which rolled in regularly, kept the island airport closed. Then another group would carry the phone out to the sailboat on the little workboat. Vinick also wanted to hire a private plane to fly overhead, but none would be available for a couple of days. Once they sighted Keiko — if they sighted Keiko — they would either leave him alone, if he seemed to be eating and keeping company with other whales, or lure him back to the pen, if he seemed distressed or lonely or hungry. By the time all the arrangements were made, everyone seemed a little exhausted, as if they had laid out plans for an armed invasion.

We took a boat out in the harbor to check on the pen. On the deck of the equipment shed was a dead puffin, probably blown sideways by the storm. Inside the shed, someone had posted a list of possible new behaviors to teach Keiko that included "Pec slap and swim," "Bubble-blow underwater," and "Swallow Jim in one piece." A crew of divers was scheduled to start cleaning the seaweed off the net in preparation for winter, although now it seemed like a bootless task, given that Keiko might never come back.

But it was a good day, all things considered. The Humane Society had just revealed that it would take over managing and funding the project, and Craig McCaw's ex-wife, Wendy, announced a grant of four hundred thousand dollars for Keiko. In the afternoon, the fog thinned, flights made their way to Heimaey, and the rented satellite phone arrived. As we loaded gear onto the workboat, a gray-faced local woman, bundled in a man's overcoat and red galoshes, hollered from the dock, "How's my Keiko? Is our star still out there?"

★ ★ ★

Call me only slightly disappointed. Who wouldn't want to have seen the great black-and-white whale? Who wouldn't want to scratch his tongue, look into that plum-size eye, take a turn around the bay pen on his back? All I saw of whales in Iceland were two humpbacks who dived a few feet from the workboat, flourishing their tails like ladies' fans. Keiko was far away by then, headed for Norway, where he panhandled from picnicking families and romped in Skaalvik Fjord. What a choice! In the entire world, the only country that allows commercial whaling is Norway, and a member of Bergen's Institute of Marine Research suggested that it was time to stop the madness and put Keiko to death. But the children who swam on his back and fed him fish reportedly found him delightful, as has everyone who has ever known Keiko. He played with them for a night and a day, the luckiest whale in the world, and the great shroud of the sea rolled on as it rolled five thousand years ago.

Shadow Memory

When my grandmother died a few years ago, I was given her formal china, her silverware, a fur-lined lap robe, and her *Webster's New International Dictionary of the English Language, Second Edition* — an old brick of a book, leather-bound, with skin-thin pages and black half-moon thumb tabs. I was more taken with the china and the silverware than the *Webster's*; after all, I had much newer dictionaries, as well as a computer that could spell and find synonyms on its own. One afternoon, in the throes of spring cleaning, I decided to get rid of it. Before pitching it into my rummage box, I riffled idly through its pages. I flipped past the color plates showing house flags of steamship lines, and the multicolumned Table of Oils and Fats, and the pen-and-ink drawings of diploids and seed weevils, and page after page of ant-size type defining "gressorial" and "sacrarium" and "tingle," until I came upon a page — "Luna Cornea" through "lustless" — that was stuck lightly to the next. I peeled the pages apart. Between them was a small four-leaf clover, all of its leaves facing upward, its long stem curving into a lazy "j." The clover was still green, or at least greenish, and the leaves were dry and perfectly flat but hardy and well attached to the stem. A little stain of clover juice was printed onto the pages it had been pressed between.

It was startling to come across these two lives, pressed between pages: my grandmother's and this weed, which she must have found — when? When she was out for a walk? At a picnic? Had my grandfather found the clover and saved it for her? Or had some other suitor offered it to her, hoping for his own luck? Had my grandmother tucked it into her dictionary and then forgotten it? Did she pick this page for a purpose? Or did she just place it somewhere in the middle of the book and fail to note the page, so that when she went back for it weeks or years later, she couldn't find it and never saw it again? Not since my grandmother died had I had such a distinct sense of her — a sense of her as I'd never actually known her, as a young woman with the time and patience to sort through blades of grass, looking for four leaves on a clover, believing in the luck one might bring her. And I believed I was lucky, too, having been so close to losing it, to discarding it, to never knowing what I had in my hands.

So this is what's left behind, these things that end up as our real inheritance — the flotsam and jetsam of life, the stuff that drifts into our hands and into history, the chance impression, the little shadow each of us casts, the fragile thing someone carefully catalogs and cares for and then forgets or maybe doesn't, the image of an image that conjures a memory that is either real or imagined — these are here, plucked and pressed between the pages, so they will stay fresh forever, or forever slip away.

Afterword

It's always a pleasure to revisit a place or, in this case, a story about a place, and it is always fascinating to see what time has done to it. I often keep track of the places and situations I've written about — they stay wired into my consciousness well after I've unpacked my suitcase, filed the travel vouchers, finished the piece. Nothing ever stays the same, of course. The story feels eternal, fixed, and complete, but it is really only a shard of a moment, and, in no time at all, the place will have transformed, the story evolved, the characters changed.

Sometimes the proof of this evolution is inescapable, such as the sad bulletin about Keiko's sudden death in Norway just a few months after I'd seen him there lolling in his fjord, when I was following up on the story "Where's Willy?" Keiko was not old for a wild whale, but very old for a captive one. Since one of the great puzzles of his existence was figuring out whether he was essentially a wild whale or a captive whale, it was hard to determine whether he should be considered not old or very old. Turns out he was very old — or at least old enough to get a bad case of pneumonia, and to suffer it secretly until it was too late to help him. So his saga ended in the fjord he'd found on his own, during that one summer when for a while it looked like Willy would finally go free.

I followed the continuing saga of Joan Byron-Marasek for months after I'd finished writing about her. After dozens of hearings and dozens of lawyers and dozens of schemes to delay the inevitable, she lost her final round of appeals, and the State of New Jersey came and took her tigers away. They are now living in a wild animal sanctuary near Houston, Texas. Animal hoarders have a staggering rate of recidivism — that is, most of them begin collecting again shortly after their animals are removed — so I won't be surprised at all if one of these days we see another story about Byron-Marasek, announcing that she has assembled another menagerie.

What else has happened since I completed these journeys? Well, Centro Vasco, the Cuban restaurant in Miami that I profiled in "The Homesick Restaurant," closed just a few months after my story was published. According to Jauretsi

Saizarbatoria, whose family owned the restaurant, Centro Vasco was firebombed after a performance there by a Cuban singer who was on good terms with the Castro regime. The Saizarbatorias suspected that right-wing anti-Castro activists were involved, and they were so disheartened that they decided they had had enough of the atmosphere in Little Havana. Midland, Texas — which was the hometown of a mere candidate for president at the time of my story — is now, of course, the hometown of the president. Herb Spitzer, owner of the Sunshine Market (from "All Mixed Up") did follow through on his plans to retire a few months after I finished my reporting; in fact, I ran into him in Florida a few years later, and it appeared that golf and real sunshine suited him even better than groceries and the Sunshine Market had. I've driven by the market a few times since the story was published, and it looks good, but much more corporate now — much less the one-man show, the neighborhood place, that it had been when Spitzer was still there.

Craig Fleming, the CEO of Thomas Kinkade's company Media Arts, was forced out just a few weeks after I interviewed him; so was the next CEO, and the next one — a sign, most likely, of some softness in the Kinkade market, which had also prompted a group of Kinkade gallery owners to sue the company for misrepresenting the value of their product. The Kingdom of Bhutan, which had been television-free at the time of my visit, has since given in to the march of modernism and decided to legalize the idiot box — and even instituted a national network, which I'm told broadcasts the Bhutanese equivalent of school-board meetings. Of the women who went on the Bhutanese fertility trip I wrote about in "Fertile Ground," one has adopted a child and another has had a baby since coming back from the Himalayas, and perhaps more are still on the way. The JonBenet Ramsey murder case, which is the story that propelled me to write about children's beauty pageants ("Beautiful Girls"), is still unsolved, although at least once a month, some wild-eyed tabloid like the *Weekly World News* claims to have exposed JonBenet's true killer. As far as I know, though, the gloom that her death spread on the pageant world has lifted and the pageants are back in full swing: babies in spangles and toddlers in ball gowns competing to be the prettiest girl in the world.

On the other hand, some things I've

written about haven't changed at all. Hervé Halfon, the owner of Afric' Music, is still threatening to leave Paris, but hasn't yet made a move; Gray's Papaya still has good deals on hot dogs and papaya juice and still has mustard that gets stuck in the spout; kids in Cuba still live to play baseball; Mount Fuji is and ever will be the pure image of everything Japanese. Pat and Jim Bannick still proudly hang on to their party line, and unless the phone company pries it out of their hands, they plan to hang on to it indefinitely. Tina Turner has still not visited my apartment. Travel around the world is hardly as carefree now as it was when I wrote about Thailand in "The Place to Disappear," but I'm sure that another generation of kids has found its way onto Khao San Road and is merrily drinking beer and watching free movies at the Khao San cafés.

What has truly not changed, and I hope never will, is my feeling that the world is an endlessly surprising and amazing place — that each time I overload my suitcase and head out the door, each time I think of something or someone I want to learn more about, each time I pull out my pen and start scribbling notes, a new adventure is beginning, I'm lucky to be on it, and wherever I am is exactly the right place.

Author's Note

Except for minor corrections, the stories in this collection are printed as they originally appeared in the following magazines:

PART ONE: HERE

Lifelike: *The New Yorker*, June 9, 2003

A Place Called Midland: *The New Yorker*, October 16 and 23, 2000

Beautiful Girls: *The New Yorker*, August 2, 1997

Party Line: *The New Yorker*, December 16, 2002

Madame President: *The New Yorker*, February 21 and 28, 2000

All Mixed Up: *The New Yorker*, June 22, 1992

The Lady and the Tigers: *The New Yorker*, February 18 and 25, 2002

Super-Duper: *The New Yorker*, February 13, 1995

PART TWO: THERE

The Homesick Restaurant: *The New Yorker*, January 15, 1996

Rough Diamonds: *The New Yorker*, August 5, 2002

Carbonaro and Primavera: *The Atlantic Monthly*, May 2003

The Congo Sound: *The New Yorker*, October 14 and 21, 2002

Like Waters and Chocolate Pancakes: *Condé Nast Traveler*, November 1994

Shooting Party: *The New Yorker*, August 21 and 28, 2000

Fertile Ground: *The New Yorker*, June 7, 1999

Do We Transcend Before or After We Purchase the Commemorative Eel Cakes?: *Outside*, October 1997

Game Plan: *The New Yorker*, September 18, 2000

The Place to Disappear: *The New Yorker*, January 17, 2000

PART THREE: EVERYWHERE

Homewrecker: *The New Yorker*, August 22 and 30, 1993

The World: *The New Yorker*, June 22, 1987

We Just Up and Left: *The New Yorker*, June 12, 1995

Art for Everybody: *The New Yorker*, October 15, 2001

Intensive Care: *The New Yorker*, June 28, 1993

Royalty: *The New Yorker*, September 10, 1990

Uplifting: *The New Yorker*, September 22, 1993

My Life: A Series of Performance Art Pieces: *The New Yorker*, December 31, 1990

Shiftless Little Loafers: *The New Yorker*, July 22, 1996

Where's Willy?: *The New Yorker*, September 23, 2002

Shadow Memory: *Flowers in Shadow: A Photographer Discovers a Victorian Botanical Journal* (New York: Rizzoli, 2002)

Acknowledgments

Many, many people have made it possible for me to have this wonderful life — to wander the world, publish my dispatches, and, finally, gather those stories into a book. My wholehearted thanks go to my editors at *The New Yorker* — Alice Truax, Virginia Cannon, Lee Aitken, and the incomparable David Remnick — who have encouraged me, supported me, and guided these efforts all along. I've been extraordinarily lucky to have the magazine behind me all these years, and to have such exceptional editors to learn from and work with. Thanks also to my editors at *Outside* — Mark Bryant and Susan Casey — who did the same, with gusto and great warmth. My team at Random House is just . . . the best. There couldn't be an editor more enthusiastic, wise, and inspiring than Jon Karp; he has piloted me through multiple books and each experience has been a delight. Thank you, Robbin Schiff, for making the book beautiful, and Dennis Ambrose for making it read properly, and to Gina Centrello, for putting it out in the world. Many, many thanks to Richard Pine, my longtime agent, friend, and adviser, whose brainstorm led to the book.

Most of all, thanks to my very dear friends (I'm happy to say there are too many to list here) and family (my parents, Arthur and Edith, and my siblings and sibs-in-law, David and Steffie and Debra and Dave), and especially my husband, John, and stepson, Jay, who are there when I leave for my travels and there when I return, and who always make me glad when I've come back.

About the Author

SUSAN ORLEAN is the *New York Times* best-selling author of *The Orchid Thief*, *The Bullfighter Checks Her Makeup*, and *Saturday Night*. She has been a staff writer at *The New Yorker* since 1992. Her articles have also appeared in *Outside*, *Rolling Stone*, *Vogue*, and *Esquire*. She lives in New York City with her husband, John Gillespie.

For more information on the author, visit www.susanorlean.com.